Internet Communication and Qualitative Research

New Technologies for Social Research

New technologies are transforming how social scientists in a wide range of fields do research. The series, New Technologies for Social Research, aims to provide detailed, accessible and up-to-date treatments of such technologies, and to assess in a critical way their methodological implications.

Series Editors:
Nigel G. Fielding, *University of Surrey*
Raymond M. Lee, *Royal Holloway University of London*

Advisory Board:
Randy Banks, *University of Essex*
Grant Blank, *University of Chicago*
Edward Brent, *University of Missouri*
Angela Dale, *University of Manchester*
G. David Garson, *North Carolina State University*
G. Nigel Gilbert, *University of Surrey*
Noel Heather, *Royal Holloway University of London*
Udo Kelle, *University of Vechta*
Edith de Leeuw, *Free University of Amsterdam*
Wim Liebrand, *iecProgramma/University of Groningen*
Peter Ohly, *IZ, Bonn*
Bryan Pfaffenberger, *Universityof Virginia*
Ralph Schroeder, *Chalmers University, Gothenburg*
Eben Weitzman, *University of Massachusetts at Boston*

Recent volumes include:

Computer Analysis and Qualitative Research
Nigel G. Fielding and Raymond M. Lee

Computer Modelling of Social Processes
edited by Wim B. G. Liebrand, Andrzej Nowak and Rainer Hegselmann

Neural Networks
An Introductory Guide for Social Scientists
G. David Garson

Internet Communication and Qualitative Research

A Handbook for Researching Online

Chris Mann
and
Fiona Stewart

SAGE Publications
London • Thousand Oaks • New Delhi

SAGE Publications Ltd
6 Bonhill Street
London EC2A 4PU

Sage Publications Inc.
2455 Teller Road
Thousand Oaks, California 91320

SAGE Publications India Pvt Ltd
32 M-Block Market
Greater Kailash - I
New Delhi 110 048

British Library Cataloguing in Publication data

A catalogue record for this book is available from the British Library

ISBN 0 7619 6626 9
ISBN 0 7619 6627 7 (pbk)

Library of Congress catalog card number 132722

Printed in Great Britain by Biddles Ltd, Guildford, Surrey

To Lynne

Contents

Acknowledgements

This book is a joint venture and I must start by thanking my co-author Fiona Stewart for the infectiously cheerful 'can do' approach she brought to all the challenges we met on the way. Even with joint authorship, individuals welcome additional intellectual stimulus. In the UK, my thanks go to Caroline Napper, who helped me to think through difficult conceptual areas in some parts of the book while offering unstinted personal support. Although she was not directly involved, I am also grateful to Madeleine Arnot whose mentorship, academic excellence, professionalism and personal charisma never cease to inspire my own work.

My own impetus for writing this book grew from the methodology I developed while conducting the Graduates of the Millennium project funded by the University of Cambridge, UK. I thank the university for funding this research into equity issues which I am proud to be associated with. Also warm thanks to Patrick Leman for our excellent early partnership in the first phase of this research. As the text of this book will show, I am indebted to the students who participated in the Graduates of the Millennium study. They taught me a lot about both equity issues and online communication, and they invested time, energy and flair on behalf of future students. I only wish I could have included many more of their brilliant comments in the book!

The juxtaposition of the online and real life world, which is such a key part of the book, also plays out with those who offered me the greatest personal support while I was writing it. Some of those closest to me vastly prefer the 3-D world of colours, scents and sounds to life on the screen. Dinah Hargreave will always seek the green thought in the green shade rather than the machine in the corner, while Patrick Brindle, Jo-Anne Dillabough, Wendy Luttrell, and Crionna McNally are likely to communicate online with the express purpose of arranging fun meetings face-to-face. Others, like Ann Tasker and Pam Cox, who first introduced me to the possibilities of the computer and the Internet, are excellent face-to-face and online friends.

My parents, in a real life world of flowers, home baking and kitchen table chat, were a loving and constantly restorative counterbalance to life (and work!) on the screen, as was my father-in-law, enthusiastically playing golf and brewing beer. The next generation, Alice and Will Mann, manage to combine face-to-face warmth, generosity of spirit, humour and intelligence with a breathtaking ease with the technical world. I never cease to learn from and to delight in all their qualities. As for Roger Mann, he is both a technical wizard and the most honourable, loving and life-enhancing real life person I know. Only he will know how great is the depth of gratitude I owe him. Immeasurable and heartfelt thanks is owed to all these people and – as Fiona and I will describe below – to new friends and colleagues found in cyberspace.

Chris Mann

Book writing is never totally solitary and I, too, have debts to a great many people. Firstly, I would thank my past colleague Dr Liz Eckerman at Deakin University for planting the seed and for working with me on the Young People and Health Risk studies. Also at Deakin I thank Pam Mulready whose technical expertise and advice was nothing short of brilliant and Anne Riggs for holding the research fort when I went into book writing hibernation. Thanks also to Bryan Turner, then of Deakin, now of Cambridge, for providing me with the professional space to undertake the whole project. At the World Health Organisation – Manila office – a special thanks is due to Rosemary Erben for bravely funding the Young Women's component of the study. Finally, thanks to Michael Santamaria who kept food the table, coffee on the desk, the dogs daily walked and me sane.

To Chris Mann I owe everything else. From a one hour beer in a quaint Cambridge pub to a 2 year online relationship. We did this book hard. 90% online and 10% f2f must set new records in collegial and intellectual endeavour. For all of that I thank her deeply and sincerely.

Fiona Stewart

We both wish to thank other colleagues and friends who have shared generously of their time and thoughts with regard to this book. Dale Spender is a tireless inspiration for us both. The series editors Nigel Fielding and Ray Lee offered many useful suggestions which we were pleased to incorporate in the book. Special thanks also go to the fellow online researchers with whom we corresponded and whose ideas inform this book; in particular, Wendy Seymour, Caroline Bennett and Leonie Daws in Australia; Anne Ryen in Norway; Paul Hodkinson, Clare Furneaux, Henrietta O'Connor and Clare Madge in the UK, and Casey Sweet and Marilyn Smith-Stoner in the US. Monika Merkes was an scrupulous proof reader to whom we are both grateful. Finally, we thank Michael Carmichael and Simon Ross at Sage Publishers. They were prepared to take on this book at a time when qualitative research using the Internet seemed a rather odd concept!

Technical Consultant: Richard Guy, of Orang-utan Productions (http://www.orang-utan.com) is a musically-inclined chemistry student who funds his wild, exciting life by computer-consulting and writing. Richard did more than simply share his sophisticated computer and Internet expertise with us – we must also thank him for his substantial contribution to the Technology Introduction and the useful feedback he gave us in the early stages of the book.
    He, in turn, thanks Julia Warren for her kindness.

1 Introduction

On 20 October 1969 the first attempt to log in to a primitive network of two computers was made at the University of California in Los Angeles (UCLA) and the Stanford Research Institute. Attempting to send a 'login' from one computer to another, the team successfully sent the letter 'L', followed by the letter 'O', but before the letter 'G' could be sent the computer crashed and had to be restarted. So the first message sent through the Internet was a cheery 'ello'.

Now, thirty years later to the day, we are writing this Introduction. That first halting attempt to communicate using computers has evolved into a worldwide, interconnected academic, business, military and scientific communications network (LaQuey and Ryer, 1993). In the view of many the Internet has become 'the 20th century's most dynamic bequest to the 21st'[1]. The increase in the number of computers connected to the Internet since 1969 confirms the view that this communications medium is so powerful 'it has a logic, a momentum, a force of its own. It's damn near unstoppable' (International Data Corporation analyst, Barry Parr)[2].

Increase in Internet hosts since 1969

1969 --@ 4
1979 ---@ 188
1989 -------@ 130,000
1999 --@ 56,218,000

Source: Hobbes Internet Timeline[3]

The driving force behind this phenomenal recent growth has probably been the recognition by business of the power of the World Wide Web to reach customers. But whatever the reason, the growth has applied equally to the potential of the Internet for communication between individuals. This book focuses on that potential and examines how the communicative power of the Internet may be harnessed to further qualitative research. We begin by clarifying what we mean by 'Internet Communication' and 'Qualitative Research'.

Defining Terms

What Do We Mean by Internet Communication?

In this book we focus on what has been called computer-mediated communication. We shall refer to this throughout the book as CMC. Following Lawley, we define CMC as the direct use of computers in a text-based communication process:

> I eliminate the communication technologies that rely upon computers for switching technology (such as telephony or compressed video), but do not require the users to interact directly with the computer system via a keyboard or similar computer interface ... Given the current state of computer communications and networks, this limits CMC to primarily text-based messaging, while leaving the possibility of incorporating sound, graphics, and video images as the technology becomes more sophisticated. (Lawley, 1994: *online*)[4]

In the light of this definition, we do not draw on previous studies that look into other electronic media such as the telephone or television[5]. Rather we concur with Giese (1998: *online*) that virtually every study looking into CMC uses, as a comparison, face-to-face (FTF) interaction. Analysis of the differing possibilities and limitations offered to qualitative research by CMC and FTF communication is a central theme in this book.

The Internet makes possible a number of types of CMC. Real-time 'chat', or synchronous CMC, refers to an interchange of messages between two or more users simultaneously logged on at different computer terminals. Asynchronous CMC, the feature of most email messaging systems, allows users to type extended messages which are electronically transmitted to recipients who can read, reply, print, forward or file them at their leisure. We elaborate on these differences in the Technology Introduction below.

What Do We Mean by Qualitative Research?

As has been frequently noted, qualitative research takes many forms, means different things to different people and has many names. A comprehensive account of qualitative methodologies, published as use of the Internet started to explode, has already concluded that, 'There have never been so many paradigms, strategies of inquiry, or methods of analysis to draw upon and utilize' (Denzin and Lincoln, 1994: 11). Although this complexity makes it difficult to reach a precise definition of the field, certain key characteristics of the research process are pertinent to discussion about qualitative research in general and the impact of CMC in particular.

Qualitative researchers use multiple methods to collect rich, descriptive, contextually situated data in order to seek understanding of human experience or relationships within a system or culture (Silverman, 1999). Processes of analytical induction from the data might then lead to the formulation of simple explanatory hypotheses or, using systematic approaches such as grounded theory, the development of complex theories (Brannen, 1992).

In this book we shall focus on the ways that *widely available* Internet technology might be adapted to qualitative methods of data collection and analysis. We accept that such technology has limitations. While new initiatives in video conferencing may eventually enable the Internet to offer innovative methods of observation, these processes are currently too expensive and exclusive to be a feasible option for most research projects and are not discussed here (Kennedy, 2000). Voice communication via the Internet is another future possibility as a research tool, but it currently requires extra technology beyond that commonly available in Internet-accessible computers[6].

But if video and voice communication are excluded, it might seem that there is little scope for qualitative investigation where the researcher is the 'human instrument' of research. Arguably, the physical presence of the researcher is too restricted. However, as we shall see, it would be unwise to dismiss data generated through use of the Internet as merely the result of a disembodied exchange of textual material. CMC has characteristics which do not fit within more traditional modes of data collection and which may challenge some standard assumptions about language use, interpersonal relationships and group dynamics. The authors hope to alert qualitative researchers to the exciting possibilities of what has been called 'the fourth revolution' in communication and the production of knowledge (Harnard, 1992).

Researching the Internet

A great deal has been published about the Internet in recent years. In addition, some of the most exciting research relating to CMC is now available in online journals and is the subject of continuing debate in online discussion groups[7]. As Murray has noted, such scholarship is 'vital to our understanding of how language, society and technology intersect' (1995: 11). Analysis and comment are wide ranging. They cover such areas as the history of the Internet; the economic, political, social, ethical and legal implications of its existence and practices; and a wide range of technical issues relating to information systems and software packages[8].

Of particular relevance to the online researcher is the transdisciplinary literature which documents aspects of Internet communication and human behaviour online. For 'computer systems render visible to researchers information about users, their attitudes, and their actions, that was previously impractical or nearly impossible to gather' (Walther, 1999: 1). Communication theorists, for example, have focused on the linguistic status and characteristics of synchronous and asynchronous forms of CMC (see Herring, 1996b; Murray, 1995; Davis and Brewer, 1997).

A second major focus has been the impact of CMC on social interaction and the presentation of the self online. One body of research has taken a largely experimental approach to these issues. Studies have investigated how people act and react in administrative, organizational and educational settings when involved in work-related tasks such as information exchange and decision processes (for example, Sproull and Kiesler, 1986; Rice, 1992; Garton and Wellman, 1995; Murphy and Collins, 1997). Attention has also been paid to ways in which social and human computer interaction in health, education and e-commerce communities might be nurtured (Preece, 1999). A naturalistic, qualitative approach is more common in studies which investigate how people act and react when using CMC in social settings. Here, the emphasis is less on task-related communication and more on CMC as a medium of human relationships (Cheseboro and Bonsall, 1989; Walther, 1992; Parks and Roberts, 1998), or as a mode for conducting online activities such as distance learning, support groups, interest groups and interaction in virtual worlds. Investigations of online activities are associated with discussions of Internet culture (Baym, 1995b; Rheingold, 1994; Turkle, 1997; Horn, 1998), and the impact of this culture, or variations of this culture (Shields, 1996), on debates around identity (Bruckman, 1992; Reid, 1995), gender (Matheson, 1992; Bannert and Arbinger, 1996; Spender, 1997; Kramarae, 1998), race (Burkhalter, 1999), cross-cultural relations (Hantrais and Sen, 1996; Stewart *et al.*, 1998) and the role of the online teacher or trainer (Salmon, 2000). However, findings in discrete areas of CMC, or insights which result from using a specific methodology, have not necessarily been applicable to CMC as a whole. It remains to be seen if claims that CMC will change the psychology and sociology of the communication process are well founded (Rice and Love, 1987). Wallace (1999), for example, has provided an excellent description of the psychology of the Internet which goes a good way towards informing this debate.

From Research About the Internet to Internet Research

It is, perhaps, surprising that the suitability of the Internet for conducting research remains relatively unexplored. While there have been some early initiatives in a quantitative research setting[9], there has been little systematic analysis of how the Internet might be incorporated into qualitative research practices. While ground-breaking books such as *Doing Internet Research* (Jones, 1999a) examine a range of theoretical and practical aspects associated with researching the Internet, they largely stop short of considering the Internet as a data gathering tool. An explicit and sustained investigation of this area has yet to be undertaken. This book seeks to provide that investigation. The authors have drawn upon contemporary research initiatives, including studies they are conducting themselves, as a means of opening up debate about the viability of CMC as a qualitative research method.

Until now, qualitative researchers using CMC have had to proceed with few practical or theoretical guidelines. For example, in the extensive literature review undertaken for this book, a single reference concerning online focus groups was uncovered (see Gaiser, 1997). Nevertheless, some pioneering research has gone ahead. Many of the qualitative studies which adopted CMC as a research medium did so because it seemed a 'logical' (O'Connor and Madge, 2000), indeed 'the only authentic and congruent' (Smith-Stoner and Weber, 2000), method of investigating different forms of Internet usage. Individual and group interviews have focused on many aspects of online experience, such as education (Smith-Stoner and Weber, 2000; Salmon, 2000); virtual worlds (Correll, 1995; Ryan, 1995); rural women's use of interactive communication technology (Daws, 1999); Web-site use (O'Connor and Madge, 2000); email-mediated helpservices (Hahn, 1998); use of virtual focus group technology (Sweet, 1999); online subculture (Hodkinson, 2000); and the empowering use of technology for people with disabilities (Seymour *et al.*, 1999). Among these interviewers there was a general consensus that, in order to interrogate computer communication, a new research methodology was required.

However, as Walther has pointed out, Internet research is not only concerned with the study of online behaviour (what people do in virtual and mediated environments). It is also concerned with using 'computer-based tools and computer-accessible populations to study human behaviour in general' (1999: 1). Some examples of the latter are: Stewart and Eckermann in the Young People and Health Risk study (see below); Anders in an international study of issues faced by women with disabilities in higher education (2000); Ryen and Silverman in a case study of an Asian entrepreneur in Africa (2000); and Mann in the Graduates of the Millennium project (see below). Here, CMC was chosen because it offered a means to minimize the constraints of time and space. It allowed the researchers to interview participants in different continents, on the one hand, and across a complex matrix of university colleges and faculties on the other. It also facilitated participation which might otherwise have been inhibited due to disability, financial constraints and/or language and communication differences. Yet other interviewers have capitalized on the anonymity of the technology to access the voices of socially marginalized communities such as gay fathers (Dunne, 1999) or participants who might have been emotionally evasive FTF (Bennett, 1998). In order to achieve their aims, all these researchers were prepared to develop their technological skills to work online for, as Denzin and Lincoln noted, 'If new tools have to be invented, or pieced together, then the researcher will do this' (Denzin and Lincoln, 1994: 2).

The authors are active qualitative researchers who acquired their current level of Internet expertise through their involvement in two separate but coterminous studies which involved CMC. The first of these studies, the Graduates of the Millennium project, is part of a large-scale longitudinal initiative, funded by the University of Cambridge, UK, with a concern for ensuring equity within the institution (Leman and Mann, 1999; Leman, 1999). Mann designed the Graduates of the Millennium project in order to look in depth at factors that might relate to differences in academic performance among undergraduates. The project was an unprecedented attempt to map the social and academic experiences of a cohort of 200 undergraduates over the full course of a degree. Rather than meeting students FTF, Mann established regular email communication with everyone involved. This was a double-pronged approach: first, a rolling programme of semi-structured online interviews; second, an additional 'diary' option which would tap into an undergraduate's different moods and states of mind on a daily basis. As Mann had wide experience of collecting written and verbal accounts using conventional methods (Mann, 1998), this allowed her to identify strengths, weaknesses and, above all, *differences* in comparative online approaches.

The second study by Stewart and Eckermann at Deakin University, Australia, comprised two substudies of health risk perceptions and practice among young women and men. These studies were Australia based although transnational in their undertaking. Data on a range of health issues and practices (smoking, alcohol/drugs, nutrition, stress and sexuality) were gathered through both FTF and virtual or online focus group discussions. The participants took part in the FTF and online focus groups from their home cities of Suva (Fiji Islands), Beijing (China), Geelong (Australia) and Kuching (Malaysia). The aims of the comparative studies were (a) to explore the globalization of risk among a small, purposive sample and (b) to test the viability of the Internet, particularly in regard to issues of gender, as part of multi-site public health research. A tertiary goal was to stimulate debate about the possible uses of CMC technology for health promotion and education initiatives.

Together with other studies discussed in this book, we hope our experiences will offer a valuable resource for extending discussion and debate about the Internet and its emerging impact upon qualitative research methods, both within and outside academic life. The studies have demanded flexibility in our expectations of what is or is not possible and the concomitant effects of that. They are also tangible examples of academic researchers 'surfing [the] wave of excitement' with regard to Internet possibilities (Thimbleby, 1998: *online*).

Towards Internet Methodologies

This book has been written, in the first instance, as a practical methods guide and, as such, it deals with pragmatic matters. Questions addressed in Chapters 2 to 5 include: What skills are required to conduct online research? What advantages, if any, does CMC offer researchers and participants? What problem areas may arise? And, finally, what does it mean to act ethically online? However, this book also seeks to look more deeply into the significance of the Internet for social science research and for qualitative research practices in particular. There is a tendency for people early in the life of a new technology 'to emphasize [its] efficiency effects and underestimate or overlook potential social system effects' (Sproull and Kiesler, 1991: 15). However, as Giese (1998) noted, the Internet is both a technological *and* a cultural phenomenon. As qualitative researchers, we consider it insufficient simply to demonstrate the technological advances the Internet might allow us to achieve. In *Internet Communication and Qualitative Research* the Internet is considered not simply as a technological tool but as a wholly new, constructed environment with its own codes of practice.

This raises a series of more theoretical questions which are addressed in Chapters 6 to 9. First, is Gaiser (1997) correct in concluding that textual data generated through CMC are not different from other forms of data? Or do data gathered in this way have a different quality from those collected orally, in handwriting, or in print form? Second, what is the impact of disembodied interaction on issues of power, gender and presentation of 'the self'? Might these phenomena have implications for data? Finally, taking everything else into account, can it be claimed that the Internet allows us to develop *new* forms of research? The final question is, in fact, addressed directly or indirectly in all chapters of the book. Related discussions suggest that the Internet will indeed have an overwhelming impact on the theory and practice of qualitative research.

We shall now move on to a Technology Introduction which has been included for readers who have very little experience of the Internet. This seeks to introduce those readers to some terms and concepts which will appear in subsequent chapters. There is a also a glossary at the back of the book which may be of use to more experienced Internet users who wish to confirm how we are using technical terms.

Technology Introduction

This section is an introduction to the basic services of the Internet. It has been written with new Internet users (newbies) in mind. Being a newbie can be an intimidating business (as the authors can confirm!), but things are rarely as complicated as they seem at first sight. The aim of this section is to provide the technical background you need in order to understand the rest of this book.

A word of warning. The Internet is an evolving phenomenon and there is already much confusing and seemingly gratuitous jargon in cyberspace (for example, 'newbie'). Different users have adopted their own terminology and there are often many ways of saying the same thing. This diversity is not only accepted but frequently welcomed, as it reflects the cultural conventions and mores of cyberspace. What is important to remember is that these are only words. One needs to be aware when duplication in terminology is occurring and how to break through it for the sake of clarity. When in doubt, refer to the glossary provided at the end of this book. See Turkle (1995) for a more in-depth discussion of the practice of online users in discriminating and/or adhering to particular meanings of terminology.

What is the Internet?

The Internet is a worldwide computer network that arose from ARPAnet[10], an American military network[11]. The core of the Internet, and the thing that makes it work, is a suite of software 'protocols' or rules that enable all of the computers on the Internet to communicate with each other. It is these protocols that enable us to access Web pages via our Web browsers, to download files, and to send and receive email.

Participating in the Information Revolution

In order to participate in the information revolution you need to connect your computer to the Internet. This need be neither difficult nor expensive. Many universities and companies have permanent, direct connections to the Internet and its use is becoming a routine part of academic and business life.

If a user is not institutionally linked, home use is possible. A would-be user will need a computer, appropriate software (see discussion below), a phone line, a modem and an account with an Internet Service Provider (ISP). ISPs sell Internet access by allowing subscribers to connect their computer to the Internet (or 'log on') using a modem and dial-up phone line. ISPs provide email services, software and often server-space for personal Web pages. Charges are typically based on the length of time for which the user is connected to the Internet, though in recent years intense competition has brought prices down and free ISPs are becoming more widespread.

Finally, for those with neither institutional nor home access to the Internet, facilities can be rented at many local libraries and 'Internet cafés' or 'Cybercafés'.

Services on the Internet

World Wide Web The World Wide Web (or just 'the Web') is a means of linking pages of information across networks and computers. It enables users to jump from one page to another by simply clicking on text or graphical 'hot spots' on the screen. The Web has been the most successful use of the Internet and *the* catalyst for increased demand for network usage. There are now estimated to be over 800 million Web pages[12].

To view Web pages you need a computer program called a Web browser. The most widely used browsers are Internet Explorer (by Microsoft) and Netscape Navigator and Communicator (by Netscape Communications), with versions existing for both PC and Macintosh computers. While browsers are free, the compulsive nature of the Web can lead to rapidly escalating connection charges.

The 'address' of a Web page is its URL (Uniform Resource Locator). Technically, these start with the mysterious characters 'http://' (for example, http://www.orang-utan.com). However, these are not required when typing a Web address into a modern browser and are usually ignored when quoting an address. Web pages are text files written in HyperText Markup Language (HTML), the language used by 'authors' to define how pages will look in terms of text formatting and graphics.

The quantity of information available on the Web is staggering. To help users find their way around it, powerful computers called search engines visit pages automatically and attempt to index their content. Well-known search engines can be found at www.altavista.com, www.yahoo.com and www.excite.com. However, information on the Web is hugely diluted and searches can return hundreds of thousands of results. Quite often the best way to use the Web can be to exchange interesting URLs with friends and colleagues or to take note of potentially useful addresses from real-life sources such as newspapers.

The vast stores of information on the Web include material which is offensive, illegal or inflammatory. As the Web is not censored, extreme political groups and pornographers may be easily located. However, with 'censorware' programs such as NetNanny (www.netnanny.com) access to Web sites can be filtered and controlled. Sites offering advice about children's online safety include ParentSoup (www.parentsoup.com/onlineguide/) and Get NetWise (www.getnetwise.org).

Email Email may be the most commonly used service of the Internet. As the name suggests, emails are letter-like documents that are typed on the screen and then mailed electronically, via the Internet, to the server computer of the recipient's ISP – a process that may take only minutes or even seconds. When the recipient next logs on to the ISP, the message is downloaded to their computer and will appear in the 'in tray' of their email program. Received messages can be read on screen, printed out or saved to a file. Email is generally an asynchronous form of communication. It operates in non-real time, with messages being written and read at different times, as well as different places.

Commonly used software packages for sending and receiving email include Eudora and Microsoft Outlook. Hotmail is representative of a range of free email services which are now also available. Hotmail is widely used by people who may not necessarily be using the same computer or ISP every time they connect to the Internet.

Emails are divided into three parts: the header, the body and, optionally, the signature. The header of the message contains the recipient's address, the sender's address, the subject of the email, and various delivery details added by the computers through which the email passes. The body is where the sender types the message. In terms of text, emails are normally confined to upper- and lowercase letters, numbers, punctuation and a few symbols. Certain 'extended' characters (such as £) can also cause problems. A signature (or 'sig') can be appended to the end of the email by the software. Typically it will contain the sender's name, address and perhaps a Web site URL or other information that the sender would like to include in the correspondence but does not want to type every time.

Email addresses take the form username@domain. Mann's address is ccm10@cam.ac.uk. The username identifies the individual or subscriber of the ISP ('ccm10' for Chris C. Mann). The domain identifies the organization to which the email will be sent and, frequently, other information about the organization (for example, 'cam' for Cambridge, 'ac' for academic institution and 'uk' for the United Kingdom). The domain is, therefore, like a street address, the username like an occupant of a particular house.

Other common domain elements include:

com	a commercial organization
edu/ac/uu	an educational organization
gov	a government organization
mil	military organization
net	network access provider
org	usually a non-profit organization

Geographic domain identifiers include:

au	Australia
de	Germany
nl	Netherlands
nz	New Zealand
se	Sweden
uk	United Kingdom

US domains do not require a geographic identifier; companies which are (or aspire to be) international prefer not to use them.

People often need to change domains when they change jobs or ISPs, but problems with extinct email addresses can be avoided through the use of email forwarding services (such as the free one provided by iName; see www.iname.com) where the address to which mail is sent does not change, but the address to which mail is forwarded can.

It is also possible to send messages anonymously. Emails sent using email software carry the name and email address of the author. However, an anonymous remailer can be used to strip messages of their original headers and replace them with something else. While the administrators of remailers are increasingly charging for their services, it is still possible to send anonymous email free of charge (see www.anonymizer.com).

But there is more to email than an interesting, electronic analogy to a paper letter. Being electronic, email has considerable flexibility and many advantages. You don't have to fuss with stamps or recalcitrant fax machines. Furthermore, it doesn't matter if the recipient is not at home or is asleep when the mail is sent because they can collect it when they are ready. You can email many people at once for almost no extra effort or cost. It can take just seconds for the email to arrive and, although the body of the email is exclusively text based, it is possible to send sound or picture files by 'attaching' them to the end. Some email programs allow textual formatting. However, this can be a problem if the recipient's program does not support these features.

One drawback about email, however, is that there is still no complete or centralized directory of email addresses. This is despite the efforts of Yahoo (people.yahoo.com) to assemble a global email directory. While organizations and email services (such as Hotmail) often have searchable email directories which can be accessed from their Web page, the best way to find out someone's email address is often to ask them.

Chat Chat is a generic term for real-time communication using computers and networks (for example, Internet Relay Chat, or IRC). Also known as synchronous communication, real-time chat is communication in which messages are written and read at the same time, though in different places.

To participate in chat, a user needs IRC software. This can range from 'shareware' software (software programs which are freely downloadable such as mIRC; see www.mirc.com) to licensed software packages such as Firstclass Conferencing[13]. While IRC enables you to talk to many people at once (as in citizen's band radio), other software such as AOL's Instant Messenger and ICQ (I Seek You; see www.icq.com) allow you to chat in real time with a group of people or one-to-one.

Participants connect via the Internet to chat servers (special computers devoted to this service) and 'chat' directly (synchronously) with other participants. What one person types is visible to everyone else on the same 'channel'. Typically, a chat program will have a conversation flow area where participants can read all contributions, as well as a separate composition area for writing their own messages. A message is 'posted' (sent) to a chat room, area or board as soon as the 'Enter' key is pressed on the keyboard.

Once connected, a user can list all the 'channels' available, and select which to join. Channels discuss a vast range of topics and there are hundreds available. IRC users are usually identified by a nickname – a 'nick'. Users chooses their nickname when first setting up their IRC software. It need not resemble their real name but it must be unique to the channel.

Conferencing Computer conferencing was first implemented by Turoff in 1970 and was intended to be a 'collective intelligence environment' (Harasim in Davis and Brewer, 1997: 72).

Since this time, conferencing has emerged as one of the most commonly used services of the Internet. Conferencing systems include: FirstClass (from SoftArc, Inc.), CoSy (from Softwords Research International) and LotusNotes (from Lotus). In addition, both Microsoft and Netscape have their own systems and distribute them widely in combination with software and system packages. Conferencing systems are also known as Groupware systems, of which LotusNotes is perhaps the most well known.

Conferencing offers the user asynchronous communication, but can also offer combined features. For example, Firstclass Conferencing has the following capacities: Security, Synchronous Chat, Large Group Discussion, Small Group Discussion, Threading and Design flexibility.

While the 'look' of conferencing systems varies, a typical conference site may be a type of folder, like the one that appears on both Macintosh and PC computer screens. For a conference to operate, participants post messages about a particular topic or topics. Like email, which is another asynchronous form of CMC, messages can be responded to by other participants at some time in the future. Unlike email, however, the conference is conducted at a 'conference site' (as opposed to individual email addresses) which can have restricted or public access. Conferencing provides an effective means of conducting non-real-time online focus groups.

Focus Group Facilities In order to conduct focus groups, qualitative market researchers often use 'facilities'. These are professional focus group companies and rooms specifically designed to conduct FTF focus groups. These facilities recruit and screen participants obtained from their own databases, and organize room rental, payment of incentives and hosting for the groups. The facility location is usually a series of small conference rooms.

For online focus groups, virtual facilities are used. Online facility services include VRROOM, W3Resources and Strategic Focus. Virtual facilities provide the same facilities as real-life facilities including 'rooms' such as a reception room, discussion room and client backroom. 'In-person' technical backup is often also available for a fee. Sweet[14] states that 'everyone enters a reception room and then the discussion room, once it is determined who will be part of the group'. Furthermore, there is no special software for anyone to download. Rather, participants sign on at a particular Web site.

Mailing Lists A mailing list is a group of email addresses that can be contacted by sending a single message to one address: the list's address. A message sent to a list address is automatically distributed to all subscribers. Managing mailing lists can be a tedious process, and a number of programs have been developed to automate subscription, unsubscription and message distribution. These include LISTSERV[15], Majordomo[16] and ListProc[17].

Depending upon the software, a participant subscribes to a mailing list by issuing a *subscribe* command to the list server. Typically this is done by emailing the word 'subscribe' in the body of the message, often along with the real-life name. Unsubscribing is done in a similar manner. The software program will usually reply by email, asking the subscriber to confirm their request. This middle step stops troublemakers subscribing their enemies to mailing lists, and thus swamping them with hundreds of mailing list messages.

On some mailing lists participants may need to be approved before they can start receiving and posting messages.

Mailing lists can be split into two categories: moderated and unmoderated. In a moderated list, the list owner or convenor will intercept a message before forwarding it to subscribers, and may weed out messages that are deemed inappropriate, irrelevant or offensive. Unmoderated mailing lists operate independently of human intervention. Some mailing lists keep copies of all the messages posted and archive them on the Web so they can searched; several examples of this in action can be found at www.ticalc.org.

Usenet Newsgroups. For our purposes, newsgroups using Usenet are just like mailing lists except that they don't take place using email. Rather, they use a special server computer. Both Internet Explorer and Netscape Navigator can be used to access these servers. There are also many free news servers. More information about newsgroups can be found on the Web at www.deja.com.

To subscribe to a newsgroup a user configures their software to download the messages from a particular group every time they log on. How this is done depends upon the software used. To contribute to a newsgroup, the user sends a message to the news server; this will have a similar format to an email,.

There are estimated to be over 25,000 newsgroups (Kennedy, 2000), although many news servers – especially those not run by ISPs – only carry some of what is available. At the current time, the major categories of Usenet newsgroups are:

alt.	alternative topics
comp.	computer-related topics
news.	recreation and hobbies
sci.	scientific discussions
soc.	cultural and social talk
talk.	an opportunity to put your views forward

Like mailing lists, newsgroups exist in moderated and unmoderated forms. To send a message to a moderated newsgroup you email it to the moderator, who will then decide whether or not to post it to the newsgroup. There is no human interference in an unmoderated newsgroup.

Compared to mailing lists, newsgroups are usually considered to be more versatile as you can request articles you may have missed for as long as they are on the news server. You may also 'kill' (not download) posts with particular subject lines or which are sent from a particular email address. However, social scientists may be more likely to use mailing lists than newsgroups to collect data because more people have email software than newsgroup software.

MU* Environments An MU* environment is a text-based descriptive environment which uses the metaphors of buildings, towns or landscapes to create an atmosphere (see Sempsey, 1997). Whilst these environments are sometimes used for intergroup, one-to-one and small-group communication, participants can also construct their own environment. MU* is an overarching reference indicating all such virtual environments (Bruckman, 1992). There are also a number of subtypes of environments with the best known being MUDs (multi-user dungeons, dimensions or domains), MOO, MUSH, MUSE, MUCK and DUM (Reid, 1994). Though there is some overlap between the characteristics of each environment, each acronym indicates the multiple environment conditions and its purposes.

MU* software consists of a series of 'rooms', 'exits' and other objects (Reid, 1994). Users connect to the database and can interact with others. Each user connects to a character (some MUDs provide guest characters for users who have not yet obtained characters of their own). Using those characters, users can move around the various rooms, talk to others, and interact with the various objects provided. Everything a user sees on a MUD is presented as text.

Multi-media Environments In addition to MU* environments there are multi-media environments. These enable text- and voice-based communication. For an example of this see www.thepalace.com. Another multi-media interactive environment is VisitMe (www.visitme.com). These environments allow real-time communication with audio and video; however this is only possible if your ISP allows this form of communication and your computer and connection speed are adequate. To communicate in this way, you will need a voice-capable modem and a camera for video communication (see www.cuseeme.com)

Behaviour and Language Online

Netiquette Netiquette is a term used (a) to describe the established conventions for communicating online and (b) to refer to the standards of being social and relating in the online environment; or online etiquette.

While netiquette is still emerging, there are already a number of recognized conventions. For example, in the public forum of newsgroups and mailing lists, it is common and acceptable practice to spend a few days or even weeks reading the postings of others before offering your own. This is called lurking and despite real-life (RL) connotations to the opposite, it is an online practice which is ethical and sometimes wise.

A good example of netiquette is that it would be unacceptable to forward a private email that you have received to someone else without first seeking the permission of the original sender. In chat and conferencing, base-level netiquette would concern a level of polite interaction. This could mean that it would be unacceptable to swear or to insult someone.

A comprehensive set of guidelines which individuals and organizations may take and adapt for their own use has been prepared by the Responsible Use of the Network (RUN) Working Group which can be found at www.dtcc.edu/cs/rfc1855.html. See Chapter 3 for a more detailed discussion of netiquette in research ethics.

Flaming Although definitions of flaming are rarely precise, it is usually understood as the hostile expression of strong emotions and feelings which can include personal abuse and harassment, slander, obscene language and topics and can even flow over to FTF contexts (Babbie, 1996). Flaming is used to hector or harangue another person electronically in response to an electronic message and is found in all types of CMC.

Abbreviations As part of netiquette and in order to reduce typing time, acronyms are frequently used in online communication. Examples include:

AFAIK	as far as I know
BTW	by the way
FWIW	for what it's worth
FYI	for your information
HTH	[I] hope this helps
NG	newsgroup
OTOH	on the other hand
RTFM	read the f****** manual
TIA	thanks in advance
TDNBW	this does not bode well (used ironically)
LJATD	let's just agree to disagree (discussion going nowhere)

Emoticons Emoticons are a form of electronic paralanguage which are used to show affect (Murphy and Collins, 1997) and to establish relational tone. They may also include verbal descriptions of feelings and sounds ('hehehe' for laughter) as well as denoting signs of affection or approval (for example, *big hugs*). Smileys are perhaps the most used of all emoticons. These indicate that a textual comment should be taken with a smile, and not too seriously – it may be a joke, or a friendly insult. Emoticons are generally read sideways, and some examples include:

:-(	sad
8-)	happy, spectacle-wearer
:-o	surprised
:-]	sarcasm
;-)	wink
@:-)	wearing a turban
(-:	Australian

A final word of warning for electronic communicators: sarcasm is particularly hard to convey using just text. If left undetected it can lead to serious misunderstanding. Here, at least, liberal use of smileys may be important. :-)

Notes

1   *Guardian* newspaper, UK, 21 October 1999.
2   Parr (1999) quoted in Lillington, K. 'Walk on the Wired side', *Guardian*, 14 January 1999.
3   See Zakon (1996).
4   The online world is a new field – not least in terms of referencing online journals and Web sites. (Guidance for Web citation can be found in Walker and Taylor, 1998.) We have included both print references and online references where both are available. When references for online sources refer to a direct quote the italicized word *online* will stand in place of a printed page reference. We are also extremely grateful to colleagues who shared their experiences and views in online dialogue. References to this kind of 'up-to-the-minute' information appear in the italicized form *personal email*.
     Another important feature of online communication is its informality. Spelling and grammatical 'mistakes' are frequently left uncorrected, or are even introduced deliberately for playful or stylistic reasons. Online extracts in this book have been reproduced verbatim to give the full flavour of the communication. Consequently, apparent 'errors' have been neither corrected nor pointed out.
5   See Sola Pool (1977) and Meyrowitz (1985).
6   See Aikens (1996).
7   An excellent and constantly updated Web site which lists online journals and email discussion groups is Stormsite at www.concentric.net/~Astorm/.
8   Some books which give an overview of this literature include LaQuey and Ryer, 1993; Kitchin, 1998; Jordan, 1999.
9   For a review of the literature see Smith (1997).
10   See Cringely (1993: 86).
11   For more information watch *The Glory of the Geeks*, Channel 4 Productions, UK. For a more general history of the personal computer (that touches the Internet) watch the equally excellent *The Triumph of the Nerds*, also Channel 4 Productions, and read the accompanying book by Cringely.
12   *Computing*, 29 July 1999, p. 16.
13   Stewart used Firstclass Conferencing (see Chapter 4). Other studies discussed in this book used Hotline Client (O'Connor and Madge, 2000) and ICQ (www.icq.com) and PowWow (www.tribalvoice.com/powwow/) (Bennett, 1998).
14   Casey Sweet is a focus group researcher who uses online and in-person methods. Contact Quesst Qualitative Research. Email: casey@focusgroupsonline.net
15   The LISTSERV home page is at http://listserv.tamu.edu/cgi/wa.
16   See http://www.speedsoft.com/ss/support/md.html.
17   The ListProc home pages is at http://www.cren.net/listproc/index.html.

2 Practicalities of Using CMC

In this chapter we begin by considering the practical advantages and challenges of using computer-mediated communication (CMC) to conduct qualitative research, as opposed to face-to-face (FTF) methods. Our focus is on online versions of: semi-structured or in-depth interviews; the 'observation' of virtual communities; the collection of personal documents; and focus groups. Some rather different issues pertain for survey research which may be needed as a complementary part of a qualitative research design (see Chapter 4).

In the first part of the chapter we shall assume that researcher and participants are able to take advantage of online facilities. However, because CMC depends on a new and by no means universal technology, an additional key question for a researcher considering its use is: What are the variations in computer and Internet access and usage? In the final part of this chapter we look in some detail at this question and the issue of who might have minimal or non-existent access to the research tool – the Internet.

Advantages of CMC

The practical benefits of incorporating CMC into qualitative research designs are wide ranging. Some of the most important gains are considered below.

Extending Access to Participants

Assuming that potential participants have the appropriate technology (see Technology Introduction), CMC allows researchers to capitalize on the ability of the medium to cross the time and space barriers which might limit FTF research. The following options become possible:

Wide Geographical Access CMC is a practical way to interview, or collect narratives from, individuals or groups who are geographically distant. It also facilitates collaboration between colleagues who may be on different sites, even in different continents (Cohen, 1996). The Internet is a global system accessing local newsgroups in many countries and in many languages, allowing cross-cultural comparisons of issues (Coomber, 1997).

Hard to Reach Populations CMC enables researchers to contact populations that it might be difficult to work with on an FTF basis, for example mothers at home with small children, shift workers, people with agoraphobia, computer addicts, people with disabilities. As one focus group moderator reported, 'in one of my groups, one participant excused himself to take a shot of his insulin and returned promptly. He, in fact, would have been unable to attend a two hour group an hour away with his unpredictable diabetes condition. He was a great participant online' (Sweet, 1999: *personal email*).

Closed Site Access CMC is a possible means of access to people in sites which have closed or limited access (such as hospitals, religious communities, prisons, government offices, the military, schools and cults). Some sites are also 'closed' to researchers with different visible attributes such as age, gender, ethnicity, or even physical 'style' (bikers, surfers, Goths, punks, jetsetters and so on). The technology can offer researchers practical access to such previously 'forbidden' sites – although there are clearly ethical considerations about disguising identity to become acceptable to insiders (see Chapter 3).

Sensitive Accounts Some personal issues are so sensitive that participants might be reluctant to discuss them FTF with a researcher. Not only does CMC have the potential to defuse the embarrassment that might be present one-to-one, but there is also some agreement between focus group practitioners that the online environment allows groups to speak about sensitive issues in an open and candid way without the fear of judgement or shyness that characterize FTF groups (Sweet, 1999).

Access to Dangerous or Politically Sensitive Sites CMC is a means of extending the possibilities of conducting research in politically sensitive or dangerous areas (see Lee, 1993; Fielding, 1982). Physical distance, and the possibility of anonymity, offer protection to both researchers and participants (see, for instance, Coomber's (1997) study of illicit drug dealers). Researchers can access censored and/or politically or militarily sensitive data, without needing to be physically in the field. They can interview people living or working in war zones, or sites where diseases are rife, without needing to grapple with the danger – and the bureaucracy – of visiting the area. Ramos-Horta noted that a great deal of information about the insurrection in East Timor came from statements from rebel guerrillas, written on laptops in the mountains. In other contexts, the disembodiment of CMC allows researchers physically to distance themselves from ideological 'camps', reducing the likelihood of suspicion and innuendo which might alienate some of the participants. Researchers could communicate with, for instance, police and criminals without being 'seen' visiting either; or could interview both Israelis and Palestinians without leaving themselves open to charges of spying.

Resistance Accounts CMC offers the possibility of resisting the status quo without excessive risk (either because accounts are anonymous or because it is difficult for the authorities to apprehend ringleaders or find the key people responsible for group narratives online). For some individuals, communication with an online researcher might present an opportunity to expose corruption or criminal activity. Political and religious dissidents or human rights advocates might choose to get involved in research as part of a drive to end the silence and isolation felt by victims of oppression. In China, Mexico and Indonesia, for example, political resistance online has led to phrases like 'Internet War'. Qualitative researchers might choose to investigate the substantive issues involved or the processes of resistance in general, or online resistance in particular.

In the examples looked at so far, CMC can be seen as an alternative method of gathering information which exists independently of the technology (although, in many cases, it is the only practical method of doing this). However, CMC has also led to the generation of a mass of new information and even new communities which are of value and interest to the qualitative researcher. CMC could be considered the natural if not the only way of accessing the following areas:

Interest Groups A variety of online formats, such as chat rooms, mailing lists, BBSs and conferences, focus on specific topics, drawing together geographically dispersed participants who may share interests, experiences or expertise (Denzin, 1999; O'Connor and Madge, 2000; Sharf, 1999). Researchers may join (or establish) a group which comes together with special interests in mind (Comley, 1996). With a growing total of over 25,000 newsgroups accessible to more than 40 million users (Kennedy, 2000), the Internet is an extremely convenient way of identifying people with similar interests. Researchers may make preliminary enquiries about the breadth and depth of messages in any newsgroup area by investigating an archive called DejaNews[2] which contains a record of every single post to any newsgroup made within the last four years.

Education, Business and Helpservices Online The exponential growth rate in distance learning worldwide will continue to spur online research into quality control (Parkany and Swan, 1999; Furneaux[3]), user satisfaction, including gendered experience (Ferganchick-Neufang, 1998; Smith-Stoner and Weber, 2000) and communication (Colomb and Simutis, 1996; Murphy and Collins, 1997) in this educational environment. The Internet is also established in business settings. It is not surprising that Comley (1996) mentioned research in business environments, research on employees, and research on early adopters of new technology as appropriate target sampling groups for data collection using the Internet. Targeting people who have used Web sites linked to work (and leisure) has been one way qualitative market researchers have recruited e-commerce clients or participants for business-to-business research (Sweet, 1999). Another growth industry is online helpservices and researchers have investigated both email (Hahn, 1998) and Web site (O'Connor and Madge,

2000) options. There are, of course, substantial areas of professional activity (such as planning a company merger, composing evidence to use against a police suspect, or interpreting a patient's medical chart) which are currently inaccessible to research using CMC. However, new technology and increasing social acceptance of CMC as a routine communication medium in most organizational settings will gradually (and probably rapidly) open up new possibilities for research in the mainstream of life (see Chapter 10).

Support Groups Support groups increasingly use the online environment to offer affirmation, consolation and understanding to individuals in distressed or vulnerable situations, such as rape survivors, cancer patients, the bereaved and individuals coping with addictions (see Wallace, 1999: 190–206). However, ethical issues arise if 'in the spirit of therapeutic alliance and human catharsis' vulnerable people share their feelings in online groups without realizing that their words may be heard, and even used, by researchers who have not sought prior permission (Sharf, 1999). (See discussion in Chapter 3.)

Outsider Accounts Traditionally marginalized social groups have seized on CMC to pursue their own interests and agendas. Gays and lesbians have found a safe and uncritical venue where they can socialize without inhibition (Correll, 1995). For emerging new subcultural phenomena, loosely referred to as cyberculture (Rucker *et al.*, 1992), the medium is integral to the development of their communities. At the same time, one of the most worrying aspects of Internet use has been the growth of groups who use the absence of censorship to express extreme forms of prejudice and deviance. As these groups exist, researchers may wish to contact them to investigate the social issues involved.

Playground The Internet offers access to previously unknown phenomena of 'virtual reality' through MU* environments (see Technology Introduction). Researchers can contact users who have taken the opportunity to play with online lives and identities in virtual sites (see Sempsey (1997) for a literature review). Such sites include a house (Bruckman, 1992), a café (Correll, 1995), towns (Horn, 1998; Rheingold, 1994) and fantasy settings such as dungeons-and-dragons games and *Star Trek* fantasy role playing (such as TrekMUSE).

Cost and Time Savings

The issue of reduced costs is one of the most powerful advantages of Internet use for qualitative researchers (and one that may increasingly encourage research sponsors to enquire whether conventional fieldwork could not be conducted through CMC). Once computer software and hardware have been bought, the principal expenses for CMC are ISP fees and telephone costs. In some parts of the world phone calls for Internet use are already free and, in a highly competitive and rapidly changing market, free ISP access is becoming increasingly available. For individuals with institutional access to the Internet (through education or employment) the cost to themselves and their project is zero. Savings for the researcher can also be made in the following areas:

Time and Travel With conventional FTF interviewing, time and travel expenses need to be considered for both researchers and participants. Often, this will lead to compromise in regard to where interviews are held and with whom. Maximum participation rates often depend on minimizing the travel costs and time input of participants. For some participants, such as senior citizens, more expensive transport such as taxis may be needed for reasons of mobility and safety. For others, such as high-level executives, it is the time element which is crucial.

These problems are compounded as the research extends further afield. Interstate or inter-regional comparisons increase time and expense as the researcher and/or participants have to travel to different locations and conduct multiple sessions. Transcultural participation and cross-cultural comparisons are not a viable option for most conventional research budgets. Online research eliminates the cost (and time) barriers presented by travel. In the Young People and Health Risk study, Internet technology enabled online focus groups to be conducted across four countries throughout the Western Pacific region with minimal travel costs.

Venue Hire Venues for FTF interviews need to be easily accessible to participants in terms of location, timing (before work, evenings, after dropping children at nursery), lifestyle (some participants may require a crèche, others may need on-site venues in businesses, schools or hospitals, others may have special needs such as sign language interpreters) and physical access (participants may need to avoid stairs or need wheelchair access). Researchers will also have their own requirements for FTF venues depending upon the nature of the research (such as on site if studying a nursing home, or in a neutral location if studying abused wives). The requirements of researcher and participant(s) can lead to costs in terms of the time to organize (and frequently reorganize) venues, as well as the hire costs themselves.

With online participation, the venue becomes the sites at which CMC is available. There may still be site hire costs (such as usage rates in cybercafés) and there will still be considerations about the impact of the venue (is computer access in a public, professional or home context?). In practical terms, however, many of the difficulties and financial considerations of organizing FTF venues disappear.

Tape Recording/Production/Transcription Costs FTF interviews require a good-quality tape recorder and a plentiful supply of tapes and batteries. For focus groups and other multiple participant interviews, the purchase and set-up of high-powered recording equipment can constitute a significant cost in the overall research budget. In almost all cases the recordings must be transcribed (typically about 4 to 6 hours' labour for a 90 minute tape). With online research, on the other hand, interaction results in the immediate production of a text file. There is no need to budget for recording equipment, transcribing equipment or transcription costs. Delays caused by transcription are also eliminated.

A Word of Caution Casey Sweet, an experienced 'in-person' and 'online' focus group moderator, has pointed out that, in large online market research studies, recruitment, incentive packages and the rental of facilities which allow virtual focus groups to take place all involve costs. In fact, the very possibility of technological access to large numbers of people may lead to initial over-recruitment as the researcher chases an 'ideal profile' for participants. In addition, the ability to act as an online moderator requires training (which can involve costs) and this might include increasing levels of computer literacy (which would not be necessary for an FTF researcher). There are clear financial savings to be made in many aspects of online research, but it would be a mistake to consider it cost free.

Eliminating Transcription Bias

There is agreement among many qualitative researchers that analysis of textual data is more effective and reliable if the text of the whole interview is available (Seidman, 1991; Briggs, 1986). Seidman claims that participants' thoughts 'become embodied in their words. To substitute the researcher's paraphrasing or summaries of what the participants say for their actual words is to substitute the researcher's consciousness for that of the participant' (Seidman, 1991: 87).

However, transcription of verbal interviews is either expensive if others are hired to do it (see above), or exhausting if researchers take on the task themselves. For instance, characteristic speech patterns (umm-ing and err-ing; stopping and starting) are difficult to transcribe because choices have to be made about whether some material is redundant. In a one-to-one interview, problems of accent or lack of clarity can lead to delay or transcription mistakes. In group interviews, multiple voices often speak simultaneously, which makes accurate transcription even harder. In view of these difficulties, a desire to save money (or a waning of enthusiasm) can tempt researchers to preselect and transcribe only sections of the interview. Seidman warns against this corner-cutting because there is a temptation for researchers to impose a frame of reference too early, and there is often a disinclination to return to untranscribed sections of the tape at a later date.

In contrast, the digitally generated script is a verbatim account of the whole interview. The script is complete and immediately available for analysis. Nothing is left out – a most unlikely state of affairs in FTF research. If participants wish to check for accuracy or if researchers wish to display their original sources to demonstrate their 'accountability to the data' (Seidman 1991: 87), there is a complete record of the original interaction.

Are there other practical benefits of this automated process? Lindlof (1995: 210) suggests that a quick turn-around time for data makes best use of the 'researcher's contextual memory'. This means that quick and easy access to the script adds to a more comprehensive understanding of the research interaction. A participant's mood and demeanour may be better recalled, as well as events preceding and following the interview and other factors which may affect the interpretation of the voices and interaction. Lindlof claims that, when the transcription of an interview is delayed, it is not unusual for researchers to change their perceptions of who said what and, more importantly, the context in which something was discussed.

With CMC, background clues which rely on visual or aural information are not available in the first place, so rapid access to online accounts offers no advantages in terms of contextual memory. On the other hand, online scripts *do* offer complete recall of online interviews. All available contextual material is located, and remains located, within the text. Online researchers might take notes about which participants asked preliminary clarifying questions (or sent post-interaction challenges or elaborations) but it is the body of the interaction, found within the individual messages, which provides content and context. CMC also offers the advantage that (deception apart) the researcher is no longer in any doubt about who said what; textual data are directly linked to individual usernames or email addresses. In addition the electronic script can provide other useful information such as the timing of messages and details of who has joined and left a forum.

An automatic script, desirable as it sounds, does not abolish all research tasks and responsibilities nor does it address all research concerns. For instance, researchers may still decide to edit texts for the sake of focus or clarity. (See also Chapter 3 for a discussion of decisions regarding the ethical editing of texts.) Most importantly of all, although CMC provides a complete script ready for analysis, we need to consider the quality of the data provided in this way (see Chapters 8 and 9).

Easier Handling of Data

Qualitative research projects usually require a great deal of organization of data. Keeping track of participants' personal information, making fieldnotes of ideas in progress and managing the data collected prior to and during analysis are paramount concerns. Many researchers are turning to computers to assist with these practical issues. In a 1991 survey of qualitative researchers, three-quarters reported using software for data entry, coding, search and retrieval, display and concept building (Miles and Huberman, 1994). Electronic software can facilitate the analysis process in various ways (Creswell, 1998; Fielding and Lee, 1998; Tesch, 1990). Fielding reviewed a range of qualitative software, and with some provisos concluded that: 'The software offers several advantages: it facilitates chores of data management which are tedious and subject to error when done manually; it makes the analytic process more "transparent" and reviewable; and it offers support for new approaches to analysis or approaches that would be very cumbersome if done manually' (1999: 96).

These possibilities are a positive feature in terms of online research. The large databases made possible when gathering data electronically makes the organization, storage and analysis of data important issues. However, the technological base of the medium means that textual data from research interactions can be moved effortlessly into other computer functions. Electronic mail has itself been defined as the entry, storage, processing, distribution and reception, from one account to one or more accounts, of digitized text by means of a central computer (Rice *et al.*, 1990). Electronic messages can be recalled on a computer monitor, printed out as hard copy or stored on floppy or compact discs. Text can be saved and accessed in word processing packages or moved directly into qualitative analysis software. Computers do not provide 'answers' for qualitative researchers but, used judiciously, they can assist research processes – and CMC, more than any other type of communication, can capitalize on the speed and flexibility computers can offer.

The Participant's Perspective

Participant Friendly CMC is user-friendly in terms of making rapid connections between individuals in an environment of their own choosing. Cambridge University students liked using email as a research method because they found it 'convenient, quite quick, available whenever we want to speak to you, environmentally not-quite-as-damaging-as-most-things, and free' (Graduates of the Millennium project (GOTM) student). Above all it eliminated the 'hassle' of finding pen and paper, buying stamps and keeping FTF appointments.

With all forms of CMC, participants avoid the problems which can complicate FTF meetings with researchers outside the house, such as difficulties in finding the venue, arranging cover for a sick child, car breakdown or traffic problems and so on. In contrast, they can participate at their convenience from their own home or place of work. Unlike the phone, electronic communication need not be intrusive or peremptory. With asynchronous forms, messages wait until the receiver is ready to attend to them. This makes it an ideal 'on the job' option. Users can do other work in between sessions of conducting conversations, since cutting off a computer conversation or delaying a response is more acceptable than abruptly interrupting an FTF conversation (Murray, 1991). One online focus group researcher recorded some of the activities that accompanied group interaction where participants were based at home. Although participants might 'have pizza delivered, braid a child's hair, yell at their husband about laundry' (Sweet, 1999: *personal email*), they were still able to take part in the group discussion.

Conducive to Easy Dialogue CMC is seen to be accessible to the everyday writer who might wish to write conversationally rather than in a self-consciously literary style. Mullan, an English lecturer, suggested that: 'The very software seems to encourage a flow of words. It allows for only the most basic text, with none of the word-processing facilities that have led us to expect a gloss finish from any transcript. There is no underlining, or block lettering, or trickery with fonts and indentation. And no spell check. Indeed, it is becoming usual for emails to leave a scatter of typos uncorrected, as if the mistakes told you of the immediacy of the message'[4]. Although it remains to be seen whether these conventions (or rather the lack of them) will change as email software develops, at the moment the method offers a minimally judgemental arena for writing styles. (These issues are discussed further in Chapter 8.)

Testing Ideas Many people see using CMC as a good way to test out ideas, form opinions, sharpen arguments and to say what they genuinely think in an informal or even anonymous setting. For instance, several students in the Graduates of the Millennium study suggested that people 'wouldn't speak their mind' in FTF interviews, which would produce 'less honest responses'. Online debates might take place between researcher and participant, or in a wider context such as chat rooms, as part of newsgroup lists, or in the more structured format of an online focus group. In addition, colleagues from different parts of the world can share research ideas and resources, allowing them to collaborate on projects and to deepen discussion and analysis (Sproull and Kiesler, 1991).

Safe Environment CMC offers women, older people and socially marginalized groups the potential to communicate in a familiar and physically safe environment. Some women to women communication has relaxed into a kitchen table atmosphere ('nattering on the net'; Spender, 1995); while lesbians have enjoyed a freedom of sexual expression online (Correll, 1995). Participants from these kinds of groups might be more inclined to open up to a researcher online than FTF.

Extending the Research Population So far we have assumed that the potential population for any research project is those people who already have access to the Internet. It would, of course, be possible to design a study which included bringing the Internet to those who do not yet have it. Clearly, this introduces problems in terms of the cost of providing equipment and training. But evidence suggests that initiating Internet use can be very successful. Even for people with low computer literacy, it does not take long to learn how to operate a Web browser, access Web pages or send an email. Specialized focus group software is designed to lead participants carefully through the interview process (see Chapter 5).

Challenges of Using CMC

Computer Literacy for the Researcher

Clearly, running a CMC-based research project requires some degree of technical expertise on the part of the researcher. The precise degree depends on the methods being used, but we would argue that, for example, using email or accessing chat groups is no more complex than word processing (although survey design is more challenging, see Chapter 4). Even if the researcher has not acquired the skills already they can be quickly learned. (Researchers' experiences of acquiring Internet expertise are discussed in Chapter 6.)

Focus Group Moderator Training

Working with real-time chat requires moderators to be reasonably fast on the keyboard. Specific data handling skills or software programs (such as for focus groups) may require additional training. The moderator has to learn all the ins and outs of a focus group facility if used (see Technology Introduction) and/or the capabilities provided by the chosen software (see Chapter 5). In this ever changing field, a moderator may also be advised to attend or participate in online research conferences to gain exposure to alternative practices and further knowledge. Although training may be expensive, many focus group moderators consider it essential (Sweet, 1999).

Making Contact and Recruitment

Establishing contact for individual person-to-person CMC usually involves a mutual exchange of email addresses (see below). Communicating with groups may involve assembling a 'list' of individual email addresses which are known only to the researcher (as Mann did in the Graduates of the Millennium project), or joining a previously established mailing list whose addresses are made available to all. A third option, adapted by Ferri (2000), is to create a closed list (only participants are subscribed) arranging for all messages to be sent to the researcher in the first instance. Ferri then stripped all messages of identifying information before forwarding them in digest form to all participants.

Recruitment from previously established lists is not without difficulties. Advertising the research in, for instance, relevant newsgroups requires a 'hook' which will attract attention. For instance, Coomber (1997) used the following subject heading when targeting drug dealers: *Have You Ever Sold Powdered Drugs? If So, I Would Like Your Help*. In a different context (an electronic support group) the following catchy heading sought the attention of readers: *My Story - My Pain - No Answers* (Galegher *et al.*, 1998). Coomber (1997) also suggested that recruitment messages should be posted on a weekly basis, as newsgroup posts are gradually replaced and new visitors visit sites all the time. Researchers with more technological expertise may also set up Web sites with 'hotlinks' that draw in potential participants (O'Connor and Madge, 2000).

Researchers could also target individuals in newsgroups by writing to the private email addresses which are generally attached to their postings. Coomber (1997) argued that this is not an unreasonable step to take as users are clearly interested in the subject area and they have provided a means for others to make personal contact. However, there can be problems if the researcher moves directly to sending research materials without first gaining each user's consent. Foster (1994) was a member of several 'list serve' groups and decided to take advantage of his membership to extend his research programme. He sent a message incorporating questions to many lists in an attempt to find possible participants. His 'cold calling' or 'spamming' met with a range of responses. In one group a 'moderator' (responsible for intercepting messages and deciding on their legitimacy in terms of the group's agenda) blocked the message. In other groups, some contacts filled out the survey, others refused politely, and others strongly objected to this use of list serve groups. One recipient suggested that a more appropriate approach would have been to send out a short message describing the study and asking interested people to request a copy of the survey via private mail (1994: 96). Given that sensitivity in making contact is a crucial aspect of building good research relationships in qualitative research, the final suggestion seems appropriate. More detailed discussion about access and recruitment is found in Chapter 4 and, for focus groups, in Chapter 5.

Finding Email Addresses

The easiest way to find someone's email address is to ask them. There is not yet a fully developed global, or even national, directory of email addresses. There is no central list of email addresses on the Net, although a few world email sites have email directories[5]. Unfortunately it is almost impossible to obtain such lists commercially (companies such as Bigfoot will not supply them). Currently no UK ISP rents out lists. One positive development, however, is that academic, business and governmental institutions now routinely add email addresses to postal addresses and phone numbers on their business cards, advertising and stationery.

There are further problems. An electronic address must be completely accurate. Common addressing problems are: mis-spellings or incomplete email names; participants giving Web site locations rather than email addresses; fictitious addresses (such as santa@greenland); or confusion caused when someone changes their ISP. With the postal system, an improperly addressed letter may still be delivered correctly, but an incorrectly addressed electronic message will either not be delivered or go to the wrong place. 'Smart software may eventually mimic the forgiving character of the postal system, but for now, accuracy in addressing is mandatory' (Morrisett, 1996: *online*). On the other hand mails with non-existent addresses do get sent back (bounce), so at least a researcher will realize the message did not arrive.

Even if a researcher has the correct email address, not all people who have an address check their email regularly. 'There are even those who actually have had an address allocated to them but have no idea how to use it' (Foster, 1994: 94).

Ensuring Co-operation

Even if the technology is available, it is important to remember that many individuals (and some nations) do not share the enthusiasm for the Internet and CMC that is suggested by usage statistics. As Fulk *et al.* discovered, some people did not enjoy electronic talk, experienced new contacts with outsiders as threatening and time consuming, and were afraid that 'creating permanent written text exposed them to criticism or perhaps ridicule' (1992: 17). Other participants might be happy in principle to work in the electronic environment, but the usual problems of ensuring co-operation in a potentially demanding area like qualitative research remain.

One key consideration is to keep in mind the 'price tag' that is often attached to participation in research (in terms of participants' time, cash and energy). In conventional market research, small rewards for co-operation are frequently offered (such as cash or free samples). These may be difficult, although not impossible, to arrange in online research. For example, Sweet (1999: *personal email*) reports that 'incentive payments' for market research can take place in a number of ways. First, cheques can be mailed to participants (if their street addresses are known). Second, special electronic arrangements can be established. Respondents might be given the equivalent of, say, $30 in credit, to be used at a specified online shopping site. Third, there could be a 'point program', where participants are able to earn points which can then be exchanged for purchases, either on- or offline

'Scholarly' research usually attempts to enlist the altruistic support of the participant (Wilson, 1996). This may have proved surprisingly easy in the early days of some online communities. The ideological stance of the original 'netizens'[6] was that users should utilize new technologies to make the world a better place by making their unique contributions available to everyone else (Licklider and Taylor, 1968). (This approach is linked to ideas of the democratization possibilities of the Internet which we discuss in Chapter 7.) However, even the most idealistic users admit that if Internet access has to be paid for, as on the commercial networks, 'the Netiquette of being helpful would have a price tag attached to it' (quoted in Hauben and Hauben, 1998: *online*).

Wilson's view is that neither market nor academic research will achieve good response rates if the research is not seen to be directly relevant to people's lives (1996: 97). However, the skills of the researcher may also have a bearing. As market researcher Sweet described, 'I am constantly asking people to discuss subjects they probably rarely need to discuss or have the inclination to discuss. Sometimes it takes people a while to warm up but once a context is set and the discussion opened there is a flow of opinions' (1999: *personal email*).

It seems that, as with most research projects, it is the subject matter of the research which will attract participants – and their experiences of the research process which will earn their continued participation (as we shall see in the following chapters). One way that researchers may ensure initial and continuing co-operation from participants is by attending to rules of netiquette which are often common across different sections of users (see Chapter 3). For instance, netiquette suggests that users do not advertise or make commercial or self-seeking postings. As we saw in the discussion of making contact above, people may become increasingly frustrated by unsolicited mail and the information overload it presents. Researchers may find they are 'simply ignored by the deluged recipient at the other end of the line' (Selwyn and Robson, 1998).

Interactive Skills Online

Until voice recognition systems become more practical, CMC is limited to participants with a certain degree of conventional and computer literacy. Even at university level not all participants have computer and Internet expertise:

> I did gather wadges of leaflets for complete beginners but they all start something like, 'Now, first your filemanager account access server must be inputted to the hardware PC installations ROM system; next, download your DOS to the main network icon drive...' ... A computer is a big beige box on another beige box with a magic typewriter in front, and what I want to know is what key to hit and what colour the screen is supposed to go. Tuesday I changed my password without realising, Wednesday I had someone else's email (?), and today I had kangaroos bounding across my screen while the message "resistance is futile!" flashed at me and the computer (apparently) trashed everything it had on it ... (GOTM student)

Low technical skills, particularly keyboarding skills, may marginalize some participants who might feel unable, or too embarrassed, to take a full part. If nervous participants do come forward, researchers can take steps to remove some of the mystique of the method. A focus group moderator can also alleviate some literacy concerns by displaying a 'welcome message' assuring people that spelling and grammar are not important.

However, even if basic levels of conventional and computer literacy are available, concerns remain relating to the interpersonal style of both participants and researcher. Qualitative research relies on the development of rapport, a mutual respect arising between researcher and participant(s). In FTF research, the establishment of rapport depends to a great extent on communication skills such as well-timed responses, appropriate vocabulary, and verbal and non-verbal paralinguistic cues. With CMC, the only effective interactive skill is verbal communication. This threatens to disadvantage researchers and participants who express themselves in different ways. 'Fine, if you like words and know how to use them to express yourself. Forget it, if you communicate primarily through facial expression, body language, voice intonation and silence.'

Similarly, in an online group context, skills in written language are the only means of ensuring participation. In oral discussions there may be a struggle to be heard, but in CMC there is no assurance that you will be read. As Colomb and Simutis point out, 'What counts as "gaining the floor" in CMC is that one's message draws a response' (1996: 208). Researchers and participants 'must make themselves heard in a situation in which no one knows they want to speak or has any obligation to notice that they have spoken' (Galegher *et al.*, 1998: 510). Messages that are most frequently rewarded by responses tend to be witty, controversial, intriguing and relevant to an ongoing discussion (which may itself be part of a cluster of concurrent discussions sometimes called 'threads'). Even when messages are sent by someone with authority, participants will not rush to gain the floor if topics are boring or not presented in a stimulating way (Colomb and Simutis, 1996: 209–210). (These issues will be discussed at length later in the book.)

Losing Access

A key challenge for online studies is to sustain electronic connection with participants for the whole period of the research (Bennett, 1998). Internet 'churn' or defection refers to people who gain, and later lose, Internet access. For example, in a recontact study in the UK and Canada, CommerceNet/Nielson (1996) found that 21% of those who had Internet access in the first period of the study were no longer online seven to eight months later. Similarly, in a survey of final year students at the University of Ulster, it was reported that even though these students enjoyed free Internet access at university, most would have lost online access completely after leaving college (Kingsley and Anderson, 1998). This happened even though a significant proportion of the students valued email, with nearly half of the sample reporting that their closest friends also held email accounts.

There are, however, some ways round this dilemma (see Technology Introduction). For example, it is now commonplace for search engines and online companies to provide email accounts free of charge (for example, Hotmail, INAME, Excite, Yahoo). Also there is a move to personal accounts which are not associated with life changes related to institutions or other sites. For many people, an email address may soon be considered a permanent feature which stays constant even when changes in employment, marriage or resettlement affect their postal address or phone number. It remains to be seen how much of a problem keeping an email address will be in the future.

Internet Access and Usage

Who Is the Potential Research Community?

The first practical consideration for qualitative researchers who are considering using the Internet as a research tool is to identify the potential research community. With conventional research participants may, in principle, be drawn from anywhere (although finance, distance and/or language differences will in practice limit the scope of the research). For research using CMC, however, the participant pool is limited from the outset. In this section we shall consider the restrictions that researchers face when designing a research project with a population of Internet users.

One difficulty in writing about this area is the sheer speed with which Internet usage has grown and, indeed, the rapid pace of change of the technology itself (Coffman and Odlyzko, 1998). Statements made now may appear ridiculous in just a couple of years time – but we shall review the situation as it appears at the beginning of the year 2000. Researchers who wish to check up-to-date demographic material of all kinds will find Web sites the most useful source of information[8].

It is the unrepresentativeness of current Internet access which remains the greatest problem for data collection. Microsoft's Bill Gates has admitted that, in terms of the Internet, the problem of 'the haves versus the have-nots has many dimensions: rich versus poor, urban versus rural, young versus old, and perhaps most dramatically, developing countries versus developed countries' (Gates, 1997: 34). As Thimbleby (1998: *online*) pithily remarked, 'serfs don't surf'. Qualitative researchers need to be aware that access to the Internet is a matter not only of economics, but also of one's place in the world in terms of gender, culture, ethnicity and language.

Variations in Usage Rates Worldwide

Given that only approximately 0.01% of the world's population is currently online, it is not surprising that some writers focus on the 'cyberspace divide' (Loader, 1998). One commentator (Hess, 1995: 16) sees the online world as 'an elite space, a playground for the privileged'. He concludes, 'There is a global glass ceiling, and for many in the world a large part of ... technoculture lies well above it'. International levels of Internet use are only beginning to be collectively published and in order to establish any global overview of usage, a range of sources needs to be relied upon. Estimates vary greatly and figures change rapidly. For example, Headcount International Communications reported 102 million Internet users in June 1998. Datamonitor[9] predicts that the number of global Internet users will reach 545 million by 2003, surpassing the number of PCs installed globally.

These numbers are spread unevenly between countries, and finance is not the only factor involved in the disparity of usage (Jordan, 1999). As English has become the dominant language on the Internet (Thimbleby, 1998), accounting for about 90% of all interaction, this presents a language barrier for many potential users (as it might for many researchers). In some countries (such as France) there is also a reluctance to participate in what is sometimes seen as US cultural imperialism with regard to the global Internet. Even in countries where there is Internet access, researchers need to examine the context in which the technology is used. For instance: Is Internet use within a country familiar or novel? Is it welcomed or viewed with suspicion (as in Japan; Aoki, 1994). Is it available to all or the province of a few? Is it expensive, becoming quite cheap, or free? Is access only institutional (available through networked academic, governmental or business communities) or public (available in libraries, computer laboratories or cybercafés) – or will individuals have the flexibility of freely available personal use (at home or, using mobile systems, anywhere at all)? These considerations will have an impact on research design, affecting its feasibility at many levels.

In the USA and much of Europe the Internet is widely seen as a mass medium. It is used by the public for business and pleasure and is no longer the specialist preserve of academics, scientists and 'net nerds'. The USA, as might be expected, has shown exponential growth in usage in both the private and public spheres. In June 1999, the number of users aged 16 years and over was estimated at 92 million (Headcount International Communications). Of these users, 27% had Internet access in their homes. In the UK there has been a similar explosion in Internet usage. For example, the *Which? Online 1999* Internet report[10] estimated that about 10 million people in the UK have access to the Internet – an increase of 50% from the previous year. A *Guardian*/ICM poll (1999) predicted that by the year 2000, nearly half of the UK population would be online, with home-based Internet access at 14%. In some Scandinavian countries, such as Sweden, home use of computers is already at 21%.

In other parts of the world such as Australasia there are expected to be 24 million users by the year 2001. In Australia itself, there are currently more than 1 million users. What is more telling, perhaps, is that this represents a 280% increase compared to the rate of usage in 1996 (Headcount International Communications). In China, there are approximately 1.2 million Internet accounts which are shared by many users; a cybercafé craze is sweeping the country and giving public Internet access to much of the population.

Nevertheless, there are many countries where using CMC as a general research tool would not be practical, although it might be appropriate for conducting email interviews with select individuals who *are* online (Ryen and Silverman, 2000). In developing nations access to the Internet is strictly limited. Contributory factors include the cost of access, limited technological skills, as well as an inadequate telecommunications infrastructure (such as unreliable phone lines and power supplies) and outdated computer hardware equipment (Ott, 1998; Holderness, 1999). Thus, despite being some of the most populated parts of the world, both Africa (see Hall, 1998) and South America currently have relatively low rates of Internet usage. For example, in December 1998 it was estimated that there were only 2 million users in South America (Headcount International Communications. See Headcount.com). In Africa, in 1999, there were thought to be 1.2 million users, but 85% of these were in South Africa (Connect-World Africa, http://Connect-World.com). Leaving South Africa aside, the possibilities of Internet use are constrained by the small number of computers in the region, with an average computer density of one per thousand (ibid.) Even where there is some access, as in Jamaica, the consideration that the technology is inappropriate in view of the country's lifestyle and local needs (Dyrkton, 1996) might deter some researchers.

In other countries government regulatory barriers form an obstacle to Internet access and/or use. Namibia has tried to quash Internet use; Syria is agonizing over whether to introduce it. China has sought to limit its use, seeing unfettered communication as a weapon of subversion in the hands of dissidents. Although Internet cafés have recently been opened in Saudi Arabia all connections are routed through the state proxy server where technicians can block 'bad sites' (in terms of politics and religious orthodoxies). Use of cybercafés reflects the strict taboo against the mixing of the sexes and special annexes allow women to surf alone, or in the company of male relatives[11]. In a contradictory stance, while planning to wire all households by 2000, Singapore has also imposed restraints upon Internet sites which have political and/or religious content (Herschlag, 1997). Even in Australia, federal legislation has recently been introduced whereby local ISPs are responsible for censoring sensitive material.

Access and Socio-economic Background

Even within countries, the Internet is not an egalitarian technology (see studies by Haddon, 1992; Kendall, 1999; Turkle and Papert, 1990; Silverstone and Hirsch, 1992). A full understanding of usage requires examination of economic and social class issues of access to technology and electronic communication (Anderson *et al.*, 1994; Teo, 1998).

Access to a computer at home and work is highly correlated with household income and socio-economic background (Graham and Marvin, 1996). In addition, as Fernback and Thompson (1995) reported, participation in CMC itself depends upon finance, the intellectual accessibility of the software and interaction – and time to take part. In one US national public opinion survey, a 'digital divide' was found with Internet users being generally wealthier and more highly educated (Katz and Aspden, 1997).

Kendall (1999) drew on a range of survey reports to compile a breakdown of Internet usage in the USA. The reports suggested that approximately half of US Internet users had some college experience; about 18–26% also had some postgraduate education. More than 60% of users were from the higher paid end of white-collar jobs. Similarly, in the UK, one in three from the professional and managerial classes were online at home compared with 16% of all white-collar workers and only 2% of the semi-skilled and unemployed (*Guardian*/ICM poll, 1999).

There were also differences in online participation at work. Kendall (1999) noted that participation in the online forum she was researching depended upon being available at the forum's most social times (weekday afternoons). She concluded that much synchronous interaction online depended upon users having jobs in which they could control the timing and pace of their work. This pointed to the participation of users with professional or technical jobs rather than occupations where there was supervision or surveillance. Reflecting on the elite nature of this professional usage, Hess described access to the Internet as 'the new secret handshake' of the business world (Hess, 1995: 474).

However, in countries where Internet access is becoming cheaper, and also associated with leisure technology like TV, the profile of users will change. European research also points to a growing trend for communities to find ways to compensate for IT deficiencies among their citizens (see the Virtual Society? programme)[12]. It is difficult now to generalize about who will make use of the Internet in the future. But it seems highly probable that, in time, researchers will have access to participants who choose to pursue a wide variety of online interests and activities in their free time – and that these participants will come from all walks of life.

Access and Gender

Our culture has created a very real difference in computer expertise: more men than women are more knowledgeable about computers. Estimates of women online vary dramatically. In 1994, a figure of 10–15% was suggested (Shade, 1994). By 1999, a study of the figures available from multiple sources indicated that between 31% and 45% of US women were online, the higher percentage possibly including women who were not active users (Kendall, 1999). In countries where Internet access is common, differentials in gender use are particularly marked in workplace and home use.

While approximately 25% of men have Internet access at work in the UK, this compares to only 18% of women. The discrepancy was particularly marked in the 25–34 year group. There is evidence that the Internet has become a work tool and pleasure toy for 20 to 30 year-old men with about 33% of this age group using it at work (*Guardian*/ICM poll, 1999). In the USA, Kendall (1999) noted that the most active participants of the online forum she was investigating were men logging on at work. Findings suggested that more men than women had sole use of a computer at home and, even in households with joint ownership of a computer, 18% of men enjoyed home use compared with only 11% of women (*Guardian*/ICM poll, 1999).

Various reasons are put forward to explain the differences in Internet use between genders. Some authors point to the fact that the Internet originated in the Department of Defense (Ferganchick-Neufang, 1998; Spender, 1997). Others suggest that it is a consequence of the masculinist nature of computer technology in general (Kramarae and Kramer, 1995; Wajcman, 1991). Some studies suggest that there are significant gender differences in use of computers, computer literacy, exposure to computers and usage motives (Bannert and Arbinger, 1996). The historical predominance of men using first computers, and then the Internet, might affect both women's desire for access and their experiences online.

> Women are currently making numerous important contributions to the computer field and in on-line communities, and the proportion of their contributions continues to rise. Currently, however, just as in our larger society, public and professional space on-line remains male-dominated ... virtual reality is still seen as a masculine space, and both real and perceived differences in computer expertise between the sexes may contribute to discrimination against women on-line ... Though the number of women on-line continues to rise ... this increase has not eliminated sexual bias and discrimination. (Ferganchick-Neufang, 1998: *online*)

If 'the stereotypes glorify men's role in and exclude women by definition from the "information age" it is not surprising that women may be more reluctant to go on-line, less confident of their abilities when they do so, less participatory in on-line group discussions' (Herring, 1996a: 105). It is clear that male domination of cyberspace might affect both the fora of interest available for qualitative study (male issues and leisure preferences) and the nature of interpersonal interaction that might arise between researcher and participants, or between participants. (These issues will be explored in greater depth in Chapter 7.)

However, there is evidence that gender balance and cultures online may be changing. The US research firm eMarketer predicts that the number of women online will rise to 51% by 2002 (Derkley, 1998). In Australia, the percentage of women Internet users doubled between 1997 and 1998 (to 37% of users). According to Derkley (1998) this suggests that women are flocking to the Net as 'the biggest and best networking tool around'. Following Spender (1997), Stewart *et al.* (1998) also noted that the Internet is eminently suitable for the conversations of (young) women. It is perhaps not surprising that studies are beginning to report not only high rates of usage for women but also their enjoyment and satisfaction. Indeed, some authors suggest that women now feel freer to express opinions online than FTF (Haraway, 1991). Although prejudice against female users is still evident in traditional male strongholds of computer science and technology (see Chapter 7), women in most areas of business and social life use CMC in the same ubiquitous and unremarked way that they use the phone. This suggests that the perspectives of women may, after all, be readily accessed through this medium.

Access and Ethnicity

Lockard (1996) claims that the online world has an unmistakable 'Euro-American whiteness', which would present a severe limitation for qualitative researchers. Partly this a question of who is online. A survey of black US hackers pointed to a prominent racial/ethnic divide between Internet-aware and non-aware respondents (Wynter, 1996). In another study, blacks and Hispanics were found to be disproportionately unaware of the Internet, irrespective of age or education, relative to whites (Katz and Aspden, 1997).

But there is also the question of online culture. Even when ethnic minorities in the USA did participate, some found that other users assumed that everyone online was part of the dominant white racial group (Kendall, 1999), a hegemony generally manifested by the noticeable absence of discussions about race and ethnicity online (Lockard, 1996: 227). Some authors argue that the command structure and logic of the Internet and its operating protocols privilege English-language users (Shields, 1996: 126). This would also have a discriminating impact on ethnic minorities within predominantly white western countries for whom English is not a first language.

However, some studies have focused on intercultural communication between, for instance, East Asian and North American students (Ma, 1996) or have looked at virtual communities within a discrete culture such as Japan (Aoki, 1994). It remains to be seen how Internet access develops for non-western populations, and western ethnic minorities, in the future.

Access and Age

Survey reports suggest that approximately half of US Internet users are under 35 years of age (Kendall, 1999). However, age and gender may interact, with most 20 to 30 year-old users being male, while 40 year olds and over are mainly female (*Guardian*/ICM poll, 1999). Internet users might cluster in the early twenties but there are increasing patterns of Internet use by children, generally in homes or schools. One report suggested that teenagers and children constitute one of the fastest growing Internet populations with 77 million under 18s expected online globally by 2005[13].

As noted above, it is often cultural enthusiasm for technology which determines the breadth of its usage. In many North American cities, the Internet is freely accessible to children (Shields, 1996: 3). In Sweden, the national post office is so sure that post will be rendered redundant by electronic mail in about eight years that a free email address has been allocated to everyone over the age of 6.

Children might also be accessible through school networks. These 'school nets' have been enthusiastically adopted by the US, Canada, Australia, Japan and the UK. The European Network of Innovative Schools links 600 schools in 19 European countries. In the UK, there are plans to connect schools to a National Grid for Learning and the Internet by 2001. Email is often the most popular application at primary and secondary level. Clearly, there are possibilities for conducting research in some locations with children who are online, but unfettered access to children raises ethical issues for qualitative researchers (see Chapter 3).

At the other end of the age scale there are the 'silver surfers', as 'little old ladies are, for once, the new frontier'[14]. In the UK only 2% of over 55s are connected. Many think they are too old and that it will be too difficult to learn how to use the technology (*Which? Online 1999* Internet Report[15]). In contrast, in the USA, the over-55 market is the fastest growing sector of the Internet population. There are already 8 million Internet users over the age of 50 in a Texas-based 'GrannysRUs Web site'. Many older people online are home users and the technology is frequently provided by relatives to open up email communication within the family (Rheingold, 1994).

Senior citizens are using the Internet in ways which offer great possibilities for qualitative data collection. Hobbies such as genealogical research and writing memoirs can trigger narratives and open possibilities for online interviews. In the UK, Wolf Fm, a community broadcasting project, encouraged older people to use the Internet in a public site. Wolf Fm later published their stories on an internationally available oral history Web site (www.wolf-fm.demon.co.uk). The emotional range of their emailed recollections point to a new genre of oral history online (see Chapter 4).

Future Trends in Technological Access

Since the computer remains a relatively expensive household appliance (or at least one with a lower priority than televisions, washing machines, etc.), uneven distribution of Internet use is to be expected. However, as costs come down and usage grows there could be a pattern of penetration more closely approximating the 90% of households in the USA with access to phones or televisions. In a TV documentary about the history of the Internet, Bill Gates claimed that we are shortly to be living an 'Internet lifestyle' where, alongside the phone and the motor car, the Internet will be expected and accepted as a given. In which case, the Internet may indeed become the first truly 'personal mass medium' (Negroponte, 1995).

For the present, however, online researchers may need to temper over-ambitious plans, while maximizing opportunities with the Internet populations which do currently exist. The rapid growth of the technology will ensure that opportunities continue to expand.

Notes

1   Ramos-Horta, J., 'Site seeing', *Guardian* newspaper, UK, 11 January 1999, p. 12.
2   Find DejaNews at www.dejanews.com.
3   Clare Furneaux is at the Centre for Applied Language Studies, University of Reading, Reading RG6 6WB, UK (www.rdg.ac.uk/AcaDepts/cl/CALS/furneaux.html).
4   Mullan, J., *Guardian* newspaper, UK, 7 September 1998.
5   World Mail Directories include: www.worldemail.com; people.yahoo.com; www.whowhere. com; www.bigfoot.com.
6   Michael Hauben, who has been involved in pioneering interactive online research since the early 1980s, brought the term 'Netizen' (to describe a citizen of the online community) into popular use.
7   Bunting, M., *Guardian* newspaper, UK, 5 January 1999, p. 18.
8   See, for instance, NUA Internet Surveys: www.nua.ie/surveys/ and www.headcount.com/.
9   *Web Site Journal*, 2(34); see: www.WebSiteJournal.com.
10 *Which? Online Report 1999* sub.which.net/producttesting/reports/jul1998wh16t20/ summary2.html.
11 *Guardian* newspaper, UK, 24 July 1999.
12 For more details about this research see: www.brunel.ac.uk/research/virtsoc.
13 Reported in NUA Internet Surveys: www.nua.ie/surveys/.
14 *Guardian* newspaper, UK, 10 June 1999.
15 *Which? Online Report 1999* sub.which.net/producttesting/reports/jul1998wh16t20/ summary2.html.

3 An Ethical Framework

The Internet was once a community of tightly knit academics and scientists with a shared social consensus and, therefore, informal rules of conduct. Now that it has burgeoned into a world of 20 million people, the same destructive and deviant behaviour found in the real world is found in the virtual one. (Murray, 1995: 161)

This quote from Murray alerts us to the fact that online research takes place in an environment with largely customary, as opposed to legally enshrined, laws. As Kitchin (1998) noted, customary laws can represent 'mob rule'. Such laws are not necessarily just and there is little recourse to legal protection if deviant or criminal activity needs to be addressed. In fact, for many, the online world is seen as a place for the transgression of cultural rules and the breaking of taboos (Murray, 1995; Shields, 1996), which raises issues of self-regulation and responsibility for the qualitative researcher. The importance we attach to the legal and ethical issues surrounding Internet research has led us to address these at an early stage in this book. However, the reader may prefer to return to this discussion after considering the methodological areas raised in later chapters.

As Kramarae points out, the nature of law is reflective and responsive, looking to history and tradition and reflecting the status quo: 'But in cyberspace, nothing has been done before. It is an entirely new entity ... electronic communication at the moment exists almost completely outside of our legal universe' (1995: 15). At the same time the Internet *is* becoming subject to legislation, even if the legal status of cyberspace is still uncertain. Many areas need further legal definition including jurisdiction, intellectual property, security (including personal security from virtual assault, harassment and stalking), encryption, signatures and certification (see Thomas *et al.*, 1998, for a review of issues to be addressed).

Why should these issues be of interest to the qualitative researcher? Ackeroyd (1988, 1991) has produced convincing and extensive arguments which address her own question, asking why:

all social scientists, and especially qualitative researchers, need to apprise themselves of the legal conditions and the actual and potential effects of data protection laws, and, in some countries of privacy and analogous laws? (1991: 89)

She concludes that, while qualitative information usually relates to individuals' behaviour, opinions and feelings, and while transcripts and fieldnotes may have different purposes and meanings to 'data' held by governmental and commercial organizations, the fact remains that qualitative material collected by, and manipulated with, computers does not fall outside the scope of the legal system. Indeed, qualitative research, by its very nature, may run up against the law, as the researcher's perceptions of events, people or processes may be seen to contain 'inaccurate information or at least "facts" whose accuracy is potentially challengeable' (1991: 91)

Ackeroyd points out that qualitative data may justify some limited form(s) of exemption from the provisions of data legislation. However, modification to research practices will depend on the legal jurisdiction under which the research falls. In some countries controls are imposed on the collection of data (for instance, researchers may need a licence). In others there may be controls of data usage, handling, security and dissemination. Data protection and privacy laws are being revised continually as law makers attempt to grasp the implications of a global network like the Internet (see Ackeroyd (1991: 94 95) for an overview of the possible content and scope of such laws). At a time of legal uncertainty, a researcher's best strategy is to make clear to participants the legal jurisdiction under which the research is being conducted. However, there may be unprecedented complications for a researcher based in one country and conducting cross-national research. The way forward here is very confused.

Given the legal complications, researchers may feel that laws principally designed to protect information that has been given compulsorily have little application to data arising from voluntary participation in research; and on the other hand, that legislation alone is an inadequate basis for ethical research behaviour. Perhaps the most pragmatic position for the qualitative researcher is to accept that legal and ethical issues intertwine, often in complex ways. In this chapter we attempt to untangle some of these complexities and to suggest ways to move forward. In the first part of the chapter we discuss the application to online qualitative research of the principles of fair information processing that were tendered by Elgesem (1996) in his discussion of computer-related legislation in several countries (cited in Sharf, 1999). In the second part we draw on this discussion to propose some practical guidelines for the conduct of online qualitative research.

Principles of Fair Information Processing Online

Personal Data Should Be Collected for One Specific, Legitimate Purpose

The collection of data in digital form poses new challenges for the qualitative researcher (see Thomas, 1996). In conventional studies, researchers make choices about how (if at all) they will present ongoing research to participants. In an attempt to be as non-interventionist as possible, researchers might disguise the research process altogether (as in participant observation), or emphasize only certain aspects of the research. With sensitive research, which threatens emotional or physical harm to participant(s) or researcher, general rather than specific information might be provided. In many qualitative studies it is difficult to inform participants fully about the research because the focus evolves and sharpens over time. For instance, as with the Graduates of the Millennium project, a contributory element of the research (in this instance the innovative methodology) might, unexpectedly, become a key area of interest.

For many qualitative researchers, the organic nature of the research process is part of its value. However, as more countries move towards regulating the collection of digital data, legislation such as the Data Protection Act in the UK[1] may stipulate that the exact purpose(s) of the research must be made clear from the outset. In the Cambridge University study, students had initially agreed to allow the dissemination of data, in anonymous form, for the purposes of the study. Once it became clear that some of the same data might be used to discuss methodology, rather than the original study issues, fresh permission had to be sought for this new purpose.

Data collection legislation is still unclear and largely untested. However, the European Union's Data Protection Directive has established a common minimum standard of data privacy protection in Europe which is putting pressure on law makers in other countries[2]. As discussed in the introduction to this chapter, researchers need to consider the long-term implications of data protection issues at an early stage – they strike at the very heart of traditional qualitative research methodology.

People Should Have Access to the Data Collected About Themselves

Issues of public access to research data are exercising the minds of researchers at the highest levels[3]. Ackeroyd (1988, 1991) has identified and explored the problems inherent in the rights of participant access to qualitative data. First, there is variation in definition of terms. In all data protection laws the critical factor making data 'personal information' is whether or not there is a link between the data and the individual. However, legal systems vary in the ways they classify criteria for 'identifiability' (see also Bing, 1980). Second, there may be technical difficulties in participant access. Qualitative software varies in the level of complexity that the retrieval of personal information presents. While hypertext systems may offer a fairly accessible 'associative trail' to personal data, other systems may make retrieval of data complex and time consuming. Third, researchers may hope to gain legal exemption from participant access on the grounds that their methods of storing and handling personal data renders the data non-identifiable. However, as Ackeroyd points out, the publication of qualitative research has often invited enough scrutiny and comment to undermine attempts to disguise identity. At the other extreme 'disguises, distortions, omissions and fabrications may affect features critical to the analysis, and may create other problems of validity, reliability and replicability' (Ackeroyd, 1991: 98).

These problems are all relevant to data which have been specifically requested from participants (through interviews or autobiographical material, for instance). There are additional problems when data are not specifically requested but are collected from online environments such as newsgroups or virtual communities. Here, debates about who 'owns' the data may further muddy the water (see below).

Existence of Data Banks Should Be Publicly Known

Large geodemographic databases are available for sale from 'data merchants' in the UK and USA[4]. Information from these databases can be used to construct extremely accurate personal profiles, 'concerning everything from finances to what a person eats, drinks and wears, as well as revealing intimate personal details' (Kitchin, 1998: 117). Although popular with market researchers, qualitative researchers in other fields have rarely used such data banks. Now, online research offers an ease of data transferability which might make these banks a tempting proposition. However, there are clear ethical considerations about using databases, as most individuals have no knowledge of where such data are stored and little power to control use of the data (see Barnes (1979: 166–168) for discussion of these issues).

Personal Data Should Be Reasonably Guarded Against Risks such as Loss, Unauthorized Access, Modification or Disclosure

In conventional research it is easy to protect data from loss or unauthorized access. The sites and/or names of participants are usually stored in an anonymous form to avoid tracing. Vital private information such as audio tapes, letters, original autobiographical material and consent forms can be locked away. Data in these non-electronic forms are generally protected from all but the most violent assault.

However, even with FTF studies, the increased use of computers for the storage and analysis of information raises the level of risk to data. Badly set-up networks, software containing bugs, guessable passwords, viruses and hackers can all compromise data (Ackeroyd, 1991). Anyone keeping sensitive data should seek advice from their system administrator, especially regarding viruses. Moreover, following standard computing practice, regular backups of all research data should be taken and kept in a secure place (see Smith (1989a, 1989b) for commonsense computer security suggestions).

While electronic communication is in transit, however, the researcher has no control over it. The networks it will pass through are owned by other people who may employ unscrupulous system administrators to maintain them. These administrators have the power to access anything they want. When service provider Prodigy faced protests for raising its charges, it intercepted, read and destroyed messages from dissenting clients and dismissed some members. The latter had no legal recourse and no way to picket the provider. If online discussion relates to criminal activity, law organizations may 'tap' the line and researchers might lay themselves open to being subpoenaed to disclose participants' identities (Coomber, 1997; see also Frankfort-Nachmias and Nachmias, 1996). Thus 'others can (and sometimes do) listen in to our electronic private conversations' (Kramarae, 1995: 23). In the USA, as Kramarae points out, unauthorized eavesdropping (including electronic messages) is forbidden by federal law[5]. However, enforcement of such laws remains a problem.

Apart from 'listening in', other users can copy and distribute messages to unintended recipients without the knowledge of the writer. The content of messages can also be changed with great ease. Even 'deleted' emails are not safe. Fileservers are always being backed up and these backups are stored for months, or even years. 'We need to remind ourselves that email is not always destroyed when we press the delete key' (Kramarae, 1995: 23).

The conclusion to be drawn from this is that, although researchers can promise confidentiality in the way that they use the data, they cannot promise that electronic communication will not be accessed and used by others. They therefore need to be careful about the assurances they give to participants about confidentiality. A more difficult question concerns the extent to which they should alert participants to potential problems, given the negative effect that this may have on participation levels (see Practical Ethical Guidelines below). The serious possibility of being compromised in these kinds of ways has already had an impact on qualitative research conducted in business environments. For instance, in market research, some participants avoid the online environment when discussing competitively sensitive issues (Sweet, 1999).

There are solutions to some problems of transit confidentiality. Using IRC the direct client-to-client (DCC) facility ensures confidentiality. DCC establishes a direct connection between participating computers which eliminates third-party interference. For email, a possible solution is provided by encryption (Forcht and Fore, 1995). Encryption involves using a computer program to convert electronic communication into an apparently random series of characters, before it is transmitted. The receiver then uses the same program to convert the characters back into the original text, but anyone who intercepts the message during transmission is unable to read it. The receiver can also store the message in encrypted form, providing ongoing security. Furthermore, messages can be digitally signed so that receivers can be sure of their origin, and that they have arrived intact. All of these things can be achieved using a freely available program called PGP (Pretty Good Privacy), which uses a system of public and private 'keys' (or codes) to ensure that messages can only be decrypted by the intended recipient[6].

However, encryption complicates a project because it requires that all interactants use email software that shares the same encryption capability. (As the various proprietary encryption systems on the market are complicated, no single system has taken off. Users fear they will be left with a marginalized technology.) More technical knowledge is required of the researcher, and participants may need training in using the software. The extra complexity introduced may be a disincentive to participants to sign up for a study in the first place, or to maintain their involvement once started. A researcher who wants to encrypt outgoing messages, perhaps because they quote sensitive information from an incoming message, will need to know the public encryption keys of all participants. And the requirement to decrypt all messages may mean that some of the advantages of easy transfer of data between systems are lost.

At this moment the situation is confusing. Encryption is still illegal in some countries. Even where it is legal some governments may view encrypted emails as suspicious and a cause for investigation. On the other hand, some evidence from the USA suggests that encryption of emails within a commercial environment is becoming routine with, for example, encryption keys being printed on business cards. It may be that, as the technology develops, the problems currently presented by encryption will cease to be an issue.

Data Should Be Collected in a Context of Free Speech

In the USA, the First Amendment of the Constitution forbids laws which prevent freedom of speech in any context. In the UK, the Race Relations Act forbids racist and sexist language in TV, books and radio, but the Internet does not have to conform to these restrictions. As a result, there are few sanctions and little legal redress for anyone who has negative experiences while participating in research online. This has implications for the personal security of both researcher and participants.

The online environment may be physically secure, but the potential in the virtual venue for anonymity (writing, speaking, or acting without being identified or identifiable) and pseudonymity (writing, speaking, or acting under a false or assumed identity) in the virtual venue opens up possibilities for highly stressful interaction. The online world has its own forms of intimidation, harassment or threat. Some people might use the cloak of anonymity to manipulate the flow and content of interviews and discussions. In areas where the research focus is private or sensitive, there is the possibility of toying with the emotions and trust of others (see discussion in the Participant Risk section below). Playing with identity makes it technically possible for researchers or participants to defame others using rumour, innuendo or lies.

Some commentators warn that researchers will meet new manifestations of deviancy, pornography, antisocial behaviour and crime. The motive for antisocial behaviour might be personal or connected to a particular world view. Some feminist authors present the online world as a very sexist and hostile environment monitored by systems operators who are overwhelmingly male (Ferganchick-Neufang, 1998; Kramarae, 1995). In addition, the growth of 'hate sites' run by the Ku Klux Klan, neo-Nazi groups and white supremacist religious groups has increased images and messages of racial and ethnic hatred and prejudice online.

Nevertheless, although unprotected by legislation, researchers and participants can afford themselves some measure of protection by deleting unwanted mail without reading it. If research is conducted in public sites, there are also hundreds (if not thousands) of witnesses who will police improprieties. Researchers may also set up private discussion sites themselves, which allows them to choose whether to display incoming messages that might insult or alienate participants. The Anti-Defamation League has developed a 'Hatefilter' which might be of use to studies which wish to avoid infiltration by extremists[7].

Open discussion of contentious and provocative subject matter presents another potential problem. As electronic communication is considered to be in the public arena, participants (and service providers) can be held legally responsible for online messages. For instance, the *Wall Street Journal* (1995) gave an example of a libel suit filed against Prodigy over a message posted by a subscriber which accused an investment firm of fraud. After 1988, when it became law, bulletin boards began to impose restrictions and post disclaimers referencing the Electronic Communications Privacy Act[8].

Personal Data Are Not To Be Communicated Externally Without the Consent of the Subject Who Supplied the Data

But who supplied the data? In some online qualitative studies the researcher will have gained the informed consent of participants at the beginning of the research (see below). However, for much online research, issues of consent raise difficult questions relating to online property rights. As Kitchin asks, 'who owns a message on a bulletin board? The system operator? The poster?' (1998: 107). Then there is the problem of cross-posting (forwarding email messages to others). Who owns these messages? These are important issues for online researchers and the ethical, practical and legal implications are still unclear. Ethical guidelines for reporting results from Internet research are still being debated (King, 1996).

Debates about ownership of digital data are often set within copyright discussions (Small, 1996; Litman, 1996). The discussion that follows draws on an outline provided by Whittle (1997). In print, copyright is a set of legal rights associated with the creation of certain intellectual work. Copyright in CMC includes the right to copy, modify, distribute, run (on a computer) or transmit a work. The first issue for a qualitative researcher is to decide whether the reflections of participants on a variety of personal and social issues may be considered in the same way as copyrightable items such as articles, essays or poems. Cavazos (1994) holds that all CMC is published written material and that to quote it without crediting the source is a violation of copyright. However, as Whittle points out, 'fair use' clauses within copyright law relax rights that might work against the interests of all concerned (for instance, quoting sections of books that give the original writer valuable exposure). Hence quoting small sections from a newsgroup discussion which was of general interest to all might be fair use. On the other hand, Whittle questions whether it is fair use for a researcher to publish a collection of discussion 'threads' from different fora.

Another factor is that absolute copyright is also mitigated by the concept of 'implied licence'. For example, each individual may own the messages they transmit in CMC, but if copyright were to be enforced literally no one could download or view the message. In sending the message there is an implied licence to read, or even archive, the information it contains. How might a qualitative researcher interpret that licence to archive (and then analyse and possibly publish) data?

Many commentators (such as Herring, 1996b; Waskul and Douglass, 1996), distinguish between data collected from private or semi-private sources (such as email or 'closed' chat rooms) and those accessed through open access fora (such as newsgroups and bulletin boards). Most qualitative researchers would strive to obtain informed consent before private and semi-private sources were accessed for research purposes. However, assuming this is not an option, one earlier precedent was to use pseudonyms to refer to participants and groups unless permission to use real names has been explicitly granted by the participants involved (Herring, 1996b: 5). A more robust approach would be simply to use the name that accompanied the original text on the grounds that, if people are happy for the Internet to see the association between their words and their name, why should they object to it in a book? But any disclosure promises to group participants would obviously have to take priority.

Paccagnella (1997) has argued that messages posted on Usenet (and, we would add, in conversation on publicly accessible IRC channels) are not equivalent to private letters. Rather, they are public acts, deliberately intended for public consumption. He concludes that, while this distinction should not lead researchers to assume that postings can be used without restriction, it does imply that they need not take more than normal precautions.

However, as Ferri[9] has pointed out, private interactions *do* take place in public places. Hence, Humphreys (1970), who exposed the private interaction of gay men in public restrooms, may be considered an (ethically challenging) equivalent situation. Ferri concludes, 'who is the intended audience of an electronic communication – and does it include *you* as a researcher? Most lists/chat rooms/and electronic spaces state an intended audience and many require you to suscribe. I have yet to see "people conducting research on the subscribers of this list" mentioned as an intended audience!' (ibid.)

One approach in a public forum is to make distinctions between messages which illustrate the phenomenon under investigation (implying a strong sense of observation on the part of the researcher) and those which are used by participants as debating positions (implying a strong sense of 'claiming their own words' on the part of the participants). Denzin (1999: 123) may be seen as identifying himself with the former position, presenting himself as a 'passive, lurking observer' who was focusing on the online text as discourse. Herring

(1996b: 6) set a precedent for the latter citing 'debating' comments as though they were public references.

Wilkins (1991: 58) has discussed in detail the 'ambiguities of research in this medium'. She had obtained data by 'lurking' on a conference site and then made her preliminary analysis of this material available to the previously unsuspecting message writers. Some of those involved objected to Wilkins' study as an invasion of privacy while others spoke positively about it. A two-week general discussion followed which concluded that 'anything posted to a publicly readable topic becomes public domain, and can be used (ported, quoted, argued, flamed, or ignored) by others so long as some form of authorship is cited, either by reference to note, number or name' (Fianna, 1986, entry no. 35, quoted in Wilkins, 1991: 58). A similar conclusion was reached by the ProjectH Research Group, a team of scholars from several countries and many universities who, in 1993–1994, collaborated on a quantitative study of electronic discussions (Rafaeli *et al.*, 1994). This group also decided that permission should not be sought for the recording and analysis of publicly posted messages. It seems that Usenet sources, in contrast to their private–public counterparts, may be exempt from the jurisdictions of institutional 'human subject' boards and ethical committees.

Practical Ethical Guidelines

We have seen that Internet use raises a variety of unresolved legal issues. However, as Thomas *et al.* point out, 'The Internet, just like the physical world, cannot rely on laws alone to keep order. There must be some level of ethics that people operate under in both these worlds' (1998: *online*). This is particularly important in the context of research.

According to Seidman (1991), the impetus towards protecting the rights of research participants is relatively recent. While this may be the case, 'ethics' is now well established as a core aspect of qualitative research (see Fetterman, 1998). However, MacKinnon (1995) has noted that there are currently insufficient ethical guidelines and very little agreement about how to proceed in a virtual arena. Because online research practice is still in its infancy, the critical researcher will be confronted by quandaries at almost every point in the research process. Email interviews, real-time focus groups or online 'observation' all present dilemmas with which the online researcher must grapple, yet there are few research practice conventions available.

In this section, we consider some practical precedents for conducting ethical research online. In doing so, we examine the standard range of features which constitute ethical practice in conventional qualitative research. We start by considering issues of 'informed consent'. Since this procedure is at the centre of the research process, whether it be online or FTF, we examine in detail the implications of obtaining informed consent when using CMC. The discussion of informed consent and related topics takes note of ethical guidelines that do exist.

These include: Schrum's (1995) recommendations for ethical research in the information age; Elgesem's (1996) six principles of fair information (see discussion above); and Sharf's (1999) five points for qualitative practice. In addition, the Internet has its own codes of practice for ethical usage and there is a general belief that new forms of online etiquette will become 'a template for relationships on the net' (Babbie, 1996: 68). However, as we shall discuss in the final section of the chapter, appropriate netiquette depends upon context of use and this is certainly the case for online research.

Informed Consent

Informed consent involves giving participants comprehensive and correct information about a research study, and ensuring that they understand fully what participation would entail, before securing their consent to take part. It is perhaps *the* key issue to be addressed anew when creating a framework for ethical online research practice.

In FTF settings, the explanation of a study is often presented through use of a 'Plain Language Statement'; that is, an outline of the aims and objectives of the study, the expected findings and the use to which such findings will be put. The consent of participants is usually indicated by their signature on an informed consent form (see Seidman, 1991). Such a form generally covers issues of participant anonymity and confidentiality, parental permission if children or young people are involved, participant risk, withdrawal (and lack of prejudice associated with such a decision), remuneration or compensation, as well as issues of secure storage of data, the destruction of data and ownership of data.

All of these elements remain salient in the online environment, although their relative importance may differ depending upon the aspect of the Internet used in the research. Furthermore, as Garton *et al.* (1999: 93) have noted, the online environment can make problematic what in a FTF context is more clear cut. For example, they ask, 'How will people know when they are the objects of a study?' The virtual environment has other implications for the gaining of informed consent. For example, with conventional FTF research, a participant is usually given the opportunity to ask questions prior to signing a consent form and before commencement of an interview. Here, points of confusion or the clarification of intent can be easily addressed by the researcher. Online, questions will probably be constrained by time. For instance, discussion may depend upon whether the participant and researcher can be online simultaneously. A participant may also be less inclined to ask questions because of the sense of formality which can be associated with the written word. In this case important aspects of consensual involvement may be neglected leading, in the worst scenario, to a participant remaining unclear about the research and therefore not truly giving their informed consent. Furthermore, because a researcher is not able to see, hear and note the embodied aspects of a participant's understanding and acceptance of the terms of participation, it may again be less clear whether informed consent is actually being achieved. Care should clearly be taken in this area.

This section examines four main services of the Internet used in online research – email, chat, conferencing and participant observation using mailing lists and newsgroups – and considers the practical issues involved in obtaining 'informed consent' in each area. The complexities of particular individual issues of consent are examined in depth later in the chapter.

Obtaining Consent for Email Interviewing

With email interviewing, informed consent can be obtained by the online researcher in a number of ways. First, a statement about the study and the accompanying consent form can be emailed as an attachment or, depending upon length, included in the body of an email to identified participants. Second, a study may have a Web site which explains its purpose, practical arrangements, qualifications of researchers and so on. This Web site could include a facility which allows an electronic consent form to be downloaded by participants and then emailed back to the researcher. These methods were used in studies by O'Connor and Madge (2000) and Smith-Stoner and Weber (2000). Third, and as long as the researcher possesses the relevant postal addresses, paper versions of statements and consent forms may be sent by conventional mail, 'snail-mail', as is often the case with FTF studies.

While the first options may sound easier, they do have drawbacks. For instance, researchers will be unable to obtain a written signature. This may or may not be important. For instance, new European data protection legislation requires researchers to obtain written consent and researchers who omit to do this may be liable to civil action. Some human subjects ethics committees, which operate to regulate research undertaken within universities and hospitals, may also insist upon a signature. In contrast, in their study of people with disabilities, Seymour *et al.* (1999) simply accepted a typed 'YES' or 'NO' response on the consent form. If there are problems, researchers may ask participants to sign physically a consent form which they obtained electronically. The form could then be faxed or snail-mailed back to the researcher. Whichever method is adopted, the key question for the researcher is whether an actual signature is required, or whether a tick in a box or typed 'YES' response is an acceptable substitute.

Written consent is associated with issues of authenticity. Can a researcher be sure that emailed consent forms come from the appropriate person? The virtuality of online research is a challenging area which will come up again and again in this book. It can present a serious stumbling block for pioneering researchers who often have to work within the constraints of institutions unfamiliar with developing norms of electronic communication. Bennett raised the following issues:

> Obtaining consent from your participants via email can be problematic depending on your institution, their views with regard to the legalities of obtaining consent in this way, and also what kind of study you are going to undertake (i.e. what is your methodology and what kind of information do you wish to obtain?). For example, is it a study which is likely to cause distress to the participants? And if so, will the ethics committee be concerned that this method of obtaining consent is going to be as legally binding as 'traditional' methods of obtaining consent (for instance, if problems come up during your research that were not anticipated)? Ethics committees are much more concerned about the legal aspects of research studies than the actual ethical issues themselves, so you must bear this in mind. (1999: *personal email*)

Let us consider how the factors identified by Bennett might work together in a real situation. Anders (2000) wished to conduct research into the issues facing women with disabilities in higher education. When she sought permission to use email as the main means of data collection from her ethics committee, she faced a long period of negotiation with her institution, which looked at the method with 'a degree of fear' (1999: *personal email*). However, several factors worked in her favour: teaching staff were extremely supportive in terms of 'what I wanted to do and how I wanted to do it'; the institution (Deakin University, Australia) had a commitment to 'flexible learning' and to disability issues; and the ethics committee also deemed that participants were mature academic women who would be less susceptible to abuse, misrepresentation or harm than most populations. As a result, Anders was allowed not only to use email but also to collect an electronic signature on an email consent form. This was in keeping with the institution's commitment to the kind of 'flexible delivery' which would allow the greatest degree of equity to all students. Consistent with this approach was the requirement that, if the women wished to participate in ways other than email, Anders would not discriminate against them. This was a proviso that Anders already firmly subscribed to:

> I am working with women who use computerised communication, as well as deaf women (who without translators I would be unable to interview), and with blind women for whom written questions would be inappropriate. Some women prefer to answer my emailed questions in hand writing, others in typed and mailed responses, or in audio taped format. (1999: *personal email*)

However, Anders had a further, most important, observation to make. Another study she was involved in, which used conventional methods, had 'a much more difficult passage through Ethics'. She concluded that she may have been successful in the former study partly as a result of giving 'a lot of background, details, etc. - because email data collection is so "new". I'm sure that helped - I think often people using more conventional methods don't really think about the ethical issues involved and I felt I *had* to!' (1999: *personal email*). Other researchers have also stressed the need to prepare a strong case when introducing online methods to committees that have to consider human subjects requirements. Anders was able to show that online methods were not merely adequate but, in fact, particularly appropriate for women with disabilities.

Other studies will have different, but equally convincing, reasons for choosing and defending CMC. For instance, Internet research has been taken up with enthusiasm by many teachers and students involved in distance learning (studies noted in this book include Parkany and Swan, 1999; Smith-Stoner and Weber, 2000; Salmon, 2000). The title of Stein's (2000) book *Learning, Teaching and Researching on the Internet* suggests that these may be complementary processes online. Indeed, both Stewart *et al.* (1998) and O'Connor and Madge (2000) used software for their research which had originally been acquired by their institutions for distance learning purposes. Research initiatives into distance learning issues need to be seen within a context of phenomenal growth in mega-universities worldwide[10]. It seems inevitable that distance learning, and research associated with it, will proliferate. There are implications here. Education 'at a distance' is already seeking ways to defend its practices without the validation of FTF interaction. In some institutions, such as the California Institute of Integral Studies to which Smith-Stoner and Weber are attached, students taking online doctorates even have the opportunity of defending a thesis online. This suggests that precedents and procedures for protecting the integrity of online practices will be established in thriving communities which 'do business' online – and that the research community will both benefit from, and contribute to, future norms in this area.

However, until online methods are more mainstream, it is the individual researcher who must take responsibility for convincing others of the authenticity and credibility of the medium when, for instance, seeking informed consent:

> As this is a relatively new way of obtaining consent, you must defend your choice rigorously. Back up your decision to use email, to obtain consent, with examples of other studies that have done so. Point out that 'traditional' methods of obtaining informed consent do not guarantee any more 'security', reliability or validity than emailed methods. Demonstrate how you intend to ensure that the emailed consent form is in fact returned by 'the participant', for example by setting up a code word that only he/she can know, or a set of questions to which only they know the answer to (and which you can return to and clarify throughout the study as a security measure). Most importantly, identify any weaknesses in your proposal to use email as a way of obtaining consent and back them up fiercely! (Bennett, 1999: *personal email*)

In Appendix A we see how Parkany and Swan (1999) prepared the ground for gaining the approval of their institutional review board for an online consent form.

Obtaining Consent for Chat

Chat is the form of CMC used to conduct real-time online focus groups. It is unlikely that a researcher will be able to obtain informed consent from participants at the moment of the actual chat session or focus group. Participants need to read, understand and, possibly, respond to a statement about the study, which will take time if they are fully to understand the implications. They may also need to complete and, in some cases, sign a consent form. These requirements would disrupt the commencement of the planned discussion, and can lead to valuable online time being used unproductively.

This dilemma can be overcome if the real-time chat is supplemented by an asynchronous conference area which allows statements to be read and agreed ahead of time, or by a consent form which is completed and returned by participants prior to the session using email or by traditional methods.

Obtaining Consent for Conferencing

Conferencing is a form of asynchronous CMC where text may be read and responded to at leisure. Because of this, there are few practical difficulties in obtaining participant informed consent, the possible need for a written signature by the participant notwithstanding. For example, a statement about the study could be posted by the researcher ahead of time, either at the Web site from which the conference will take place or in the conference area within the designated software facility. Participants would post possible questions back to the researcher or, if particularly personal, could email them. The asynchronous mode of conferencing allows much of the information which is central to a researcher obtaining informed consent to be dealt with ahead of time.

Obtaining Consent for Participant Observation

Mailing lists, newsgroups and BBSs constitute several sources of information for the online researcher. As we noted above, debate about use of this material is active, with researchers beginning to rule not only that such sources sit within the public sphere of Internet services but that they can be freely referenced (see Herring, 1996b). Of course, there may be constraints which reflect the concerns of individuals using a particular environment. For example, on the all-women discussion list *'Systers'* those who join, and hence those in a position to conduct research, must agree never to share information received from the list with others without the express permission of the author of the message containing the information (Winter and Huff, 1996).

Unless there are such clear guidelines, researchers who want to make use of newsgroups and mailing lists as participant observers must decide how they tackle the issue of gaining consent from those who post to such lists and, indeed, whether consent needs to be obtained (Reid, 1996). There are parallels here with the conventional FTF context where consent is usually not obtained. For example, as Garton *et al*. (1999: 93) ask:

> Must researchers identify themselves if they are only participating in the electronic equivalent of hanging out on street corners or doughnut shops where they would never think of wearing large signs identifying themselves as 'researchers'?

Given the lack of consensus in this area, it is not surprising that researchers do not always declare explicitly whether they obtained permission for their logs of study (Reid, 1991). However, there are some research precedents. For example, in regard to his own participation on a list, Denzin (1999: 123) has stated: 'I never identified myself to the group, nor did I obtain permission to quote from postings, thereby violating many of Schrum's (1995) ethical injunctions for electronic research'. Similarly, Hodkinson did not officially announce his participant observation of Goth[ll] sites to users, but he did intend to gain their permission before reporting findings:

> I was advised that this might be a bad idea by certain off and on-line respondents who felt this was liable to cause exclusory measures by certain individuals. Posting an announcement of my presence as a social researcher on a newsgroup could be compared perhaps to making similar announcement over the PA of a nightclub in which I was conducting ethnographic work. As well as creating possible hostility it might well distort the 'natural' interactions I am seeking to observe and record. Rather, I shall obtain permission from individual posters whose comments I reproduce or quote from. (1999: *personal email*)

Paccagnella (1997) also noted that, even when a study is neither hidden nor concealed, users may not necessarily be aware of the use of particular data. Clearly, the ethical conventions surrounding the use of material from online public sites need to undergo further refinement before they can be considered satisfactory.

Parental Permission

Where research involves children and young people, the process of obtaining informed consent can have additional complications. One of the potential advantages of the Internet for conducting research is that, because of its popularity with young people, it makes contacting child participants directly relatively easy. But, in view of the ethical difficulties of conducting research with a disembodied child whose maturity, personality and possible vulnerability may be unknown, researchers must consider whether they should eschew direct contact and only contact participants through parents or schools. In certain jurisdictions, or as a requirement of institutional ethics committees, it is already standard to obtain informed consent not only from younger people but also from their guardians or parents. This requirement could be simply addressed through the provision of extra electronic consent forms. However, given the difficulty of verifying the originator of electronic communication (unless, as we discussed earlier, software allowing digital signatures is used), the ethical researcher might consider that consent for research involving children should always be obtained from adults in paper form.

Participant Risk

A further key aspect of obtaining informed consent concerns clarification of any possible risks in involvement for participants. One view might be that a text-based research tool diminishes the possibly exploitative aspects of interviewing. Alternatively, human subjects review boards and ethics committees might decide that online research represents a greater threat of harm to participants than FTF studies.

For example, as discussed in Chapter 7, participants in CMC studies may face the risk of online harassment and abuse. This may particularly be the case when groups of people are involved, as with online focus groups. However, even in one-to-one studies, if participants' email addresses become known to one another there is a danger that these will be used for purposes unconnected with the study. In the Graduates of the Millennium study, students in one department discovered each other's names and set up an informal communication network in which messages were copied to all participants. Although no harassment took place, the volume of messages being received caused two students to drop out of the study.

Another cause for concern might be the temptation for users to treat CMC in an unguarded way – rather like 'a conversation on a train':

> Although the medium seems inherently impersonal, there have been many cases observed or reported by the participants of the most intimate of exchanges taking place between persons who have never met face-to-face and probably never will. Revelations about personal inadequacies, deviant preferences, past love affairs, and serious personal problems ... have passed through the [computer conferencing] system as private messages to strangers who were 'met' on the system. (Hiltz and Turoff, 1978: 28)

A belief that the Internet is an uncensored, unpoliced environment may also make participants more willing to admit to illegal drug use or petty crime (see Coomber, 1997).

The ambiguous public–private nature of almost all services of the Internet is, as we discussed, now widely acknowledged. Sharf (1999) argues that researchers must be aware of the potential for public exposure of participants, particularly when sensitive topics and highly personal information are involved. Interviewers must also be aware of their reduced ability to protect participants who are straying into dangerous areas. In FTF interviews, researchers can intervene in three ways to prevent damaging admissions from becoming public. They can warn participants that they may be revealing more than they intend; turn off the recording equipment if participants continue; or choose not to transcribe parts of the recording. In CMC these options do not exist. By the time researchers see potentially damaging contributions they have been typed and sent – no protective intervention is possible. A researcher's only course of action is to try to delete the message, though this is not without its ethical problems and, as discussed earlier, complete deletion is impossible.

Accordingly, the ethical researcher's role should be to emphasize the public nature of CMC to participants before they give consent, and perhaps to re-emphasize this during the study, despite the adverse effect this might have on participation rates and free discussion. Participants must be allowed to protect themselves, by considering carefully whether they are prepared for each message to be made public before they send it.

Despite the care taken by researchers, human subjects committees may remain uneasy about the risks associated with online research. There is some genuine cause for concern. Social psychologists, for instance, face strict professional guidelines when working FTF. These are to ensure that misleading participants about the true purposes of research (in order to access 'natural' behaviour, for instance) does not lead to ill effects. On the Internet, as Wallace (1999) points out, there are no formal guidelines and few insights into the possible impact of research deception. Yet this is an environment with great potential for dissembling. The psychiatrist who masqueraded as a woman to tap intimate confessional stories is a case in point. Van Gelder (1991) described the feelings of women who had been communicating via a national computer network when they discovered that a group member, who had presented herself as a severely handicapped woman, was in actuality an able-bodied male. This persona, known as Joan, was adopted when the psychiatrist discovered that women were much more open and intimate with him when they mistook his computer identity as female. When his true identity was revealed some women described this experience as 'mind rape, pure and simple' – a cheat and a fraud. (However, deception in FTF settings is not unknown either – see Chapter 9.)

There are further difficulties relating to, for instance, cross-national research. Sheer distance might preclude an FTF debriefing. While an online briefing may well become acceptable in the near future (see the earlier distance learning discussion) some ethics committees may be reluctant to agree to it at this stage. For example, Anders (2000) was required by her committee to make sure that she could organize counselling in the state/country of each of her far-flung participants should it become necessary.

However, it would be unwise to exaggerate the risks of CMC research. The online environment may be new to many but people rapidly become accustomed to its norms and this, of course, will accelerate in the next few years. As

Wallace (1999) has noted, even children are learning quickly to protect themselves online. She cites Tapscott (1998), who has described the results from online research projects that involved many discussions with children and teenagers who use the Internet regularly. The N-Geners, as he calls them, were surprisingly relaxed about the 'dangers' of the Internet and many expressed the view that adults were overreacting to the risks of online interaction. This robust view of a technology that is becoming everyday to many suggests that risk in research should be seen in the same careful but sensible way that it is approached FTF. Each study needs to be considered individually, and distinctions can then be drawn between research designs that are innocuous, acceptable or suspect.

Participant Withdrawal

Participant permission to withdraw from a study at any time and without prejudice are central elements of the informed consent platform (Seidman, 1991). In FTF research, withdrawal can take place by a participant leaving a room, or not honouring an appointment in the first place. Similarly, a participant may phone a researcher or simply never respond to an invitation to participate.

While these latter two measures may also apply to online research, the physicality of leaving a room, for example, does not. A virtual room can of course be left, but it is not so obvious. Unlike FTF, where it is difficult to leave an interview without saying something (although not necessarily giving a reason), a virtual participant may, quite simply, disappear. If this is the case, the researcher will be left wondering why. Did communications get confused, were instructions not clear or is this a failure of technology? Depending upon the nature of the contact details that a researcher has about participants, the circumstances surrounding participant withdrawal may never be fully known.

The apparent withdrawal of a participant introduces a new set of ethical challenges. For example, how should a researcher follow up a participant who has disappeared from the screen? How many follow-up emails would constitute harassment of that person? Is a researcher permitted to try to find out why a person may have left a study, when further online communication is the only means they may have at their disposal? In particular, how can a researcher know whether follow-up emails will be perceived as a welcome reminder or an unwelcome intrusion?

There are few clear answers to these questions. However, to provide as much scope as possible for sensitive handling of such issues, we would recommend that a researcher always tries to gather a combination of contact details from a participant. These could include street addresses and phone or fax numbers. On the other hand, participant anonymity may be contravened in the process.

Financial or In-kind Payment or Compensation

As noted in Chapter 2, participants usually decide to volunteer for studies for either altruistic or financial reasons. Ethical perspectives concerning whether or not to offer payment to participants does not differ from the FTF context. However, the online researcher does need to ensure that, if payment is promised, then that promise is honoured. For example, if participants are offered shopping credits, the researcher needs to be confident that the sites chosen will remain online for a reasonable time so that the credit can be used. Whatever approach is chosen, and if payment incentives are to be effective, online researchers will need to be knowledgeable and organized in regard to this area of online practice.

Confidentiality

As we saw in the first part of this chapter, ensuring participant confidentiality in conventional FTF research is relatively easy to achieve. For example, the use of pseudonyms, the changing of any identifiable personal details, including names of places, institutions and times, the assigning of code numbers, the secure storage of data and the destruction of such data (often after a set period of time) are all mechanisms whereby participant confidentiality may be protected.

In the online context, however, issues of confidentiality become problematic. As we have seen, electronic data are subject to multiple risks. For example, would it be appropriate for researchers to offer confidentiality if they were unable to provide encryption? There is no easy answer. The most honest response may be for researchers simply to make clear to potential participants that they are unable to ensure total confidentiality. At the same time they could emphasize that they would take every precaution within their power to act ethically (that is, ensure confidentiality) in their research undertakings. It is possible that, if a researcher were to make this admission, institutional human ethics committees might intervene to prohibit the planned research from ever taking place because participant confidentiality is such a key element of informed consent. However, it could be argued that there is still a range of measures that the researcher can adopt to maximize confidentiality. We now turn to those options.

Anonymity

In social science research, the use of pseudonyms has always been a valuable means of preserving a participant's identity in research reports. Working online, such changes are also worthwhile but may need to occur at a number of levels. For example, with email (and asynchronous conferencing), real names, user names, domain names, signatures and even ISPs may all need to be adjusted. Paccagnella (1997) has argued that just because particular online sources may be public, this does not mean that people have waived their rights to remain anonymous, nor that the identity of an institution and/or list should be exposed. Walther (1999) has noted that publishing research that discloses even the name of a site can lead to repercussions in terms of a flood of visitors to the site or battles within the site over who allegedly did what. Such is apparently the case at the MU* (see Technology Introduction) called LambdaMOO after publication of Dibbell's (1993) article 'A Rape in Cyberspace'. For a similarly unfortunate aftermath in an online group, see Reid (1996). However, Walther points out that such disruption can be avoided. Alternative research precedents have already been provided. For example, Kendall (1999) changed all names in her research including the name of the forum and people's online pseudonyms. Turkle made her own position clear, as follows:

> In reporting cases of people who have part of their identities on the Internet, I follow the same policy as for other informants: I protect confidentiality by disguising identities. This means that among other things, I change MUD names, character names, and city names. In the case of the WELL [an online town emanating from California], there is a clear community norm that 'You Own Your Own Words'. I have asked contributors to WELL discussions how they wish to be identified. Different people have made different choices. When I use materials from publicly archived online sources I simply indicate the sources. (1995: 324)

In the context of chat, the issue of anonymity may be problematic. For example, chat usernames can be assigned by either the researcher or participant. These usernames may bear no relationship to the identity of the user and hence might be used in research reports without modification. On the other hand, where usernames (such as nicknames) are chosen by participants there may be no requirement for them to provide their real-life (RL) names. If this is the case, the researcher may never know the 'true' or RL identities of participants: anonymity has gone beyond the point of hiding identities in a research report and become perfect anonymity where identities are hidden even from the researcher. But if the researcher does not know who the participants in a particular study are, how can the researcher convincingly claim informed consent? Turkle decided that she would not report on her findings unless she had met the Internet user 'in person rather than in persona', but she added that 'researchers with different interests and theoretical perspectives will surely think about this decision differently' (1995: 324).

A further, related issue is that of researcher identity. In conventional research there are limits to the identities that the researcher can negotiate with subjects: 'Ascribed characteristics such as age, gender, "race" and ethnicity limit the sort of person the researcher can become and also the sort of relationship that can be developed with subjects. They may also restrict access to settings and to data' (Foster, 1996: 72). In CMC, these limits need not apply. Even when researchers are attempting to be as authentic as possible in their presentation of self, they still face ethical decisions regarding the amount of information about themselves that they should make known to participants. For, just as researchers may not be sure of the precise identities of their participants, so may participants be unsure as to the identities of those conducting the research. As one student in the Graduate of the Millennium study said, 'you may have worries about dealing with virtual students but what about us? We have to deal with a virtual researcher!'

Decisions regarding the ethics of self-presentation (which might be made on a study-to-study basis) tie in with the challenges of presenting self online (which will be discussed in Chapters 6, 7 and 8) and also the implications for data of research practice in the virtual field (which are discussed at length in Chapter 9).

Netiquette

Outside of the research context, many attempts are being made to identify common standards of etiquette for the Internet. As discussed briefly in the Technology Introduction, 'netiquette' can be understood in two ways. First, it can mean a set of conventions and rules which structure online practice in all kinds of fora. Second, it is often used to refer to standards of politeness and courtesy in the online environment. Hundreds of specific netiquette suggestions are published, with service providers, employers and governments all offering suggestions for appropriate use (Scheuermann and Taylor, 1997).

It is clear that some aspects of netiquette offer online researchers the beginnings of an ethical frame in which to conduct their research. Of particular use are sets of principles, such as Rinaldi's (1996) Ten Commandments for Computer Ethics, which would be acceptable in most situations. However, many rules of netiquette will almost inevitably differ depending upon the forum or Internet service in question (as one of the most useful online netiquette guides describes)[12]. The following section outlines some of the netiquette issues which are likely to inform online research practice when communication is one-to-one (like email, chat), one-to-many (like mailing lists and newsgroups) and many-to-many (like real-time chat focus groups).

Email Netiquette

Researchers using email will reshape conventional rules of one-to-one netiquette to suit the purposes of a study. For instance, although some netiquette articles promote emoticons such as smileys (see Technology Introduction) to replace facial expressions and body language, and urge users to be relaxed about spelling and grammar, these characteristics would not be suitable in emails that seek to establish first contact with participants. The early exchange of messages would be more akin to introductory paper correspondence, and would generally adopt a conventional, even formal, tone. It is only later on, in some but not all circumstances, that more informality would be appropriate. In addition, the establishment of relationships in a global context requires researchers to be aware that another person's culture, language and humour may be different from their own.

Nor would it be useful for qualitative researchers to follow standard rules of short-sentence messages in, for instance, an in-depth interview conducted by email. The researcher may actually prefer an extended discursive exploration of issues rather than the recommended 'brief well-written note'. Rather than trying to define the tone of communication (as much netiquette does) CMC in some research settings would need to be fluid, context dependent and possibly changeable over time. For example, as we shall see in the discussion of CMC as a mode of language (Chapter 8), email may have a greater or lesser association with conversational or written norms depending upon context, and its tone will also depend upon the interpersonal relationships of the interactants.

Netiquette injunctions to avoid interfering with someone's computer work or appropriating their intellectual output (Rinaldi, 1996) have obvious implications for research. It would be clearly unethical for a researcher to take email comments out of context, either by inappropriate cutting and pasting of sections of an interview or by neglecting to outline the wider context of the research. To do the latter adequately in online research a researcher might need to provide more information than that required working FTF. For instance, a researcher might include such details as the number of emails exchanged with an individual and the level of anonymity involved (was a participant ever seen FTF, known by a real verified name, writing under a pseudonym?), as well as giving the usual methodological and theoretical context for the research.

Chat Netiquette

One-to-one chat involves two people having an interactive dialogue using CMC. The netiquette for this form of communication differs in some ways from email. Chat software may 'ring' the recipient (rather then waiting for a reply) so, like the phone, issues of intrusion may apply. Netiquette urges against, on the one hand, reringing too frequently if a response is not immediate and, on the other hand, assuming that there is a personal reason for non-response (it is more likely to be a technological problem). In this online mode, typos and other mistakes are more acceptable (even at an early stage in the research relationship) because the rules of conversation are paramount. Mistakes are seen as the textual equivalent of 'umming and ahhing'.

The netiquette of many-to-many chat shadows the etiquette or group rules which can apply to FTF focus groups. For example, the online facilitator can outline a series of expectations of the group, the language to be used, any topics which would be considered unsuitable for the group to discuss and the requirement of respect for fellow participants. In addition, the netiquette requirement for administrators of chat groups to have written guidelines for dealing with improper or illegal messages might also be adopted by focus group facilitators.

One directive which would be clearly inappropriate in the rules of netiquette would be an FTF facilitator's insistence that participants should not interrupt each other. In the online environment of chat, interruptions are difficult to avoid as distinctions between questions and responses become blurred during high participant interactivity. However, the online equivalent for 'no interruptions' could be a rule that no comments are left ignored; that is, that all participants must engage, where at all possible, with the comments of others.

As with email, the scripts of online focus groups must not be inappropriately edited for publication and a comprehensive description of the virtual research context should be provided. There is, however, a further complication. In real-time chat focus groups, the researcher must be prepared to structure the interaction of the group (see Chapters 5 and 6). For example, the facilitator may need to reprimand particular participants or to regulate overbearing or even rude participants (those not displaying sufficient netiquette). However, any involvement of the researcher automatically becomes part of the electronic script and therefore part of the dynamics of the session. While FTF a tape or video recorder could be stopped in order to allow an issue to be sorted out, in the disembodied online environment, where text is the only means of communication, any altercation would be recorded. Researchers would need to make case-by-case decisions about whether editing out this material would be interfering with a participant's 'own words'.

A final issue in chat netiquette concerns the researcher's own treatment of the research participants. In this regard, welcoming messages placed in asynchronous areas (as discussed in Chapter 5) are extremely useful ways for researchers to set a framework for group practice. If rules and expectations are outlined from the beginning and, if necessary, participants are given the opportunity to respond to these statements, then the researcher can be seen to be involving and even empowering the participants in the study. Heavy-handed facilitation may constitute unethical practice, particularly if it leads participants to feel that their opinions are neither valued nor valuable.

Conferencing Netiquette

Many of the netiquette issues discussed so far also apply to asynchronous conferencing. The main implication for netiquette in these non-real-time focus groups is the absence of the facilitator. Because it is impossible for the facilitator to be online all the time, effective netiquette must emanate from a self-governing group (Gaiser, 1997). However, if a researcher felt that the group might not be aware of common rules of netiquette, or that extra admonitions might be necessary, one possibility would be to transmit rules for participation (for example, not flaming) ahead of time, in a welcome or introductory message.

A more reactive solution is to use software to censor particular topics and words so that the rapport of an online interview or focus group is not disrupted (Sweet, 1999). For example, with the package W3Resources, words can be censored. However, as Sweet was to discover, this software may be configured to pick up certain letter combinations and is then unable to distinguish their significance when they stand alone as compared to when they are part of a larger word.

Usenet Netiquette

Unlike the forms of Internet communication discussed so far, which are all 'semi-private', the newsgroups and mailing lists associated with Usenet are a public area. Usenet netiquette is therefore qualitatively different. Above all, Usenet netiquette is concerned with self-preservation in an environment where a message might be read by several thousand people who might be paying phone and online charges for the privilege of reading it. At a practical level, researchers who intend to participate actively in this environment would benefit from using widely accepted forms of Usenet netiquette, such as reading a group's Frequently Asked Questions (FAQ) file, and lurking online for a while to get acculturated, before asking a question, posting a message, or presuming to solicit help or information. Admonitions to avoid flaming, criticizing or humiliating others seem self-evident in a research context (unless a study of escalating aggressive behaviour is planned). It would also seem good research practice, as well as being good netiquette, to start a reply to a message in a many-to-many context by summarizing, or including just enough text of, the original message, to contextualize the reply.

Researchers should also observe Usenet netiquette by avoiding the accidental mixing of public and private messages. Certainly, if a researcher were to send a personal message to a list or a group inadvertently, an apology would be in order. Similarly, some mailing lists or newsgroups are private (as was the case with *Systers* mentioned above) and netiquette would preclude researchers from posting messages from there to a wider Usenet audience – although, as was indeed the case with *Systers*, the researcher may be granted permission to publicize some internal messages for research purposes (Winter and Huff, 1996).

Conclusion

Most professional ethics committees require that researchers seek all reasonable means to ensure the rights of participants. They recognize that studies cannot legislate against illegal interventions and look to legal systems to redress wrongdoing. Undoubtedly, as computer and information technologies continue to grow, legal precedents will be established. For instance, while netiquette may have begun quite informally, there are signs that it may increasingly be given some legal force[13]. In the meantime, qualitative researchers can benefit from reading debates about handling ethical and legal problems (see Ackermann, 1995). They should also be aware that good-practice norms for online research are being adopted as mandatory requirements by funding bodies[14] and institutional review boards[15]. It would be politic for a researcher who intends to work online to find out about top-level discussions that would impact on their research design at an early stage.

However, whatever future rules or laws are proposed, decisions about ethics in the online environment are and will remain the responsibility of researchers themselves. Above all, the priority in qualitative research is to protect the well-being of participants. It is not a question of asking 'what methods can I use online and how can I justify the ethics of using them?' In the last resort, 'Someone is not going to be there to look over everyone's shoulder to make sure that they make the right decision. It is up to us to do what we feel is right' (Thomas *et al.*, 1998).

Notes

1   For more information about the Data Protection Act, see www.open.gov.uk/dpr/dprhome.htm
2   Kaplan, C., 'Strict European Privacy Law puts pressure on U.S.', Cyber Law Journal, *New York Times*, 9 October 1998 (www.nytimes.com/yr/mo/day/tech/indexcyber.html).
3   The Scientific Freedom, Responsibility and Law Program within the American Association for the Advancement of Science (AAAS), the world's largest multi-disciplinary science association, felt it necessary to write to the Office of Management and Budget, USA, to 'Request for Comments on Clarifying Changes to Proposed Revision on Public Access to Research Data', published in the *Federal Register*, 11 August 1999. For the text of the letter which outlined its concerns, see www.aaas.org/spp/dspp/sfrl/projects/omb/ombltr2.htm.
4   Examples are CACI in the UK and TRW and Trans Union in the USA: www.caci.co.uk; and www.transunion.com.
5   In 1986 Congress passed the Electronic Communications Privacy Act (ECPA). The Act prohibits anyone from intercepting, using and/or disclosing email messages without the sender's permission. However, the Act does give permission to a system operator to access a user's email if it is necessary for the operation or security of the system.
6   See www.pgpi.orgh for more details of how Pretty Good Privacy works.
7   For details about 'Hatefilter' see www.adl.org/hate-patrol/info/.
8   For more information about the Electronic Communications Privacy Act see www.law.vill.edu/vcilp/fed_leg/ecpa.htm.
9   Message posted to OnlineRsch@ onelist.com, 19 October 1999. See also Ferri (2000).
10   *Guardian* newspaper, UK, 30 November 1999, p. 19. See also J. Daniel (1999) *Mega-universities and Knowledge Media*. London: Kogan Paul.
11   The Goth scene emerged in the UK in the early 1980s, and involved the fusion by certain bands, their fans, and indeed music journalists, of elements of punk, glam rock and new romantic into a distinctive style of music and fashion. The music is often described as dark, macabre and sinister, and the style is most obviously (though not exclusively) seen in black clothes and the wearing by males and females of distinctive styles of makeup (Hodkinson, 2000: Introduction).
12   Responsible Use of the Network (RUN) Working Group of the IETF. 'Netiquette Guidelines: RFC 1855'.
13   'An argument for "netiquette" holds up in court', Cyber Law Journal, *New York Times*, 16 July 1999 (www.nytimes.com/yr/mo/day/tech/indexcyber.html).

14 The Economic and Social Research Council, which is a core funding body for social science research in the UK, has already responded to European Union data protection legislation with a guidance document relating to copyright and confidentiality.

15 The Scientific Freedom, Responsibility and Law Program within the American Association for the Advancement of Science (AAAS) convened a workshop in 1999 to examine the challenges facing scientists conducting Internet research involving human subjects. The outcomes of the workshop deliberations will be used to draft a chapter in the *Guidebook for Institutional Review Boards on Internet Research* produced by the NIH Office for Protection from Research Risks (OPRR) in 2000. For the latest information, see www.aaas.org/spp/dspp/sfrl/projects/intres/main.htm.

4 Introducing Online Methods

The main tools of data collection favoured by qualitative researchers are interviewing, observation and document analysis.

Interviewing is the most widely applied technique for conducting systematic social enquiry in academic, clinical, business, political and media life (Holstein and Gubrium, 1997) and qualitative research is well established in this area. 'Interviewing' can take a number of forms, so it is perhaps better thought of as a collection of related methods. The primary distinction is between standardized (structured) and non-standardized (unstructured) interviews. Non-standardized interviews can be further subdivided into individual (or one-to-one) and group interviews (often called focus groups). A wide range of techniques for generating and analysing data from FTF interviews with individuals and groups has been developed over time (see Fontana and Frey, 1994; McCracken, 1988; Briggs, 1986; Lincoln and Guba, 1985).

Observational techniques are also widely used in conventional qualitative research, frequently in conjunction with some form of interviewing. Finally, there are forms of data collection where there is a lower level of interaction with the researcher and a stronger emphasis on documentary analysis, such as journals, diaries and autobiographical approaches (see Flick, 1998; Chamberlain and Thompson, 1998; Reinharz, 1992; Gluck and Patai, 1991).

These different research methods have costs and benefits at both practical and methodological levels, and one of the main purposes of this book is to investigate whether, and to what extent, CMC can reduce the cost of these methods and/or increase the benefits. In this chapter and the next we shall begin this investigation by considering:

- how these methods are used in a conventional format;
- the advantages and disadvantages of attempting to conduct such methods online.

An essential aspect of this discussion is the place of practical expertise. When collecting data, the qualitative researcher-as-*bricoleur* picks and chooses from the tools of their methodological trade (Denzin and Lincoln, 1994: 2). In most forms of conventional research, methods of data collection are well established and training manuals and courses are readily available. However, there are additional challenges for researchers who wish to collect data online.

Researchers may have differing levels of experience with computers. In addition, technology is progressing very quickly. As we have seen in Chapter 2, there are pros and cons associated with the use of electronic interaction in a research design and some studies would clearly not be suited to this medium. However, once a researcher has decided that CMC is the way forward, the first practical step is to ensure that the researcher and all respondents have access to the required technology and the confidence to use it (see Technology Introduction). Then researchers need to consider the logistics and mechanics of arranging and conducting qualitative research online with individuals and groups.

In this chapter we discuss such issues in relation to:

• standardized interviews in the form of email and Web-page-based surveys;
• non-standardized forms of online one-to-one interviewing;
• 'observation' of virtual communities; and
• the collection of personal documents online.

In the following chapter we discuss the specific factors that pertain to virtual focus groups.

The aim of both chapters is to provide sufficient information to (a) spur online research initiatives and (b) give a basis for methodological discussion of online research.

Standardized Interviews

In structured interviews, interviewees are asked standardized questions with a limited set of response categories. Conventional surveys often take place FTF or over the telephone; others may be in the form of a self-completion questionnaire. Responses are recorded according to a pre-established coding scheme and are generally analysed statistically (Fontana and Frey, 1994). Frequently, and especially when paper based, standardized interviews are referred to as 'surveys'.

There has been a long history of debate regarding the place in qualitative research of methods which have been characterized as involving numbers rather than words (Miles and Huberman, 1994: 15). Beginning with Max Weber (1922), some qualitative researchers have not excluded quantitative measurements a priori, but have used them where appropriate and with necessary caution. Epistemological and philosophical discussion relating to qualitative and quantitative research continues (Becker, 1996; Bryman, 1988). Recent formulations suggest that, when 'method' is understood as a procedure, tool or technique, there is no one method or set of methods which would define an enquiry as qualitative (Schwandt, 1997). If we distinguish qualitative research questions as those which focus on the form/nature of phenomena, there will be times when additional contextual information is relevant. Allowing that apparently simple, factual questions can be more difficult than they seem (see

Wilson (1996) for a discussion) qualitative researchers may still have recourse to, for instance, demographic information.

While some researchers retain a qualitative–quantitative distinction at the level of practical data collection (May, 1993), many others are prepared to combine methods in the research design if this strategy addresses the research question (Brannen, 1992; Miles and Huberman, 1994). A qualitative researcher may purposefully adopt 'multiple research strategies' (Burgess, 1993) as part of a process of triangulation (Denzin, 1970), or as part of a cumulative process in the search for qualitative understanding (Reinharz, 1992). Williams *et al.* (1988: 15), who consider methods for new media as mainly extensions of existing methods, also suggest that 'the new media researcher should consider alternative methods, or even multiple methods, and attempt a triangulation of methods'. (See Mixed Methods section later in this chapter.) Accordingly, as some qualitative researchers will include standardized interviews in their repertoire of methods, we shall consider the impact of CMC on this form of data collection. The challenges faced by researchers who have attempted structured interviews online have been more extensively documented than many of the other methods we discuss. Studies of online surveys began to be published from the end of 1995 (for reviews see Comley, 1996; Witmer *et al.*, 1999) and offer considerable practical insight for any researcher who intends to use CMC in this way.

Email Surveys

In an email survey the questions are usually sent to respondents as the text of a conventional email message. To complete the survey, respondents use the 'reply' facility of their email system and add their answers to the text of the returned message. (Examples of a text-based email survey and a response are given in Appendix B.) The answers received can then be typed into an analysis program in the same way as for a conventional survey. Alternatively, a program can be written that interprets the emailed responses and reads the answers directly into a database, offering signficant savings in terms of data entry. Commercial survey creation programs[1] are available that, as well as assisting in producing the text of a survey, can carry out this interpretation of replies, provided the survey has been completed correctly (see also Smith, 1997).

Text-based email surveys are convenient for the respondent because they require no facilities or expertise beyond those that they use in their day-to-day email communication. However, because only text can be used, the survey can appear dry and uninteresting. Email in its simplest form cannot be used to transmit extended characters such as pound signs (£) and does not allow formatting of text (such as bold and italics, different fonts, etc.). In addition, although the researcher may ask the respondent to use a particular format for the reply, this is completely under the control of the individual and cannot be imposed. There is nothing to prevent the user from answering outside the boxes, from selecting three choices where only one is required or from deleting questions or altering their format. The researcher may still be able to interpret what the respondent means, as with a badly completed paper questionnaire, but the need to edit responses removes the advantages of automated data entry and can greatly increase the per-case costs.

If all potential respondents are using more modern email systems that can understand HTML[2], then these problems can be alleviated by using an HTML-based email survey. Because HTML only uses standard text characters, the survey is still sent as the text of an email. But because the email system interprets the HTML commands, the message can be laid out in an attractive way. In addition, the researcher has control over the user's responses: answers can only be typed in text entry boxes and, if only one choice is required, only one will be accepted. HTML-based email combines these advantages of Web-based surveys (see below and Appendix C) with the direct response of email. However, until HTML-enabled email systems become more common, these benefits are only possible if the survey will be covering a defined population where the researcher knows what system respondents are using.

A third possibility is to present the survey not as the email message itself but as a file (for example, a word processor document or a spreadsheet) which is attached to the email. The respondent opens the attached file, completes the survey using the relevant program, saves the file and then attaches the saved file to a return email. This gives control over the appearance of the survey, but completion and return require more technical ability of the respondents. In addition, respondents must all have access to the program (such as Microsoft Word or Microsoft Excel) in which the attached document was created. As with HTML-based mail the approach is only suitable for a defined population where the researcher knows the abilities of respondents or can provide training and support.

Some of these problems can be overcome by using survey creation software to produce a self-contained interactive survey program[3]. The program file is emailed as an attachment. Respondents run the program (for example, by double-clicking the attachment icon) and are then shown the survey questions in an attractive graphical interface which most users should find easy to understand. The program may be able to check users' responses and may allow personalized routes to be taken through the questions, producing an elegant, responsive and efficient survey. No other software needs to be available on respondents' computers, and the survey program can produce a formatted answers file which can be mailed back to the researcher for automated input to a database. However, there are a number of limitations. A program created for the Windows operating system will not run on a Macintosh and vice versa. This limits the number of respondents who can use the program, or introduces numerous complexities associated with having two versions of the same survey program. Even with a single operating system there may be unexpected technical difficulties when trying to run the program on the wide range of computers likely to be used by respondents. (Couper *et al.* (1999) found problems with all seven of their pre-test subjects). The program files produced may be large (in the case of Couper *et al.*, approaching 1Mb) which may result in unacceptable volumes of Internet traffic and may be beyond the size permitted for incoming email attachments. Indeed, some organizations may prohibit the receipt of any programs as email attachments because of fears about viruses.

Because of these problems, most of the email surveys reported to date have used the straightforward text-based route. Email surveys have been used to study small-scale homogeneous groups of online users (Parker, 1992; Smith, 1997; Tse *et al.*, 1995; Winter and Huff, 1996) and, more recently, as a method for administering a large national survey in the USA (Sheehan and Hoy, 1999). Studies report widely differing comparative response rates between postal mail and email survey returns (Sheehan and Hoy, 1999; Smith, 1997; Witmer *et al.*, 1999). Sheehan and Hoy suggest that lower email response rates may be associated with the unfamiliarity of the technology – but this is rapidly changing, and among some sections of society use of email is already almost universal.

Schaefer and Dillman (1998) conducted an experimental study in which they compared three mixed mode, multiple contact email procedures with a survey using conventional mail methods. The population for the experiment, the permanent faculty of Washington State University, received four contacts: a prenotice, the questionnaire, a thank you/reminder and a replacement questionnaire. One group received all contacts by email, a second group received the prenotice on paper and all other contacts by email (unless they responded by requesting a paper survey), a third group received the thank you/reminder on paper and other contacts by email, and the control group received all contacts on paper. The authors reported no significant difference in the response rates of the all-paper and all-email groups (both around 58 per cent), though the email questionnaires were returned significantly faster. Email responses were more complete, especially for open ended questions, and the email survey achieved much longer responses to open ended questions than the paper version (a finding of particular interest to qualitative researchers). Schaefer and Dillman concluded that, 'this study suggests the viability of a standard E-mail method based on techniques found successful in mail survey research' (1998: 392), though they recommend that it be combined with paper methods in a mixed-mode design to ensure that respondents who do not have (or do not wish to use) email are not excluded.

However, Couper *et al.* (1999) reported less successful results from their comparison of mail and email surveys of employees of five US government agencies. Their methodology was similar to Schaefer and Dillman, though their questionnaire was longer. Couper *et al.* reported an overall response rate of 71 per cent for the paper questionnaire sent by conventional mail but only 43 per cent for the email version, with very different patterns between different agencies. The difference in response rates may have been partly due to the fact that many employees, despite being automatically allocated an email address, did not in fact use email and hence never received the questionnaire. (Schaefer and Dillman, on the other hand, were able to validate the addresses of their email sample by a number of means.) Couper *et al.* also put part of the variation between agencies down to technical problems; some agencies use an email system which converts messages over a certain size (such as the questionnaire) into attachments, and a number of employees reported that they had received attachments but didn't know what to do with them. (This problem was also reported by Comley (1996) who had to split his survey into two emails.) About 21 per cent of all email respondents did not make use of the reply feature as intended, using a word processor or text editor instead. Twenty seven per cent of responses required editing before they could be added to the database, leading the authors to conclude that, 'we did not experience the cost savings expected from e-mail' (1999: 53).

Despite these problems, Couper *et al.* 'remain optimistic about the potential for e-mail as an alternative to the traditional mail survey' (1999: 54). As they point out, the success of an email survey may depend on many factors and there is a need to explore in greater detail the factors that affect nonresponse and measurement errors in email surveys.

Web-page-based Surveys

Schaefer and Dillman commented that their experiment with email surveys 'revealed the possibility that [these] represent only an interim surveying technology' (1998: 392). Many researchers are turning their attention to the World Wide Web as a more suitable medium for administering questionnaires[4] (for further information see Comley, 1996; Kehoe and Pitkow, 1996; Coomber, 1997; O'Connor and Madge, 2000; and for a comparison with email surveys, Patrick *et al.*, 1995).

A Web-page-based survey (see Appendix C) has the advantage that it appears identical (subject to the browser used) to all respondents. The survey can be given an attractive appearance utilising text formatting, colours and graphics. It is also easy for respondents to complete, typically by selecting responses from predefined lists or entering text in boxes and then simply clicking a 'Submit' button when finished. The data received by the researcher are in a completely predictable and consistent format, making automated analysis possible without the editing that may be necessary with text-based email.

The disadvantages of using the Web relate to the technical knowledge required to set up the survey. The researcher must have (or be able to call on) expertise in HTML[5] in order to create the Web pages. Survey creation programs[6] can provide 'what you see is what you get' editing of pages, removing much of the mystery of HTML, but identifying and learning a suitable program presents another hurdle to be overcome. Once the pages have been created, space on a host Internet server[7] must be arranged (this may be available as part of an ISP package) and the pages must be uploaded to the server. Uploading usually requires an FTP (file transfer protocol) program; a possible source of this may be the ISP, or the relevant facilities may be provided as part of the survey creation program. A numeric address and password for the server will be required (obtainable from the ISP), together with a steady nerve in the face of advancing jargon. Finally, it will be necessary to identify the full, correct URL (http:// address) for the Web pages so that respondents to the survey can find them.

Unfortunately, that's not quite it. When the user clicks the 'Submit' button on the survey page it activates a small program, known usually as a 'script', that transfers their answers to the host server. The script is held on the host and the page designer must ensure that the correct script is being used by the Web page, and is in the correct place on the server. Advice can be obtained from the ISP or other sources, but will usually include the terms 'CGI' or 'Perl' and by now the avalanche of acronyms may have overwhelmed the courageous researcher. As Smith (1997, *online*) concluded in her review of online surveys, 'the lack of standardization among operating systems, servers and browsers creates a challenging milieu in which a researcher must be technologically savvy as well as methodologically sound'.

Despite these problems, Web-page-based surveys offer significant advantages (which we discuss next) in terms of reach, speed and economy. Consequently they seem certain to become more and more common, especially for commercial market research. Smith (1997, *online*) predicted that Web survey software would soon become an indispensable research tool, 'along with or even instead of analytical tools like SPSS'. It may not be long before the creation of Web survey pages is routinely taught in social science research methods courses.

Advantages/Disadvantages of Conventional and Online Standardized Interviews

When we consider the advantages/disadvantages of conventional and online standardized interviews, it is in terms of their narrowly defined role in qualitative research. We suggest that, for qualitative researchers, structured interviews are useful when focused and specific contextual information is required and cost, time, reach (possible range of context) and/or anonymity are an issue. Accordingly, we shall compare and contrast conventional and online versions of this technique in terms of these four factors.

Cost Discussions about cost are relevant within and between conventional and online standardized interview methods. Conventional self-administered questionnaires are generally considered more economically viable than labour-intensive FTF or phone interviews. However, CMC can cut costs further. Email offers substantial savings as it eliminates paper and is cheap to send. Although Web-based surveys can involve initial start-up costs, once these have been met the costs for implementation and analysis of the survey are minimal (Sheehan and Hoy, 1999). However, researchers need to ensure that both they and the participants understand what is involved in terms of the costs of acquiring expertise.

Time Within conventional methods, self-completion surveys are considered time effective. But CMC offers even greater time benefits. Comley's (1996) study directly comparing email, postal mail and Web survey options showed that increased speed was a major advantage in the use of email. Schaefer and Dillman's (1998) study confirmed that email questionnaires were returned faster than their paper equivalents.

Web-page-based surveys can speed up responses even further (Comley, 1996; Smith, 1997); studies have shown that hundreds of responses may be generated over a single weekend (Sheehan and Hoy, 1999) and there are anecdotal accounts of 'thousands of responses' being received within a few hours (Gjestland, 1996). However, researchers may need to set aside a considerable period of time for solving technical problems before implementation of an online survey (Couper *et al.*, 1999) and even during it. Smith remarked with frustration that, in her Web-based survey, a Javascript[8] pop-up 'thank you' message did not work (although it had worked when initially tested) and respondents did not receive acknowledgement that their data had been successfully submitted. She then had to spend time deleting redundant information. She added:

> One respondent reported that every other question in Part 1 of his questionnaire was missing ... This remains a mystery. (1997: *online*)

Email surveys can also consume time if the researcher has to search around for addresses, if many addresses turn out to be invalid and if the form of the survey has to be explained to participants.

Reach (extension of context) One drawback to all FTF interviews is that they generally involve organizational problems. If qualitative researchers want to set in-depth studies within a wider context, arranging multiple standardized FTF interviews may present logistical problems. Phone interviews (Cannell, 1985; Sykes and Hoinville, 1985) have the potential to increase the geographical reach of researchers, but there are financial considerations, and problems remain when interviews need to cross time zones.

With the caveat that Internet use is variable worldwide (see Chapter 2) Web-page-based and email surveys offer considerable advantages in terms of increased reach by collapsing boundaries of time and space (Bachmann *et al.*, 1996; Mehta and Sivadas, 1995). Email surveys can only be sent to known addresses; but if that address is a group, a single transmission can reach many people. A drawback to this is that surveys posted to one population (a newsgroup, for instance) may be forwarded to other populations resulting in confusion about the source of responses (Coomber, 1997).

Use of the Web is growing rapidly as the information available on it proliferates, but the very attractiveness of the Web is causing some employers, in particular, to consider controlling access to it. Evidence at present is anecdotal but it seems likely that, in a work setting, fewer people have access to the Web than to email. The Web is arguably now the most popular application on home computers, but since completion of a Web-page-based survey requires the user to be online the whole time it may be less attractive than an email survey which can be completed offline. On the other hand, since access to Web pages is usually available to anyone who knows (or finds) their URL, it can be difficult to prevent people who are not part of the target population from completing the survey, or to prevent multiple submissions by the same person. Pages can be password protected, but this adds another technical challenge for the researcher and complicates the administration of the survey.

Nevertheless, because they can be completed by anyone who accesses the relevant page, Web-based polls generate very high rates of response (Kehoe and Pitkow, 1996). This points to increasing reach in terms of the potential diversity of participants (Sheehan and Hoy, 1999). On the other hand, it may be supposed that respondents are homogeneous in terms of their familiarity with Web usage – in which case online surveys may only offer understanding of limited, and specific, contexts.

A further complicating factor is the strong bias against survey research among some computer cultures that has been reported by Kendall (1999) and Paccagnella (1997). Paccagnella noted that many of the most interesting virtual communities are proud of their exclusive culture. A stranger wanting to do academic research is sometimes seen as an unwelcome arbitrary intrusion. Kendall concluded that her research about 'mudding' (use of MU* environments; see Technology Introduction) would have been unlikely to have received sufficient responses following a rash of poorly conceived surveys sent out by mudding college students (1999: 71).

Finally, if the aim of the survey is to provide a wider context, it is essential to ensure that desired participants do actually respond to research enquiries. This begins with recruitment. Simply advertising the research on a Web page is not sufficient. The researcher would need to be pro-active by, perhaps, posting information to appropriate online groups (see Coomber, 1997). Decisions would have to be made regarding the use of specific survey clearing house sites, invitations to participants posed to user groups, and direct email contact (see Walther and Boyd, 2000).

In sensitive areas response rates will also be related to the next factor we consider: concerns about anonymity (Coomber, 1997).

Anonymity The focus of some qualitative studies emphasizes the need for anonymity. When sensitive information is needed from a wide range of people, an anonymous survey may be a suitable complement to the in-depth component of the research.

Here privacy is a paramount concern. In a virtual environment, where an 'aura of suspicion' surrounds the stranger-to-stranger communication associated with survey research (Smith, 1997), research trust and credibility are essential. Smith noted that many of the respondents in her email survey had been 'extremely interested' in how she had acquired their names and addresses, and many had verified her identity and credentials before participating. Another practical difficulty is that participants using BBSs and IRC may fail to complete surveys correctly (or at all) because it is the anonymity of the medium that they most value (Myers, 1987).

Reviewers of survey research distinguish anonymity issues for email and Web-page-based standardized interviews (Smith, 1997; Sheehan and Hoy, 1999) with email being seen as a less protected medium. When respondents use the 'reply' function of their email programs to return completed surveys, the message carries their name and email address in its header. It is possible to send messages through an anonymous remailer which strips messages of their original headers and replaces them with something else, so that the originator of the message becomes virtually untraceable (Lee, 1996)[9]. Unfortunately, this anonymity may then act as a cover for multiple responses from one person.

In principle, Web surveys allow for anonymity since respondents can choose whether to include their names. Once again, this can become a problem as 'ballot stuffers' can make multiple responses. In addition, as the Web is an open medium, unwanted participants, who are not part of the target sample, might respond. If these problems are circumvented by employing password protection of a survey site, anonymity again becomes an issue. Practical details for setting up a Web survey when anonymity is a paramount concern are discussed by Coomber (1997).

Different issues of anonymity may come into play when researchers are investigating virtual communities in which participants adopt online personae. For instance, standardized interviews may be used as part of an ethnography of virtual communities. Here, personae responding to standardized interviews may be 'deliberate and elaborate fabrications' (Walther, 1992: 3). Paccagnella has questioned the meaning of socio-demographic data obtained through structured online questionnaires in these circumstances:

> What is really happening, for example, when SweetBabe, a regular participant in IRC channel #netsex and one of the hypothetical cases from our survey sample, tells us that her real name is Mary, she's thirty years old and she works as a secretary? It is wise to suppose that, more than providing us some (if any) actual information about Mary's real life, such an answer could help to understand better SweetBabe's symbolic universe, her online self-representation, her social values and relationships ... from a phenomenological standpoint, SweetBabe and her social world are for us much more real than this supposed Mary about whom we actually know absolutely nothing. (1997: *online*)

In fact, issues of anonymity and authenticity remain the core methodological stumbling block for researchers using online methods (see discussion about obtaining informed consent in Chapter 3). We shall discuss the implications for research practice of collecting data in virtual venues in Chapter 9.

In structured interviews the researcher attempts to control the interview by standardizing questions and constraining responses. It is in non-standardized interviews that the focus moves from the pre-formulated ideas of the researcher to 'the meanings and interpretations that individuals attribute to events and relationships' (May, 1993: 94). It is this emphasis which leads many practitioners to refer to such interviews as qualitative – and it is to these methods we now turn.

Non-standardized Interviews

Once we move outside tightly structured survey interviews, the interview continuum is very wide (see Briggs, 1986; Lincoln and Guba, 1985). These methods offer different levels of qualitative depth as, depending upon the interview form, participants have more or less opportunity to answer questions in their own terms (May, 1993: 92–94). The choice of interview method usually depends upon the research question itself, or upon the qualitative approach which informs the overall research design (for classifications of qualitative studies see Creswell, 1998; Tesch, 1990). Working online, less structured interviews with individuals are usually conducted by email, or by 'chatting' one-to-one using real-time software (see Technology Introduction). Less structured interviews with groups are discussed in detail in Chapter 5.

The Qualitative Interview Spectrum

At one end of the non-standardized interview spectrum is the semi-structured interview. This may be fairly formalized, using an interview protocol organized into specific thematic areas, or it may branch out tangentially from a small selection of more open-ended questions. Such interviews are more like conversations between equal participants than standardized interviews (Garfinkel, 1967). Supplementary questions (sometimes called probes) are introduced in a spontaneous manner to seek further clarification and elaboration of answers (Wilson, 1996). The main advantage of such interviews is to offer 'purposive topical steering' (Flick, 1998: 106) as the format allows interviewers to track the issues which are of most interest to themselves. In contrast, 'squarely at the qualitative end of the research spectrum' (May, 1993: 94), unstructured or 'in-depth' interviews place greater emphasis on the subjective experiences of individuals (Denzin, 1989; Clandinin and Connelly, 1994).

Interviewers who favour in-depth methods are often sceptical about how far subjective experiences may be accessed even in relatively flexible semi-structured interviews (Flick, 1998: 98). There is a concern that the interview may reflect the researcher's own agenda too closely. With in-depth interviews, it is participants who structure the form and content of extensive reflective responses (sometimes called narratives) evoked by a broad initial enquiry from the interviewer. Although the interviewer provides the focus of the interview, there is generally an emphasis on the 'stories' that people tell, the 'voice' of the person within the story, and the narrator as the prime 'knower' of self (Seidman, 1991).

There are also differences of style and emphasis between in-depth interviews depending upon the purpose of the interview, and its place within different disciplines. Methods include such forms as the long interview (McCracken, 1988), oral history (Portelli, 1998), the life story (Chanfrault-Duchet, 1991), the psychological voice-centred interview (Brown and Gilligan, 1992), feminist personal narratives (Middleton, 1993; Gluck and Patai, 1991), and the narrative interview (see Flick, 1998). Cross-national, interdisciplinary perspectives and debates about research practice in a variety of these approaches may be found in Chamberlain and Thompson (1998).

Non-standardized Interviews Online

Debates about qualitative interviewing are not only relevant in terms of discussing conventional methods, but also inform discussion about the possible place of the Internet as a research tool. For instance, we have seen that a key challenge in the design of a qualitative study is to find a balance between interview methods which give participants 'the floor' and those which allow the interviewer to pursue their own research enquiries.

The experiences of researchers who have used CMC to interview illustrate that, as in conventional studies, it is possible to achieve different degrees of balance online depending on the purpose of the study and the methodological perspective of the interviewer. O'Connor and Madge (2000), who carried out semi-structured online interviews with real-time focus groups, reported being delighted with the results because the groups successfully developed key themes introduced in an earlier questionnaire. Here the emphasis is on the interviewer's purposes. Bennett, who conducted in-depth interviews, also used real-time chat (one-to-one). She found she preferred chat to either FTF or email alternatives because it enabled an equitable research balance to be established from the beginning of the interaction. She valued the immediacy of the real-time response not only for the speed with which her own enquiries could be addressed but also because it allowed a negotiation of meaning between herself and her 'co-researchers' (while also avoiding the potential embarrassment of FTF interaction).

Researchers who have carried out non-standardized interviews using asynchronous CMC are divided about their success. Hodkinson (2000) experienced semi-structured email interviews as excessively question structured and formal. He felt unable to achieve the fruitful mutual interaction he enjoyed when conducting in-depth interviews FTF. Partly as a consequence, a number of his email interviews involved few exchanges and participants did not become as engaged as he hoped. In contrast, in the Graduates of the Millennium project, Mann was confident that semi-structured email interviews conducted sequentially over a three-year period had allowed both the student participants *and* herself to explore their own agendas.

Ferri, who focused on women with learning disabilities, and Anders, who investigated women with disabilities in higher education, both sought 'invisible' stories of women's experience within a frame of identity politics. Here, the emphasis of the research balance was firmly on the subjective experiences of participants. Anders conducted email interviews over a full year. Although discussions developed broadly from three 'staggered' questionnaires, the women were invited to reshape/reframe these questions in any way they preferred. Anders was delighted with the richness of the resulting dialogue (between 10 and 100 hours with each individual over the year). Finally Ferri (2000) set out to explore 'the potential of electronic mail to transgress boundaries between the researcher and the researched, and the product and the process of constructing knowledge'. She regularly collected messages from each participant in her 'closed' discussion list and then circulated everyone's contributions with all identifying material removed. The ensuing asynchronous discussion fora yielded 'very interactive, complex and rich data'. Ferri found working online 'an amazing way to bring people together and to facilitate participatory research' (1999, *personal email*). The studies described in this section suggest that CMC can be adapted to interviews across the qualitative spectrum. However, as we shall discuss in Chapter 6, the level of qualitative depth either aspired to, or achieved, will depend upon a variety of complex factors.

Practicalities of Organizing Non-standardized Interviews

A number of challenges are shared by all non-standardized interview approaches using CMC. As discussed above, there are considerable logistical difficulties with structured interviewing and many of these issues carry over to less structured methods. Whether working online or FTF, there are practicalities of accessing, financing and having the competence to use the relevant technology, whether recording and transcribing equipment, the phone, or the Internet. Similarly, whether using standardized or non-standardized methods, all interviewers have to make choices about sampling, gain access to participants, make initial contact, give a rationale for the investigation, build trust or credibility, persuade participants to respond, and give clear instructions about the interview process. However, at almost every stage of the interview process there are vital procedural differences which distinguish interviews which seek qualitative depth from those which identity the frequency or distribution of phenomena. We shall discuss these differences in terms of sampling, access, making contact and giving instructions in non-standardized one-to-one interviews.

Sampling Strategies in Non-standardized Interviews

As we saw above, surveys tend to focus on numerical 'reach'. In qualitative interviews sampling is more focused; the challenge is to find individuals who have experienced the phenomenon under study and are prepared to be involved (Miles and Huberman, 1994: 119). Rather than looking for representativeness 'purposeful' sampling strategies are generally adopted (see Patton, 1990). The interviewer's 'purpose' is associated with the methodological approach taken (Creswell, 1998: 112–113). For instance, a biographical interviewer might seek a unique individual, an ethnographer might seek a cultural group to which they are a stranger, a case study researcher might seek a sample showing the widest range of relevant characteristics (the 'maximum variation' of sites or participants). Purposive sampling is often constrained by logistical difficulties and traditional and online methods have different strengths and weaknesses in this area.

Considerations in Conventional Sampling

In conventional research, sampling decisions involve geographic and other practical considerations. In most studies, interviewers need to: make travel arrangements; schedule (and frequently reschedule) the times, dates and venues of meetings; set up recording equipment (often in less than ideal environments); and keep in mind transcription costs. These issues may dictate choice of site. Multiple sites increase organizational complexities which might deter the interviewer working alone. Even within single sites [10], the research design might point to multiple interviews, with the potential for further logistical problems if different participants are available for interview in the same time slot.

Arranging 'sufficient' interviews is a further serious methodological and hence logistical challenge in different approaches to qualitative interviewing (Creswell, 1998). Researchers seeking the maximum variation of characteristics between sites, or between participants, may realize that the number of planned interviews is escalating. Sometimes a decision is made to limit the scope of the enquiry if the interview arrangements threaten to become too costly or timeconsuming. There is some consensus that theoretical sampling approaches such as grounded theory require between twenty and thirty hour-long interviews and these are often on different sites to allow comparisons to be made (Creswell, 1998; Douglas, 1985). In-depth interviews might require fewer people but each interview may be time consuming (McCracken, 1988). As one researcher involved in narrative interviews commented, 'the problem of telling one's own life is that one knows too much' (Larson, 1997: 456). When 'long' interviews can last from two to four hours, ten participants might be considered reasonable (Creswell, 1998), but this is a conservative estimate. In a study of female academics in Canada, a group of five interviewers conducted 200 such interviews (Acker and Feuerverger, 1999).

In addition, there may need to be flexibility with regard to extending the interview base. For instance, with grounded theory, data are collected from a range of interviews until a particular theoretical category is 'saturated'; that is, until nothing new can be learned (Glaser and Strauss, 1967). Apart from the original interviews arranged, the researcher might need to move quickly to set up new interviews if a theoretical category needs to be refined further. The analysis of 'sufficient' numbers of interviews also involves financial considerations. With in-depth interviews the financial burden of recording, transcribing and analysing huge amounts of unstructured rich textual material is often underestimated. It is also a common place for budget costcutting.

Another consideration for conventional researchers is to be able to offer a secure, private and familiar environment where personal issues might be explored. This is particularly the case when the interviewing is sensitive (Lee, 1993). For instance, Wilson (1996) chose to interview people who had been in long-term residential care in their own homes. However, in some situations, participants might be cautious about inviting interviewers into their homes (women, the elderly, people who fear public exposure) or might not have access to private living space (if living in prisons, refuges, etc.). In conventional interviewing the alternative is usually to meet in public places, which can be noisy and lack privacy, or in non-familiar settings organized by the researcher. These options are clearly not ideal for conducting non-standardized interviews which seek to explore subjectivities in depth.

Sampling Online

How might online interviewing address these problems? Assuming that both interviewer and participants have ready access to online communication, many of the factors discussed above are not an issue when using email as an interview method. The interviewer rarely needs to travel; organizing recording equipment and costing for transcription is unnecessary; the asynchronous nature of most email interaction allows participants great flexibility in terms of the frequency and length of their responses; access to a computer in a personal environment can offer both privacy and familiarity; and, in areas where email use is ubiquitous, techniques such as 'snowballing' (finding one participant through another) can locate additional interviewees with the minimum of time and energy. So, in the online environment, there are fewer of the constraints associated with conventional research as many of the difficulties of accessing multiple, and geographically disparate, real-life sites disappear.

In addition, the global range of the Internet opens up the possibilities of studying projects which might have seemed impracticable before. In one study, CMC allowed the interviewer to widen the geographic scope of her in-depth interviews with gay fathers to include participants not only in the UK, but also in New Zealand, Canada and the USA (Dunne, 1999).

Online interviewing was also an appropriate choice for studying the trans-local and transnational subculture of the Goths (Hodkinson, 2000). In this latter study, the global reach of the research, and the established Internet culture of the participants, meant that purposive sampling was like fishing in a very big pond. If participants did not respond, or dropped out after answering an initial set of questions, Hodkinson merely tried somebody else.

However, the overall patchiness of computer access and skills (see Chapter 2) would certainly limit the possibility of purposive sampling in many areas of real life (although not of course of virtual communities). It might well defeat the aim of some interviewers, particularly in areas like oral history, to actively seek out lives in order to open up the possibility for self-expression among previously marginalized groups such as women in the family, the old, the institutionalized and hospital patients (Bornat, 1994). Even if some individuals had occasional use of email, time constraints on computer access could mitigate against longer interviews and, if computer access were limited to public venues, issues of privacy remain. Although silent communion with a computer screen in a cybercafé might attract less attention than an FTF interview in a coffee bar, the possibility of passers-by reading intimate thoughts may inhibit many potential participants (Creswell, 1998).

There is another aspect of access which has a deep resonance for online research. In principle, the virtual interviewer could camouflage aspects of personal identity such as class, age, gender and ethnicity in order to make previously limited or proscribed access possible. However, as we shall discuss at length in Chapter 7, there is strong evidence that people do make attributions about others from information which is inadvertently (as well as consciously) transmitted online.

It is possible to circumvent social cues which might be suggested by names or email addresses by, for instance, opening an 'iname' account. This allows the user to choose a context-free username (which can be almost anything) together with the domain name: iname.com [11]. Another possibility is to interview in teams. Here, characteristics such as age, gender and ethnicity may be variously represented. In the Graduates of the Millennium project, the two interviewers initially involved were a young man and a middle-aged woman. Both names were appended to all emails so the identity of an individual participant's interviewer was unclear. However, other interviewers may prefer to utilize CMC as a cloak for the real-life self and this clearly involves ethical considerations (Chapter 3) as well as implications for data (Chapter 9). We discuss possible 'democratizing' advantages/disadvantages of taking this route in Chapter 7.

Problems of Access in Non-standardized Interviews

A consideration related to sampling decisions is whether the site(s) chosen require the researcher to go through a gatekeeper who controls access to participants. Gatekeepers can grant or withhold permission to conduct research in their jurisdiction, be that a prison, a family, a golf club, a student society or a multi-national business. In their concern to protect their own interests and those of the group, gatekeepers may refuse access altogether or restrict it to particular areas, times or events (Foster, 1996). This may be less of a problem if the experience or process being studied takes place in multiple sites. Because the research is not focused on a particular site it may be acceptable to contact participants directly (Seidman, 1991: 35).

These issues take on different aspects in online research. As we have seen, using email makes the option of using multiple sites more feasible so, if avoiding one key all-powerful gatekeeper was a priority, there would be fewer logistical problems to prejudice that option. In addition email permits direct access to individuals without the use of intermediaries. This is particularly the case where researchers are investigating public sites with which they are already familiar, such as specific academic or business environments. There are also special interest sites where users consciously seek to make contact with each other. As Hodkinson noted:

> I used a combination of Web-searches and hypertext links, to collect the e-mail addresses of several Goth bands from various parts of the world, and then sent them all an e-mail which introduced my research, and requested an online interview. In fact, finding e-mail addresses was one of the most convenient aspects of using the net. Every Web-site and every e-mailing list post contains the address of the individual responsible for it, making it possible to make contact instantly. The interconnectedness between E-mail addresses, Web site URLs and newsgroups were especially useful. (1999: *personal email*)

However, it can be much more difficult to access individuals outside familiar contexts. As it is unlikely that an accurate national, or preferably international, register of email addresses will be established, problems of access remain. In the online world both moderators (the people who intercept and decide on the legitimacy of messages sent to a newsgroup or mailing list) and Webmasters/postmasters (the people who run www/email servers and have the power to give away email addresses) have the potential to act as gatekeepers.

For instance, when Foster (1994: 94) attempted to contact people through mailing lists and interest groups some moderators, 'quite rightly, took the view that my survey was not germane to the main business of the group, blocked it, and courteously informed me of this'. In another study, Smith-Stoner and Weber (2000) had to persuade teaching universities to announce their desire to interview women distance learning students through 'system wide broadcasts' in their institutions. Some institutions refused to do this. Cole (2000), however, was successful in gaining permission from the Web site manager of the US 'Promise Keepers' movement, allowing him to follow up email addresses for potential participants. As we shall see in the next section, where we discuss how a researcher might make contact with participants, the relational style of a qualitative researcher might have an impact at each stage of the access process.

Making Contact in Non-standardized Interviews

The question of *how* to gain access to participants is more crucial in qualitative than quantitative approaches to interviewing. The stress placed on the researcher as the human instrument of research means there is a greater degree of closeness and personal involvement between interviewer and participants. This relationship is crucial to the success of the research and it develops from the very beginning of the research process. As Seidman (1991: 31) noted, the way interviewers gain access to potential participants and make contact with them can affect every subsequent step in the interviewing process. To a much greater degree than in standardized interviews, the 'communicative competencies' (Flick, 1998: 55) and the perceived social and personal characteristics of the researcher are salient issues.

Current research suggests that interviewers experience email as an easy and efficient means of initial communication with contacts, whether they are subsequently interviewed in person or online. Cole (2000) arranged his FTF interviews with Promise Keepers in this way. Similarly, Hodkinson arranged offline and online interviews with his Goth contacts, through formal and informal email networking:

> One e-mailing list appeal for volunteers for off-line interviews resulted in my conducting two tape recorded group discussions. In another, numerous e-mail exchanges with an individual I met fleetingly at a Goth festival resulted in a place to stay, and a guide for an important off-line research trip to Leeds. I have found that the Internet is particularly suited to establishing the first contact in such eventual networks of respondents. (1999: *personal email*)

Another approach is to place strategic advertisements in appropriate newsgroups, mailing lists or BBSs. Bennett (1998) found her male participants by advertising in groups such as alt.acadia and soc.men, stressing that she was seeking extended interaction in a confidential one-to-one exchange. Dunne (1999), who was seeking a generally invisible population marginalized in both mainstream and gay culture (gay fathers), included her email address in publicity leaflets and journals.

Locating participants is only the first step. Given the emphasis on relationship building, a key consideration in online research is whether text-based email communication is able to establish sufficiently close contact with potential participants, in the early stages of the research, to secure their collaboration (Seidman, 1991: 31). In conventional research, making initial contact with participants usually involves writing a letter or phoning, often followed by a first contact visit. These introductory moves can be a daunting experience if interviewers are shy, have difficulties in self-presentation, or act awkwardly on the phone (Seidman, 1991). Making first contact using CMC might alleviate these pressures slightly: email is a less intrusive medium than the phone as it almost never interrupts the receiver (possibly minimizing the chance of an initial irritated response), and it requires less attention to formalities than a letter (although in some situations formality would remain the most suitable approach – see also the discussion of netiquette in Chapter 3).

It could be argued that email messages at least hold their own with the phone and the letter as a means of projecting an ideal introductory style, incorporating, 'seriousness but friendliness of tone, purposefulness but flexibility in approach, and openness but conciseness in presentation' (Seidman 1991: 38).

Giving Instructions in Non-standardized Interviews

A final step in the early stages of arranging qualitative interviews is conveying the form and purpose of the research to new recruits. Whether the preliminaries are discussed by letter or phone, the interviewer using conventional methods is generally able to clear up any remaining misunderstandings FTF. Qualitative interviews which are arranged and then conducted online have to rely on text to put across the broad and finer points of the research, to spell out the interview protocol and to arrange any other 'housekeeping' details such as flagging the arrival of follow-up information (Foster, 1994).

In one study where semi-structured online interviews were to follow a brief online demographic survey, the researchers stressed that 'advance organizers' were essential to clarify the research procedure. Phrases such as: 'This is the second step in the interview process. After you return the survey we will begin the interview' were used to talk participants through each stage of the research (Smith-Stoner and Weber, 2000: 6). However, the interviewers found that, because online instructions required more context and explanations than conventional research, there was a danger that the interactions became too long and convoluted:

> Two computer screens full of text seems to be most effective in getting respondents to explain and elaborate on responses. Scrolling back and forth on the screen with longer posts can become confusing and result in topics being missed. (2000: 9)

Another issue, which is clearly relevant at all stages in online interviewing, is the precise verbal formulation of instructions and questions. As Smith-Stoner ruefully reported,

> We are used to saying 'A picture paints a thousand words'. In reality, online, 'A word paints a thousand pictures' (quote from Eric Berkowitz, a fellow student) so we have to allow for that. We asked people about 'meaningful learning' and they said they didn't understand the questions. When we eliminated that as a question and asked: 'What were you passionate about?' they used the word 'meaningful'. So we had to tinker a lot with the words. (1999: *personal email*)

As we have seen, there are problems with some aspects of setting up online qualitative interviews for, as with conventional research, 'various methods may produce different problems, suspicions and fears in different persons' (Flick 1998: 58). However, in suitable contexts, online qualitative interviewing does seem to offer the possibility of minimizing some logistical problems in the research design. This is important because, 'every step the interviewer takes to ease the logistics of the process is a step toward allowing the available energy to be focused on the interview itself' (Seidman, 1991: 39).

Observational Techniques

For the qualitative researcher, observational work offers another means to understand the social meanings which are constitutive of and reflected in human behaviour. Observational work can have advantages over interviews. Foster's (1996) comprehensive overview of these advantages suggested that: information about human behaviour can be recorded directly without having to rely on the retrospective or anticipatory accounts of others; observers may see the familiar as strange, noting features of the environment/behaviour that participants may not be able to see; patterns and regularities in the environment may be observed and analysed over time; observation can give access to information about people who are busy, deviant or hostile to taking part in research (Foster, 1996: 58).

With these aims in mind, there are multiple options for observational approaches. Researchers may 'themselves participate in the activities of the group they are observing (participant observation); they may be viewed as members of the group but minimize their participation; they may assume the role of observer without being part of the group; or their presence may be concealed entirely from the people they are observing' (Frankfort-Nachmias and Nachmias, 1996: 207).

Clearly, currently available text-based CMC is not an appropriate method for research which seeks to observe the 'real' world. However, recent studies, which focus on *virtual* communities, begin to challenge the basis of terms such as 'observation' and 'natural contexts' as used in traditional research.

Observation of Linguistic Behaviour

How might we begin to conceptualize observation of the constructed environment of the Internet? Let us consider the foci of observation in real life. Frankfort-Nachmias and Nachmias, (1996: 210) identified four areas of observational interest: non-verbal behaviour (body language and particularly facial expressions), spatial behaviour (issues of physical closeness and distance), linguistic behaviour (both what is said and how) and extralinguistic behaviour (rate of speaking, loudness, tendency to interrupt, pronunciation). Using currently available technology only one of these four options, that is linguistic behaviour, seems to be a clear focus for observation via the Internet. Indeed, for these purposes, 'the Internet is a research setting par excellence, practically irresistible in its availability' (Jones, 1999b: 13). Although researchers and participants are not 'visually or auditorially present' (Ferrara *et al.*, 1991: 14), researchers may also observe non-verbal and extralinguistic behaviour exhibited in 'emoticons' (Metz, 1994) and paralinguistic and non-linguistic cues such as 'electronic paralanguage' (see also Chapter 6):

> expressives such as used in comic strips (eg, 'humpf'), multiple vowels to represent intonation contours (eg, 'sooooo'), multiple punctuation marks (eg, 'well how did things go yesterday????' (to express exaggerated questioning or surprise), use of asterisks for stress (eg 'please call - we've *got* to discuss'). (Murray, 1988: 11)

Language Analysis in Experimental Settings

Assuming that a qualitative researcher sets out to 'observe' linguistic behaviour online, a key methodological issue becomes relevant. Qualitative researchers focus on 'natural' as opposed to contrived research settings. The preference is to observe participants in the 'field', which is generally interpreted as the site where social action takes place whether the researcher is there or not (Schwandt, 1997). To observe participants in artificial settings is seen to diminish the possibility of attaining *verstehen* or empathic understanding.

However, a great deal of the research which has looked at linguistic behaviour using CMC has been conducted in experimental settings. Paccagnella (1997) has given a detailed and insightful review of literature which has identified the limitations of experimental designs from the perspective of qualitative researchers. For instance, Baym (1995a) points out that experimental findings rarely draw attention to: the nature of the group or the individual participants who have taken part in interaction; the task the group was required to accomplish; the kind of CMC used (particularly if it was synchronous or asynchronous communication); and the time the group spent interacting. As Paccagnella (1997) notes, time constraints seem to be a particular source of flaws in experimental studies.

A meta-analysis of previous research (Walther *et al.*, 1994) argues that time-controlled group interaction (communication exchanges were often only 30 minutes long) could be held responsible for the different way that CMC has been characterized in artificial as opposed to field studies. These authors conclude that being asked to complete a task in a given time, in a context where participants have minimal knowledge of the other people involved and little expectation of future interaction, can hardly be considered a parallel to observing the social richness and interactional complexity of an established online group. Paccagnella concluded his review of experimental observation of discourse in online communities with the following words: 'the invitation issued by Robert Park in the first half of this century to get the seat of our pants dirty by real research conducted out of the classrooms and laboratories is still valid' (1997: *online*).

Discourse Analysis in Naturalistic Settings

Can studying the 'naturalistic' linguistic and extralinguistic behaviour of interactive online communities further the deeper aims of qualitative research, which are to study participants' 'ideas, attitudes, motives and intentions, and the way they interpret the social world'? (Foster, 1996: 61).

Ethnomethodological approaches to social enquiry, such as conversational and discourse analysis[12], are broadly concerned with how people construct their own definition of a social situation (see Schwandt, 1997: 44–45). These methods focus on ordinary, mundane, naturally occurring talk to reveal the way meaning is accomplished by everyone involved. Qualitative researchers with an interest in these approaches can 'observe' the natural conversations of various kinds of newsgroups, synchronous conferencing (using real-time chat), and of MU* formats (see Technology Introduction). By 'lurking' unseen they are able to watch the interaction without intervening in any way.

Some examples of studies which have observed conversations online are: Denzin (1999) who used conversational analysis to interpret the gendered 'narratives of self' in a newsgroup focusing on 'recovery' from alcoholism; Rodino (1997) who looked at the multiple, sometimes contradictory, ways in which users 'performed' gender on an IRC channel; and Paccagnella (1997) who studied the 'logs and messages' of an Italian virtual community named Cyberpunk. There are differences in scale in such research. Paccagnella recorded and archived messages every month for eighteen months. He was then able to conduct searches for particular situations, for example the dialogues between specific groups of actors, in a given period, on a particular topic. His constructivist interpretation of Cyberpunk involved analysing nearly 10,000 messages from 400 users. Rodino qualitatively analysed text from observations made over a much shorter ten-week period:

Most of these observations were recorded. I made observations by entering chat channels and lurked (entered no text). I watched interactions on chat channels: #boston, #chat, #chatzone, #gaysex, #hottub, #ircbar, #romance, #talk, #teenchat, #texas, #truthdare. (1997: *online*)

Denzin (1999) also intensively analysed threads of conversation as particular topic areas in a newsgroup were elaborated by participants.

All these studies sought to understand cultural meanings and the complexity of daily social experience through dense deep readings of cybertext discourse. This observation of online communities attempted to 'make visible the cultural apparatuses and biographical histories that allow such talk to be produced and understood' (Denzin 1999: 122).

However, Paccagnella (1997) has identified some ways in which qualitative analysis of online discourse might lack some of the analytic breadth that is possible when FTF conversations are observed. Referring to Marvin (1995), he points out that, as in FTF interaction, there is a dynamic dimension to conversational turn-taking in CMC. The time taken typing, and the delays between turn-taking (which can be a few seconds in synchronous CMC or several days in asynchronous options), can shape the mood of the interaction. This information is often lost in the analysis.

Second, the logs or messages ignore the context of speech: 'the actual experiences of individual participants at their own keyboards in their own rooms all around the globe'. Finally, Paccagnella cites Reid (1995) who points out that CMC discourse is not intended for people uninvolved directly in the interaction. Perhaps even more than in FTF conversation, CMC loses part of its sense and meaning when reread afterward by those who had not been involved.

Clearly, CMC offers an excellent site for qualitative researchers who 'observe' discourse online. While some discourse analysts (like Denzin – see Chapter 3) lurk (observe unknown), others (like Paccagnella) participate in the online interaction. Participant observers of virtual communities may emphasize dialogue or may seek an ethnographic account of specific online cultures.

We shall now discuss how qualitative researchers might investigate virtual communities as cultures. For, in cyberspace as in real life, 'man is an animal suspended in webs of significance he himself has spun' (Geertz, 1973: 5).

Participant Observation

One definition describes FTF participant observation like this:

As a methodology for ethnographic field work, participant observation is a procedure for generating understanding of the ways of life of others. It requires that the researcher engage in some relatively prolonged period of participation in a community, group, and so on ... Broadly conceived, participant observation thus includes activities of direct observation, interviewing, document analysis, reflection, analysis, and interpretation. (Schwandt, 1997)

What would it mean to understand a way of life in a virtual community? Kendall identified the following areas where the social meanings of online participants might be explored: (a) changing meaning and perceptions of Internet usage for various groups, (b) cultural and subcultural affiliations of Internet users, and (c) explorations of political action and affiliation online (1999: 63). In all these areas participant observation of CMC interaction is seen to be a key way forward (Sharf, 1999: 244), a view stated strongly by Kendall:

> Much as my personal biases lead me in that direction, I would never have the audacity to suggest that all social science research projects ought to include participant observation. Yet with regard to research on interactive on-line forums, I recommend just that. (1999: 57)

Certainly data that give insight into online groups from the perspective of those involved are becoming increasingly available. At some level all researchers who comment on virtual communities of which they are part are participant observers (Horn, 1998; Rheingold, 1994; Turkle, 1995). Findings from some qualitative studies emphasize the ethnographic status of their descriptions of specific virtual worlds (for example, Baym, 1992; Kendall, 1999; Meyer and Thomas, 1990; Myers, 1987; Reid, 1991; Sharf, 1999). As with FTF research, online participant studies will be extended in time (often over years) for:

> Reaching understandings of participants' sense of self and of the meanings they give to their on-line participation requires spending time with participants to observe what they do on-line as well as what they say they do. (Kendall, 1999: 62)

The cultures which are investigated may be as diverse as a Usenet group devoted to discussing soap operas (Baym, 1992, 1995b); a breast cancer mailing list (Sharf, 1999); an online version of a real-life subculture (Hodkinson, 2000); and an interactive social forum (MU*) conceptualized by participants as a virtual bar (Kendall, 1999). (For further discussion of research into the cultures of online communities see Chapter 9).

Negotiating Access in Participant Observation

Participant observation is, above all, concerned with access. There are some immediate practical bonuses about making initial access to venues in cyberspace. In contrast to the real-time world, it lends itself to 'hanging around' (lurking) in situations where a person's presence is normally brief or transient (Foster, 1996). In conventional observational research there are also practical difficulties in recording and writing about a setting at the same time as observing it, and time lags in recording observations can allow inaccuracies and distortion. This is clearly not a problem online.

In cyberspace the physical presence of both researchers and participants is concealed. For instance, this allowed Sharf (1999), out of general interest and curiosity, to subscribe to, and to lurk on, a mailing list called the Breast Cancer List. After a few weeks she began to collect interesting postings but without any specific objective in mind. Some months later, when she realized that her casual interest had turned into a developing research project, she became an 'active' participant of the group. Sharf's experience has parallels with FTF participant research, where a researcher may pose as a real participant (perhaps a novice) – or, if more openly, as an 'acceptable marginal member' (Hammersley and Atkinson, 1995).

However, there are clear differences in FTF situations. Here, even more than with interviews, ascribed characteristics such as age, gender or ethnicity might limit access, or contribute to the researcher being defined as an insider or outsider. For instance, in J. Foster's (1990: 168) ethnography of petty crime, 'being small, young and female was a decided advantage', while in Liebow's (1967: 249) study of street corner men in the USA, 'colour' was a non-negotiable factor. 'They saw, first of all, a white man. In my opinion, this brute fact of colour, as they understood it in their experience and as I understood it in mine, irrevocably and absolutely relegated me to the status of outsider'. P. Foster (1996: 72) accepted that, 'as a 40-year-old white male, I would find it difficult to present myself as a young 'rap' music enthusiast, or develop close peer-type relationships with school pupils, or directly access the world of radical feminists'.

The potential for moving beyond these limitations is certain to become a central issue in qualitative online research in general, and in participant observation in particular. As Turkle (1995: 228) has noted, 'Life on the screen makes it very easy to present oneself as other than one is in real life', allowing identities to be 'flexible, swappable and disconnected from real-world bodies' (Shields, 1996: Introduction).

Hodkinson's online participatory study of Goth culture provided an intriguing counterbalance to accepted conventional research practices in which gaining acceptance might involve dressing in acceptable ways and/or behaving in ways that don't alienate the group. Although some researchers might see online participation as a means to move beyond the signs and significations of appearance, Hodkinson showed that this could work the other way:

> The most obvious badge of subcultural status - one's physical appearance - becomes devoid when one is communicating with a group of strangers communicating only by e-mail. Therefore, in such forums, the purple and pink streaks in my hair, my piercing, make-up and subculturally distinctive clothing, which have been so useful to most of my research became redundant. In such a

situation one must establish subcultural capital - or insider status - only through what one writes. (1999: *personal email*)

At a later point in his research Hodkinson found a way of bringing his appearance back into the equation by publishing photographs of himself on his own Web site, and advertising it on Goth fora.

In conventional research, access may also be difficult if a physical environment or certain forms of behaviour are inaccessible or difficult to observe. Many people assume that the social world of cyberspace is readily accessible once there is technological mastery but, once users have more experience, they begin to realize that the online world also has its hidden areas. These may be areas of place.

For instance, Kendall (1999: 70) investigated an online forum known as 'BlueSky'. In the course of her research she realized that some participant observers may have made limited assumptions about the character of online communities because they had never penetrated beyond the most public and easy-to-find interactive 'rooms' and had only interacted with other 'newbies'. She pointed out that, 'regulars who seek a quiet place to convene with friends build their own rooms, which allows them to control access'. It is only researchers who both 'find' these secret places, and who then negotiate access, who begin to grasp the boundaries of the community.

There may also be hidden areas relating to the levels of insider status which are reached. Hodkinson discovered that his ready acceptance as a Goth in real life did not give him immediate access to Goth behaviour online:

> Regardless of one's involvement in the Goth scene off-line, acceptance in their exclusive on-line forums can take considerable time to earn. Furthermore, it requires the learning of particular sets of norms for on-line behaviour distinct from the values of the subculture as a whole. Nevertheless, on-line forums are useful in that one is able to 'lurk' (read without posting) for a period of time, and pick up the described norms of behaviour. Having done this, I gradually became more adept and confident at communicating with the groups in a way which was consistent with these unwritten rules. Furthermore, I found that I became able to convey written details which revealed my status as a subcultural insider. (1999: *personal email*)

As Hodkinson grew to delight in and to accept his new status as a Cybergoth it would seem that (as in some FTF studies) he did risk 'going native'. In other words, the changed balance of insider–outsider might have an impact on the ways he finally described and analyzed data (see Kerr and Hiltz, 1982).

Issues of identity penetrate all levels of CMC research but, with regard to participant observation, they have also been a pertinent issue for FTF research. In sensitive or volatile real-life settings there may be very real difficulties in coping with the consequences if a researcher's identity and purposes are discovered. Some commentators suggest that, in the online environment, people need not fear any 'real' repercussions from their actions. The way seems open to participate in any virtual community, and to publicize findings from any kind of participant research, without considering the possibly painful outcome of personal exposure. However, there is no doubt that if online research focuses on such areas as money laundering, bribery in global companies or terrorism the researcher could not rely on the dubious security offered by electronic communication systems for protection from the consequences of deciding to 'publish and be damned!' (see Chapter 3).

Ethical Issues in Participant Observation

Complete participation in field research has been justified on the grounds that it makes possible the study of inaccessible groups or groups that do not reveal to outsiders certain aspects of their lives. However, in CMC, as in FTF research, there are serious considerations regarding the invasion of privacy. As discussed above, Sharf did not set out to study the Breast Cancer mailing list. Once she realized that her research interests were being engaged she decided to 'contextualize' herself by mailing posts explaining that she was interested in breast cancer as well as being an academic researcher, for:

> In retrospect, I believe I had a sense early in that it was prudent to let fellow list members know that I had two reasons for participating in this forum. (1999: 249)

Sharf's sensitivity to the ethical dimensions of participant research was sharpened by her understanding of the highly personal nature of the Breast Cancer List postings and the fact that many subscribers were coping with the disease themselves. Yet, even without these additional dimensions, ethical issues relating to the secret collection of data remain (see Chapter 3).

Collecting Personal Documents

While subjective experiences may be collected from interviews (see above), qualitative researchers also use personal documents to increase their understanding of participants who shaped history and culture and were shaped by it (Chamberlain and Thompson, 1998). Such documents might include (a) diaries or journals which can record day-to-day events or fragments of experience and (b) written autobiographies. While diaries and journals are 'ongoing records of practices and reflections on those practices' (Connelly and Clandinin, 1988: 34), autobiographical writing attempts to 'write' the whole life. Researchers use autobiographical materials to find a written record of someone's life in the person's own terms (Creswell, 1998). They seek someone 'distinctive for her or his accomplishments and ordinariness or who sheds light on a specific phenomenon or issue being studied' (Denzin, 1989: 111).

Solicited Documents

Personal documents can be solicited from participants in many walks of life. In conventional research they have been used to record the subjective experiences of participants whose unfamiliar lifestyle, or whose individual responses to a way of life, may be outside the experience of and/or inaccessible to the researcher. For instance, they allow a researcher to explore young people's experences of education and the family (Mann, 1998), or an inmate's subjective experiences of imprisonment (Cohen and Taylor, 1977).

One practical benefit of this approach is that different participants can record events that may be in a closed access location, or going on simultaneously in a single location. When life histories, autobiographical material and diary work are requested and presented online these benefits increase: access to participants (and hence range of experience) is wider and multiple sites and/or locations may be involved.

Soliciting personal documents in conventional research also has disadvantages. Some authors have noted that the method asks a great deal of participants. They are, in effect, asked to be 'co-researchers' (Burgess, 1993); a commitment like writing a diary on a regular basis can become onerous and people may give up (Lee, 1993: 115). There are also communication difficulties. On the one hand, a participant's handwriting may be difficult to read. On the other, the researcher may need to put across detailed instructions about how to focus observations.

How might these challenges transfer to an online context? Clearly, handwriting would no longer be an issue. Some issues, such as gaining and retaining the co-operation of participants, remain (see Chapter 2). As with conventional research, the effectiveness of the method would depend, to a great extent, on the personal response of participants to the whole idea of writing in this way. Not everyone would want to do it and, from a sampling point of view, there may be differences in those who do. Here are a range of responses from some Graduates of the Millennium students to a general query about whether they might be interested in keeping a journal of their university experiences:

> I spend a lot of time E-mailing and so I think the diary approach would be a fairly good idea for me. Just let me know what aspects of my life at Cambridge and my thoughts on them you're interested in, and I'll let you know.

> I am sure I will be far too busy or at least absent minded to keep up any sort of diary response, but I shall be happy to answer all of your specific enquiries.

> Sorry - I'll have zero initiative about topics myself but I'll answer any questions y'all might have.

I'll do it - But just remember to give me a prod now and then to get me thinking. Writing a commentary on life to someone who will listen to whatever you say is surprisingly difficult.

Diary methods have been used by university staff to monitor the well-being and intellectual progress of students involved in long-distance learning[13]. As with Mann's study, not all students volunteered to participate and some (the minority) kept a handwritten diary, which they submitted at the end of the course module, rather than sending regular email entries. This has enabled Furneaux, the lecturer and researcher involved, to compare traditional and email diaries, identifying the pros and cons she associates with using the diary as an interview method:

Pros
- Subjects can dash off a few thoughts as they occur to them; it doesn't require a lot of time on any one occasion.
- It's easy to set up and does not require subjects to expend much energy to send you your data.
- They don't have previous diary entries in front of them as they write, so you get authentic thoughts at that point of time, 'unpolluted' by previous entries.
- You get insights into individual students' thinking/lives you rarely get on a campus-based course (and we are a department that has a lot of staff/student contact and support). They mention minutiae/details they'd never tell you in a tutorial, especially about their personal lives/circumstances.

Cons
- Receiving regular entries from subjects, it is tempting to 'reply', if only to acknowledge receipt of the e-mail. This can turn into more of a two-way correspondence than a diary and can interfere with the methodology. Also, if for any reason the researcher stops replying then the entries can stop too.
- Subjects write more in conventional diaries, and can look back at and refer to what they have written previously - it makes for a more coherent whole to analyze.
- It's a new genre for everyone and some people take to it more readily than others. Some write a glorious 'stream of consciousness flow' - everything and anything that occurs to them at that point in time. Pure gold! Others can write a rather stilted cross between a factual narrative and a report about the study they have done/plan to do. This is not very informative!
- You are asking quite a lot of people - they have to remember to keep sending dairy entries at regular intervals over a period of time. Some send more than others, which makes it hard to compare them for analysis purposes, as you have entries from different people on different occasions.

(1999: *personal email*)

Furneaux concluded that traditional diaries give a sense of a story unfolding, while emailed entries are more like 'snap-shots' at particular points in time. In addition, while some traditional diary entries were very short – 'I didn't do anything today' – all emailed entries were at least a paragraph long. This suggests that the rapid note-taking style of much email correspondence might diminish the feeling of being burdened by the task of writing journal entries regularly.

Furneaux and Mann both recognized the relish, depth and flair shown in the outpourings of some email diarists (see also Chapter 8). Although an online journal/diary is not always appropriate, it may offer some participants a highly successful vehicle for being deeply reflective. There is a general awareness that people are often more willing to 'interface' with a computer screen than talking directly (Thu Nguyen and Alexander, 1996). Why should this be? Why is it a commonplace experience that 'it is much easier to articulate thoughts to a screen than a person' (GOTM student)? Thu Nguyen and Alexander (1996) claim that it is human–computer interaction which allows individuals to project and realize their thoughts. Matheson and Zanna (1990) suggest there are two reasons for this. Computer users are relaxed and reflective because they feel less inhibited by the possible evaluation of others. They also seem more aware of their private selves. The intimate nature of typed, informal communication seems to increase a person's concentration on their own reactions and opinions. In particular people seem to be in tune with covert aspects of themselves, such as personal feelings, attitudes, values and beliefs (Matheson, 1992).

There is certainly empirical evidence supporting the view that users may experience a sense of symbiosis with the computer. 'Rather than the computer/human dyad being a simple matter of self versus other, there is, for many people, a blurring of the boundaries between the embodied self and the PC' (Lupton, 1995: 98). Some authors describe the loss of self-consciousness as they write and the deep connection with the screen:

> A pen now feels strange, awkward and slow in my hand, compared to using a keyboard. When I type, the words appear on the screen almost as fast as I formulate them in my head. There is, for me, almost a seamless transition of thought to word on screen. (Lupton, 1995: 97)

> I don't even feel I am typing ... I am thinking it, and there it is on the screen ... I feel totally telepathic with the computer. (Quoted in Turkle, 1984: 211)

A student from the Graduates of the Millennium study echoes these sentiments: 'in a way, although it's a computer screen, it brings out a lot more than speaking to someone does'. It seems that, for a certain period, a totally absorbed writer may be only marginally aware of the eventual participant. As Gibson noted some years ago, 'everyone I know who works with computers seems to develop a belief that there's some kind of actual space behind the screen, someplace you can't see but you know is there' (cited in Kitchin, 1998: 17). It seems possible that the 'space behind the screen' may be a way of conceptualizing an individual's dialogue with their own mind. 'We are searching for a home for the mind and heart. Our fascination with computers is more erotic than sensuous, more deeply spiritual than utilitarian' (Heim, 1992: 61, cited in Lupton, 1995). As thoughts, hopes and history are typed onto the keyboard they reassemble as neat, accessible text on the screen. This ability of the computer to reflect a person back to themselves opens up the possibility that for some individuals CMC journals may be an ideal method to generate rich data about the subjective self, a self accessed in what may be experienced as an almost transparent process of relating to one's own consciousness.

Unsolicited Documents

Personal documents in conventional research may also be obtained from other sources such as private collections, archives and libraries. Access to personal documents in CMC is at a stage of transition. While extended texts (such as autobiographical writing) might be consciously stored on a computer or as print-outs, 'letters' written online have a more ephemeral quality than those written on paper. One example of a series of letters and journal entries which were stored and later published is Ruth Picardie's reflections/correspondence written in the last stages of her illness (1998). However, the Internet offers huge advantages in terms of finding unsolicited materials from public online sites. For instance, DejaNews (see Technology Introduction) allows an archival search for all recorded newsgroup entries to be conducted. On the Web, hypertext links also allow users to look deeper into aspects of the content made available in any one document. In addition, innovations in methods of electronic storage and dissemination of written materials may eliminate the challenge of collecting written documents from geographically dispersed sites, or those to which access is limited or forbidden. On the other hand, issues of copyright remain and may present even greater problems than documents retrieved in more conventional ways, as the legislation is constantly changing (see Chapter 3).

In terms of documentary analysis, conventional methodological challenges relating to the authenticity of documents (forgery, mistaken authorship, falsification, propaganda) and the agenda of the writer remain (Finnegan, 1996; Scott, 1990). However, there are exciting prospects for discussing these issues online with enthusiasts all over the world.

Mixed Methods

Many qualitative researchers use a multi-method approach in their investigations in order to examine different levels of the same situation or to focus on different aspects of the same phenomenon (Luttrell, 1999; Dillabough,

1999; Mann, 1998). However, CMC studies may offer further opportunities and challenges for mixed-method research. Above all, informed commentators (Fielding and Lee, 1999: *personal email*) identify the development and convergence of technologies as a major opportunity for future research.

As data become increasingly digital in form the boundaries between data sources and manipulation processes will weaken. Qualitative software packages already have SPSS export facilities, survey researchers are more aware of automatic text processing, and qualitative and quantitative data taken from the Web can be 'dropped' into analytic software with ease. The technological developments are crucial as researchers who study interaction on the Internet itself tend to use a combination of methods (Rice and Rogers, 1984; Garton *et al.*, 1999). For instance, Garton *et al.* suggest that forms of self-reporting (such as interviews and diaries) may readily access perceptions of media use, while observation or electronic data gathering may be better for measuring actual use of the Internet (see Schiano, 1997).

There are other mixed-method precedents. In some studies questionnaires, in either conventional (Dunne, 1999) or online versions (Smith-Stoner and Weber, 2000; O'Connor and Madge, 2000; Seymour *et al.*, 1999), may be followed by online semi-structured interviews. Semi-structured interviews may be combined with solicited diary materials (Mann, 1998). Online interviews, or participant observation of groups online, may be accompanied by 'documentary' analysis of newsgroup or list materials (Paccagnella, 1997; Sharf, 1999) or popular conventional journals (Cushing, 1996). Mixing CMC methods with FTF methods may be particularly important if researchers wish to investigate differences and/or similarities between online and offline interaction. For instance, Stewart *et al.* (1998) were able to compare the efficacy of FTF and virtual focus groups with young people. By using FTF and email interviews Hodkinson (2000) was able to access, and make comparisons between, a subculture which had real-life and virtual domains.

Alternatively, researchers may seek to access, in real life, participants who frequent virtual worlds (Turkle, 1995). Correll (1995) used a three-way methodology to study an online community and its processes. First, she observed the daily traffic between patrons at a virtual café, occasionally asking them to explain various actions or conversations. Second, she interviewed twelve patrons using semi-structured interviews via private email. Finally, she interviewed eight patrons in two FTF group sessions. Similarly, Kendall (1999) combined three years of participant observation and analysis of online documentary material with FTF interviews and participation in FTF gatherings. Kendall noted that, 'The ability to access off-line environments provides useful information between online and off-line interaction, but such access may not always be feasible' (1999: 71).

Conclusion

This chapter is advisedly called an introduction to online methods. We have attempted to contextualize online approaches within the conventional research canon, but we are aware that we have only mapped in the possibilities for Internet research at the most superficial level. Different disciplines, and different traditions within these disciplines, will, no doubt, capitalize on innovatory practices discussed here and take online research into hitherto uncharted territory. The potential for development and diversity is immense. We shall now turn to another area where the flexibility of the new technology offers exciting alternative forms to a well-established research method. As we shall see, the focus group can now become 'virtual'.

Notes

1   In March 2000 these included MaCATI (www.senecio.com), Survey Internet (www.aufrance. com), Survey Said (www.surveysaid.com), Survey Select (www.surveyselect.com), Survey Solutions (www.perseus.com) and SurveyTracker (www.surveytracker.com). MaCATI's editing program is for the Macintosh only and it has versions of its data collection program for the Mac, Windows and Java. All other programs run under Windows only. Smith (1997) has pointed out that, while Web survey development software is increasingly available, packages have huge variations in terms of price, function and server compatibility. It remains to be seen which, if any, of these packages will become the standard.

2   HTML stands for HyperText Markup Language – the coding system used to create pages which can be displayed by Web browsers. It consists of a series of 'tags' which give instructions to the browser about how to display the text. For example, the text 'bold words and <i>italic words</i>' would be displayed by a Web browser (or HTML-enabled email system) as:
    bold words and *italic words*
    However, if the same text was read using a standard email system, all the characters would be displayed exactly as typed:
    bold words and italic words
    HTML documents were originally created by typing the tags using a text editor. However, it is increasingly common to create HTML using 'what you see is what you get' editing programs where the author applies the formatting required (such as bold or italic) and the program automatically adds the relevant tags.

3   For example, Perseus SurveySolutions Interviewer; see www.perseus.com.

4   The best-known Web survey is Georgia Tech's Graphics, Visualization, and Usability Centre (GVU) which uses repeat participation to map current and changing Internet user characteristics and attitudes (see Kehoe and Pitkow, 1996, and www.gvu.gatech.edu/user_surveys/). Over 55,000 respondents were involved in the first five surveys and new versions of the survey are sent out biannually.

5   See note 2.

6   See note 1.

7   In this context, a server is a large computer which forms part of the worldwide network of permanently-connected computers that is the Internet. Your pages are held on your host server. When someone requests a page, the request is routed to your host server and the page information is passed back to their computer via the network.

8   Javascript is a programming language which can be used to make Web pages more interactive.

9   Increasingly, the administrators of remailers are charging for their services. However, it is still possible to send anonymous email free of charge – www.anonymizer.com offers this service.

10 A single site is one where 'an intact culture-sharing group has developed shared values. beliefs, and assumptions' (Creswell, 1998: 114).
11 For more details see: www.iname.com.
12 See Silverman (1993) for a summary of differences between approaches.
13 The study was carried out by Clare Furneaux at the Centre for Applied Language Studies, University of Reading, Reading RG6 6WB, UK (http://www.rdg.ac.uk/AcaDepts/cl/CALS/furneaux.html).

5 Online Focus Groups

In recent years, focus groups have become a well-known instrument in the toolkit of qualitative research. Used in both market and academic research, they are a specific type of group discussion which is usually conducted in an FTF format involving between five and ten participants. Although there is no universal direction as to how focus groups should be conducted (Krueger, 1988: 103), they are characterized by open-ended questions, which are arranged in sequence, yet which have scope for flexibility in format. The freedom and spontaneity which characterize the successful focus group have been described as being more akin to brainstorming than a structured group discussion (Krueger, 1988: 29).

There can also be many permutations in the use and nature of focus groups. They may be held over single or repeated sessions. They may be held before, after or alongside other methods (for example, questionnaires). Participants may be recruited using means ranging from snowballing to random sampling from telephone and/or other directories. The defining feature of focus group participants is that they are from all walks of life. The participants of any single focus group, however, can usually be characterized by their homogeneity. Depending upon the topic, the participants of a focus group will be of similar profile in terms of age, gender or experience.

The Focus Group Method

Morgan has suggested that the main feature of the focus group method is that it is 'interaction focused' (Morgan, 1988: 9). It is this interaction which is thought to illuminate *what* people feel or think as well as *why* they may feel or think in that particular way. According to Krueger: 'Focus groups provide a special type of information ... They tap into the real-life interactions of people and allow the researcher to get in touch with participants' perceptions, attitudes, and opinions in a way that other procedures do not allow' (1988: 177).

Unlike individual interviews, focus groups are thought to be about model and consensus building, as particular attitudes are pursued in discussion and agreement or disagreement noted. Their ability to capture the process of opinion formation makes focus groups unique among investigative techniques (Morgan, 1988: 17). The inductive analysis of focus group data also allows for a variety of findings on a wide range of possible issues. The ability for the results to be presented in a concrete and understandable manner makes focus groups relevant to a diversity of situations and contexts (Krueger, 1988: 39).

Advantages/Disadvantages

Morgan and Spanish (1984: 260) have suggested that focus groups represent a 'compromise between the strengths found in other qualitative methods'. Like participant observation, they allow access to an interactive process. Like in-depth interviewing, focus groups allow ready access to content. Speaking more broadly, Morgan (1988: 15) has argued that the main advantage of focus groups is the large amount of data that may be collected in a relatively short time period. In contrast to individual interviews, focus groups provide the researcher with insights into the opinions of many people, after a single interview session. In these respects, focus groups provide a cost-effective means of obtaining data which are rich, detailed and contextual (see Krueger, 1988).

Like any research method, however, focus groups are not without disadvantages. While the interactivity of the focus group can be a positive aspect it can also lead to discussions which are disparate in focus and which produce only surface data. The involvement of multiple participants can also lead to difficulties as the role of the facilitator is challenged when discussion diverges, particular participants are domineering while others are quiet, or differences of opinion become extreme or not different enough. The need for focus group participants to meet at a common place and time, in an environment which is conducive to uninhibited discussion, can place further demands upon the researcher. These requirements can be difficult to meet.

Innovation in the Focus Group Technique

Although focus groups continue to be conducted largely using an FTF format, they are also open to innovation (see Krueger, 1988). Telephone focus groups are one such standard innovation. These are more cost effective than FTF groups, and allow researchers to assemble people in a variety of locations whom it would otherwise be hard to reach. However, the telephone focus group method has a number of disadvantages including the absence of non-verbal communication (such as head nodding, eye contact), and a reported reduction in richness of evidence which is characteristic of 'in-person' or FTF focus groups (Krueger, 1988: 168).

Nevertheless, Krueger (1988: 169) has advocated that the researcher should be encouraged to 'twist it a bit' and discover just how robust and hardy focus group interviews really are. In the decade since this advice was given, advances in communication technology have made possible a further twist: the online focus group. If, as Morgan (1988: 23) has suggested, 'the key question' of focus group operation is 'how actively or easily can participants discuss a topic of interest?', then online focus groups represent an important avenue for further exploration.

Online Focus Groups

Despite the vast proliferation of chat rooms and Usenet services such as mailing lists and newsgroups, and MU* environments, the use of digital media such as the Internet in group research is still fairly novel. To date, little has been written about the use of online focus groups, despite their suitability for providing a virtual 'twist'. In a rare 'early' article about online focus groups, Gaiser (1997) suggested that the online environment represents vast opportunities for methodological innovation, with our own imagination the only limitation. He went on to say that, since there are no established guidelines for most online activity, debate about what can be achieved and how it can or should be done is currently wide open.

The Internet constitutes an important new domain in which the focus group method may be adapted and even transformed. The remainder of this chapter examines the elasticity of the focus group method where the Internet is concerned and looks at theoretical and practical issues including:

- types of focus group: synchronous (real-time) or asynchronous (non-real-time)
- access requirements for participants
- the online venue and environment
- the recruitment and participation of focus group members
- topic choice
- self and other disclosure
- issues of rigour and validity

Types of Online Focus Group

As with their FTF equivalents, online focus groups can take a variety of forms. In all cases, the type of focus group may be determined by the nature of the topic for discussion and the number of participants required; but online focus groups have additional issues for consideration. The most important of these is the question of timing. Online focus groups may be conducted in 'real time' (synchronous) or in 'non-real time' (asynchronous) or using a combination of both.

The Real-time Focus Group The decision that is made about timing has significant implications for the functioning of the group and the conduct of the research. The real-time focus group is conducted synchronously: all participants are online at the same time and the transmission of messages between them is immediate, or thereabouts. The text which one participant types in at his or her keyboard is immediately transmitted to the group as a whole. Other participants can read the message as it is typed or as soon as the 'return' or 'send' button is pressed. Participants can 'reply' to any message immediately upon its receipt.

Examples of synchronous CMC systems include the Relay program on Bitnet, IRC on the Internet and 'interactive talk' on bulletin board systems (BBSs) (Ma, 1996: 174).

Regardless of system, real-time focus groups can be fast, furious and highly interactive. You need not wait for others to comment in order to send further messages. The participant who is most proficient at typing is the one with the 'power' to 'say' the most. Important questions which need to be asked here include: who is replying to whom? Is the term 'reply' of relevance at all? In the real-time chat of an online focus group, the distinction between replying and sending becomes blurred as the interactivity defies conversational turn-taking.

The Non-real-time Focus Group The non-real-time online focus group is conducted asynchronously, with no requirement for participants to be online at the same time. Like email, which is also an asynchronous form of CMC, the sender transmits a message which can be responded to by other participants at some time in the future. Unlike email, however, the non-real-time online focus group is conducted at a 'conference site' as opposed to individual email addresses. A conference site can be a type of folder, like the one that appears on both Macintosh and PC screens for the storage of files. A conference folder is a specific space where participants can 'post' (send) messages about a particular topic or topics. Conferences can have restricted or public access. While messages in a conference scenario can be posted and read by participants in real time, this is not usually the case. In conferencing, all messages posted are archived in the folder and can be opened and responded to by other participants whenever they are online.

Non-real-time focus groups can overcome differences in time zones. They can also overcome the disadvantages which participants with low typing skills may experience in a real-time group. Likewise, and akin to email interviewing, non-real-time focus groups may be particularly valuable when detailed and highly reflective comment is sought.

The decisions which researchers make about whether to conduct their online focus groups in real or non-real time carry important ramifications. For example, the nature of the data generated by real and non-real-time online focus groups will be qualitatively different. Similarly, the rapport between participants will vary as will the technical aspects of how members come to participate in the online focus group. Whether an asynchronous focus group is still in fact a focus group is a further issue for discussion. Theoretically, at least, a non-real-time focus group could even be conducted using email, as long as the facilitator and all participants posted all of their individual messages to all other participants and the facilitator. These issues are returned to later in this and other chapters.

Set-up and Access Requirements

As with FTF focus groups, online focus groups have a number of logistical requirements. Depending upon how the online focus group is to be conducted participants may also need specific conferencing software, as discussed below. However, the software requirement may be simply a Web browser. Both real-time and non-real-time focus groups can operate from particular Web sites; to locate a focus group, participants only need know the relevant Web address (for an example of this see www.hbs.deakin.edu.au/women2010/). A further possibility, often used for commercial qualitative research, is the hire of virtual facilities (see Technology Introduction).

Conferencing Software

Online focus groups can also make use of specific conferencing software packages. A range of packages are currently available and appropriate choice of software can ensure that the specific needs of a study are addressed. For the Young People and Health Risk study, the package 'Firstclass Conferencing' was used. This software has provisions for private and public communications in both asynchronous (non-real-time) mode, which is available via conference areas, and synchronous mode, available via chat areas. The communications of Firstclass Conferencing are text based.

Firstclass Conferencing had been purchased by Deakin University for online and distance teaching requirements (see http://www.deakin.edu.au/firstclass/). For the Young People and Health Risk study, the software was used under the Deakin University licence and was made available to the other participating study sites through the registration of users onto Deakin's server. Usernames (user identification), password details and the Deakin Web address were emailed to the study co-ordinators prior to the online link-up. The usernames and passwords allowed the participants to be members of the visitor category of a privilege group on the Deakin Firstclass Server.

The on-site study co-ordinators in each of the participating countries downloaded the software from the Deakin University Web address and installed it on the computers with Internet access that were to be used in the online focus group link-up. To use Firstclass (both the asynchronous conference folder and synchronous chat rooms), each participant needed a username and password. These were required because the chat room and conference areas were configured to allow access only to the nominated participants of the study. A total of forty-nine usernames and passwords were issued (forty-eight for the participants and one for the facilitator/controller). Participants opened the Firstclass software by double-clicking its icon on their respective computer desktops. Prompts then asked the participants for their usernames and passwords. Once these were entered, the participants entered the online area through double-clicking the 'Risk Study' icon.

Once inside the Riskstudy conference, the participants were presented with the computer desktop shown in the chart below. The 'red chat', 'blue chat', 'green chat' and 'yellow chat' marked the real-time chat areas. These chat rooms constituted four online focus groups. These areas were mutually exclusive but were operated simultaneously. The coloured conference folders were the non-real-time areas.

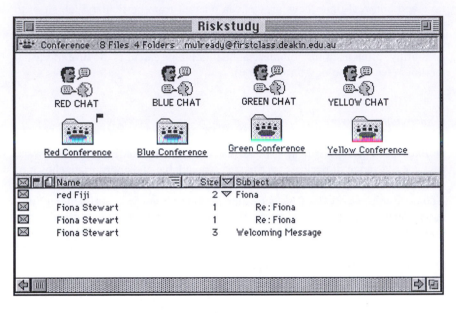

Although the Young People and Health Risk study had both synchronous and asynchronous facilities, the online focus groups were conducted in the synchronous chat areas. All discussion took place in real time. The non-real-time conference area was used for the posting of a welcoming message by the facilitator. This message was awaiting participants when they first entered the study area. Had the young participants enjoyed continued Internet and Firstclass access, the focus group discussions could have taken place in the conference areas on an ongoing basis.

The Implications of Software Choice

In deciding which approach to adopt, there are several issues which a researcher needs to consider. First among these is the issue of privacy. Many Web sites have universal access, so that participation can be open to anyone who comes across the site. However, some Web sites are 'closed' and can require a financial subscription or password in order for users to either read and/or contribute to the content of the site. In contrast, a researcher who uses conferencing software is immediately restricting access to those to whom the software is available. For example, in the Young People and Health Risk study, there was no possibility of participation unless one had access to the Firstclass Conferencing software.

There is usually a financial cost attached to use of a software product. Providers of virtual facilities will also expect to charge for their services. Cost, therefore, is a further issue which a researcher needs to consider in deciding how to conduct online focus groups.

In this respect, the principal benefit of linking an online focus group to a Web site, irrespective of its timing, is the minimal cost involved. This approach may be cost effective for the researcher because it does not require the researcher to purchase or pay licence fees for a software product. It does, however, incur the expense of setting up the Web site itself. Knowledge of computer languages used to create Web sites (such as HTML and Java) would also be required.

On the other hand, the cost to a researcher of a conferencing software product may be borne by the researcher's host institution. For example, researchers who are attached to a university or other institution may find that a suitable conferencing product is already available under the institution's generic licensing agreement for staff use. Cost is likely to be more of a problem for the non-affiliated researcher who has little access to technical and financial infrastructure support.

The Online Venue and Environment

Site Selection

The issue of focus group venue is a key consideration for researchers wishing to conduct focus groups which are dynamic and in which participants are comfortable and uninhibited in their contributions. In the FTF context, focus group site selection is usually based upon several key requirements. When the focus group goes online, the issue of site selection assumes new meaning as old definitions need to be reworked.

Krueger (1988: 86) has suggested that the FTF focus group venue needs to be (a) easy for participants to find, (b) free of distraction and interruption, (c) relaxed and informal, and (d) quiet. Concurring with Krueger, Morgan (1988) advocates that the chosen venue needs also to represent a 'neutral' space. He suggests that the physical environment of the focus group should be known equally to researcher and participants. Unlike individual interviews which tend to be conducted at the homes or workplaces of interviewees or in the offices of the researcher, the site of a focus group should be 'on the patch' of neither the researcher nor any participant. A neutrality in venue is thought to maintain the space as non-hierarchical. It is also an attempt to ensure that participants feel they have equal footing.

For Lindlof, however, it is the naturalness of the venue in qualitative research which is important. He argues (1995) that the habitat of the culture members is significant. In the context of FTF focus groups, group rapport and an atmosphere conducive to uninhibited discussion may depend upon non-alien (read natural) space.

The costs and benefits of 'neutral' as opposed to 'natural' sites continue to be debated. It is in the context of such debate that the online environment can represent a welcome addition. As Gaiser has suggested, 'conducting research online is as close to a natural setting as one can get without conducting participant observation' (1997: 136).

In the online situation, the concept of space defies easy categorization. While Meyrowitz (1985) argues that cyberspace constitutes a blurring of boundaries between public and private space, Horn, the founder of the MU* Echo in New York, suggests that cyberspace provides us with 'the perfect combination of distance and intimacy' (1998: 295). Depending upon the 'set-up' of an online focus group, participation may emanate from sites which are both natural and neutral.

For example, the 'site' of the online focus group may be considered natural if the computers that are to be used are located at the participants' homes, offices or another familiar environment. In the FTF context, the issue of neutrality of site can also be problematic. For the online focus group, however, a sense of neutrality is almost inevitably ensured. Because participants are unlikely to be aware of the nature of the location and physical environs of any of their co-participants, feelings of bias or alienation may be minimized. (Although deliberately encouraging participants to share this kind of information can also be effective – see Chapter 6.) In these two important respects, the existing tenets which guide the conduct of FTF focus groups need a radical rethink. Online researchers should not bypass such concerns. Rather, they should remain cognisant of the unique challenges which these issues present in the 'new' environment of cyberspace. The virtuality of the online focus group serves not only to challenge traditional focus group practice, but can go some way towards alleviating the dilemmas noted about the organization and conduct of FTF focus groups.

An Appropriate Environment

Scholars of focus group methodology have also cited the creation of a comfortable environment as a further important criterion for a successful focus group. In the context of FTF focus groups, this can be achieved in a number of ways. For example, the provision of refreshments, name tags, a room which does not alienate and the strategic alignment of chairs and tables have all been noted as going some way towards ensuring that the 'non-expert' participants of focus groups are made to feel comfortable (see for example Frey and Fontana, 1995). However, rather than simply ensuring that the physical surrounds of the group meeting are comfortable, Krueger (1993: 68) has suggested that participants should be made aware that their comments are welcome, valued and that their active participation will be encouraged. The emotional and/or psychological atmosphere of the group in question will also be considered important. Krueger concludes that this 'appropriate environment' should likewise reflect the socio-political ambience of the research.

In the context of FTF focus groups, an appropriate environment is also a 'permissive' one. This means that the atmosphere of the FTF group permits and encourages self-disclosure as well as uninhibited discussion of particular knowledge. Krueger (1988) has argued that this environment is facilitated not only through the words of the discussion but through body language such as head nodding, smiles, facial expressions as well as verbal expressions of encouragement. When the focus group discussion is virtual, new challenges are clearly introduced.

In the online focus group, the body is absent or, at most, virtual. With the exception of emoticons (see Technology Introduction), the development of an online environment, where participants feel free to contribute, relies solely upon textual communication. Although real-time and non-real-time focus groups will present different requirements in regard to a permissive environment, the role of the facilitator will be qualitatively different to that for FTF focus groups. 'Lacking the visual and verbal cues that would be available to them in a conventional setting to encourage them', Gaiser (1997: 140) has suggested that online focus group 'participants have little information to ensure [sic] them they are performing as expected'. In the initial stages of an online focus group, there is little space for passive facilitation. The online focus group facilitator will usually need to take a pro-active role to establish a permissive and friendly atmosphere.

The Welcome Message

In order to create a permissive environment for the online focus group, regardless of the timing chosen, several steps need to be taken. First, 'lacking the visual and verbal cues', facilitators need to be pro-active in introducing themselves. They should also be quick to outline the nature of the group and, as the researchers, their expectations of it. These tasks can frequently be combined. For both real-time and non-real-time groups, an introduction can be easily and quickly given using a pre-scripted message posted in the asynchronous conference area.

This was the case in the Young People and Health Risk study. Although the focus group discussions of this study were conducted in real time, the facilitator posted a 'Welcome Message' in the linked, non-real-time conference area of the study. Once participants came online in the chat room areas they were asked to enter the conference area and read the welcome message. At the end of the message they were requested to return to their designated chat rooms and begin the group by introducing themselves. In the context of a non-real-time online focus group, the posting of such a message is of course essential.

Example

Welcome Message which was posted in the asynchronous conference area of Young Women and Health Risk Study

Hello Everyone,

Welcome to the Young Women and Health Risk Study. We are glad you made it online. Before beginning your discussions, I'd like to introduce myself. My name is Fiona Stewart and I am the researcher who has organized this study - I am in Melbourne. I know in each of your countries you have your own organizers and we are all working together.

When you have read this message, can you please leave this area and go to the chat rooms. Your organizers will have decided which colour teams you should belong to. To begin your discussions, can you introduce yourselves to each other. You might like to tell the girls in the other countries how old you are, what your hobbies are and what you are studying at school. After doing this you are free to begin discussion. Remember, the purpose of this linkup is for you to tell each other what you talked about in your morning discussion groups.

From time to time my name will appear on the screen and I will enter your chat room. Don't worry about me, I am not checking up on you. I just want to make sure everything is running smoothly. I will not interfere in your discussion.

One last thing, please be polite to everyone, if you disagree with something said, tell the others so, but please do it nicely. Oh, and remember everyone have fun, this is not an exam!

All the best,

Fiona

The posting of a welcome message is useful because it provides participants with background information about the study at hand. The introductory outline of the FTF context is usually more than simply information giving in purpose. It is usually recognized as an effective mechanism to relax participants and engender a permissive group atmosphere, prior to the formal commencement of the discussion. In the online context, the intent and effect are similar. As well as being informative, an online welcome message can help set the tone of the online group. In the absence of FTF contact of body language, refreshments, name tags and informal chatting, this is of obvious importance.

The welcome message also presents an opportunity for facilitators to say something about themselves. One direct result of the virtual environment is that the personal characteristics of the researcher (such as gender, age or race) are not obvious. Making these explicit in either broad or specific terms may help the participants to know who they are dealing with and to feel comfortable (also see the discussion of ethics in Chapter 3).

In the Young People and Health Risk study, the combination of time areas meant that the welcome message had particular advantages. In this study the online link-up was scheduled for a Saturday afternoon. There was only a three-hour time difference between countries. The link-up followed the morning conduct of FTF focus groups. The welcome message proved an effective mechanism for linking the morning and afternoon sessions. Because the message was pre-posted in the asynchronous conference area, it was waiting for the participants as they each came online. In this situation, a combination of real-time and non-real-time area can work well to create a welcoming and comfortable atmosphere.

A welcome message can also be used to encourage participants to introduce themselves. As in FTF focus groups, online 'small talk' can help focus group participants to feel at ease with each other and the group situation. During such a period of small talk, the facilitator can notice individual characteristics (albeit as they appear in the text) prior to the commencement of the group. For example, the first messages could be taken up with the participants giving their names and a brief outline of their occupation, marital status, family life and so on. Participants could also outline why they have volunteered to participate in the focus group. In the Young Women and Health Risk study the following introductions occurred:

Yellow Oz: Hello. We are the Yellow Oz team. Our names are Jenny and Sarah
Yellow Beijing has joined the chat.
Yellow Oz: I'm Jenny and I am 13. I enjoy sport and music
Yellow Beijing: Sorry we are late. we just finished the face to face discussion.
Yellow Oz: Thats Ok. We haven't been waiting long.
Yellow Oz: Hello my name is Sarah. I like playing sport and talking to my friends on the phone
Yellow Beijing: hello,my name is Luo xuan, I am 12, I study at no.35 high school of FeenTai of Beijing , China.my hobby is music,and making friends.
Yellow Oz: Our first discussion was about smoking what did you talk about first
Yellow Oz: Some of us learn Chinese, do you learn English?
Yellow Beijing: I am zheng Man, I am 12 and study in the no. 23 middle school.
Yellow Oz: hi zheng Man
Yellow Oz: hello Luo xuan are you still there?
Yellow Beijing: I like singing,and I like to make friends with you

---

Just as Krueger (1988) has noted the value of small talk in the FTF focus group context, so it is useful and possible in the online environment. However, small talk may be less likely and less appropriate if the online focus group is conducted in non-real time. Online small talk may be most possible (and useful) in the real-time environment where interaction is immediate and undelayed.

In the online environment the facilitator may also need to reassure participants, particularly in the early stages of an online link-up. For example, in her focus groups Casey Sweet (1999) needed to reassure participants that they were in the right place for the discussion and that their contribution was welcome. The following extract was taken from an online focus group with participants in various American states and cities:

> 01:21:20 PM Casey: HOW MANY TIMES HAVE YOU PARTICIPATED IN AN ONLINE FOCUS GROUP FOR WHICH YOU WERE PAID?
> 01:21:32 PM Sue: 3
> 01:21:52 PM Cheryl: Am I in the right place now?
> 01:22:18 PM Cheryl: none...could you tell from my difficulty in getting in the right place?
> 01:22:44 PM Casey: APPROXIMATELY HOW MANY TOTAL PERSONAL AND BUSINESS HOURS DO YOU SPEND ONLINE MONDAY THROUGH FRIDAY?
> 01:22:50 PM Edward: I've done 1 previous online focus group. This is my 2nd.
> 01:23:01 PM Lisa: 35
> 01:23:04 PM Casey: CHRISTINE -- YOU'RE DOING FINE.

A Permissive Environment

In an online focus group, it may be likely that a permissive environment will take longer to establish, although once it is established it may become even more permissive in atmosphere than a traditional FTF focus group. While Morgan and Krueger caution against expecting focus group participants to talk about 'anything and everything' (1993: 7), the online environment can produce discussion of a nature which is not accessible elsewhere. Sex educator David Schnarch writes about precisely this when describing his experience of discussing sex, intimacy and relationships with four adolescent boys in an America Online chat room. He concludes: 'It was an opportunity for me to look beyond textbook theories and learn ... Those boys and I briefly crossed the age-appropriate realities about sex, intimacy, and relationships' (Schnarch, 1997: 15–16). Schnarch suggests that, even if possible, it would have been unlikely for such discussions to have taken place in an FTF context.

Horn, too, has argued: 'Nowhere else in life do we have a place that gives us just the right distance and time to negotiate such new territory' (1998: 95). On the basis of a 1995 poll of 209 members of her online town 'Echo' (by definition also a MU*), she reports 42% claiming to have 'said things on Echo [that] you wouldn't say to anyone or only to your closest friends?' (1998: 195). The potential for a heightened permissive online environment is, arguably, a unique aspect of CMC and one which alters the ways in which focus group discussions can be conducted.

Selecting Online Participants

As with FTF focus groups, the selection of participants for an online focus group depends upon the purpose of the group and the study for which the group is being conducted. Regardless of the format of the focus group in question, there are several features to consider in regard to its participants.

First, although focus group participants may vary from group to group, they are usually all non-experts (Krueger, 1988). This means that almost anyone can participate in a focus group discussion depending upon the topic. Second, focus group participants can come from all walks of life. In this respect, they are each expected to bring specific knowledge to bear on the discussion (Morgan, 1988). It is precisely because focus group participants come from all classes and occupations, are male or female, young, old or in between, that each can offer a unique contribution to the focus group discussion. Third, participants of any specific focus group are likely to be relatively homogeneous in some way. While they may vary in age and gender, they will have similarities in experience or life situation which render them suitable for a focused group discussion.

The requirements of participants for online focus groups are little different to those for conventional groups. It is the recruitment of online participants which may vary.

Recruiting Online Focus Group Participants

Participants for FTF focus groups can be recruited by a range of means. For example, if conducted as part of a larger, multi-method study, focus group participants may be selected from the sample of respondents who completed an earlier questionnaire. If focus groups are the sole method of data collection for a study, participants may be recruited through snowballing or through a random sample taken from any number of directories, consumer mailing lists, school or university attendance lists, membership lists, organization records, referrals and telephone screening (Krueger, 1988).

In addition to these conventional recruitment practices, participants for online focus groups can be contacted online. Depending upon the purpose of the focus group, participation may be serendipitous and coincidental or organized well in advance. Chat rooms and conference areas which are linked to Web sites may invite participation from anyone who happens to 'surf' or 'lurk' around the site. For focus groups conducted using specific conferencing software, participation may be more exclusive, as was the case in the Young People and Health Risk study. Given that focus groups, by definition, focus upon a narrow range of topics, suitable participants may be recruited from pre-existing Internet chat rooms, conference groups and listservs, both public and private. For example, researchers who wish to conduct a focus group on the topic of men's health may benefit from a search of chat rooms, Web sites and Usenet services which already exist in that area. Resourceful use of the Internet can expand the boundaries of how participants for focus groups may be contacted and recruited.

Identifying Online Focus Group Participants

Unless researchers arrange to meet their online focus group participants physically as well as virtually, they cannot be completely sure of whether or not their participants are who they say they are. For example, in the Young People and Health Risk study, Stewart and Eckermann have been asked on numerous occasions about the verifiability of the young women and men who participated. In this particular study, however, they were assisted by three additional on-site co-ordinators in the participating countries. Without these co-ordinators they would have been unable to confirm the demographic profile of who was participating.

This may be a particular problem when it is important for groups to be homogeneous.

Arranging a Homogeneous Focus Group Sample

People in focus groups have been found to 'disclose more to others who are similar than to people who differ from them' (Jourard, 1964: 15) or who have a commonality rather than diversity (see Krueger, 1988: 26) and this represents both a potential problem as well as a welcome challenge for those conducting online focus groups. The need for focus group participants to be suitably similar (see Morgan, 1988) can be problematic when participants are recruited online. This is for obvious reasons. Unless online focus group participation combines the textual dimension of chat rooms or conferencing with the visual dimension of digital cameras and/or voice, the researcher will be unable to be sure that the focus group really is comprised of, for example, adolescent girls.

The severity of this as a problem depends upon the criteria established by the researcher for the particular focus group at hand. However, if focus group participants are recruited from a particular Web site or listserv and the focus group is to be about a topic linked to the site or list, then this may not be a problem. For example, if a focus group is to be conducted on the issue of the chronic illness colitis, recruitment of participants from linked listervs and mailing lists may be viable since all those contacted could be expected to have an interest in or knowledge of that illness.

Morgan has suggested that a key question in regard to good focus group operation must be, 'how actively or easily can participants discuss a topic of interest?' (1988: 23). If the answer is 'very easily', then the precise identity of focus group participants may be less important than it is conventionally assumed to be. In this definition, a 'successful' focus group, need not necessarily depend upon the homogeneity of the participants involved.

Number of Participants

As with FTF focus groups, the number of participants in online focus groups is a key factor. However, whereas in an FTF environment the voices of more than ten participants can mix into each other and shy participants tend to be silenced, in the virtual environment participants cannot be drowned out. The fact that each individual has a computer ensures that group members always have 'voice'. The danger of jeopardizing the interaction of the online focus group exists in other areas. The first of these areas is the time sequence of the group in question.

Participant Numbers and the Real-time Focus Group When an online group is conducted in real time, the number of participants is particularly important. Too many participants can create a group discussion which moves so rapidly (high interactivity) that it skims over otherwise complicated issues. One result of this could be that participants are denied the space to respond to the issue in question. As Horn has noted, 'because the conversation is live [in chat] you can only talk as fast as you can type' (1998: 63). Those who can type fastest will be those who dominate the dialogue. They will also be those who have most control over the tone and direction taken by the focus group. This dilemma is redolent of the frequent problem in FTF focus groups where the participation of some group members is hampered by the lack of 'sufficient pause' in discussion (see Krueger, 1988: 27).

The role of the facilitator can also be made difficult if a real-time focus group contains too many participants. The more participants, the more interactive an online focus group discussion may be. The more interactive a focus group, the harder it may be for the facilitator to control and/or structure the dialogue. This is particularly the case when it comes to ensuring that adequate time is allotted for each topic and that the nature of the discussion is both appropriate and useful. That some participants are bound to be more vocal and more skilled at typing than others is an important element to consider when deciding upon the ideal number of participants for a real-time online focus group.

Participant Numbers and the Non-real-time Focus Group When the online focus group is conducted in non-real time or asynchronously, many of these problems disappear. For a non-real-time focus group, the number of participants is almost limitless. For example, an asynchronous focus group, perhaps linked to a Web site, means that participants can contribute and respond at leisure and when the topic at hand is of interest. While in practical terms there are no limits to the number of members that can be incorporated into an asynchronous group, if the virtual environment is to be made comfortable, permissive and conducive to ongoing self-disclosure, then a very large number of participants is clearly not advisable.

Regulating the Numbers of Non-real-time Focus Group Participants The ideal number of participants for an asynchronous group will depend upon both the researcher's aims and the nature of the study. Furthermore, it is likely to be the result of trial and error. What is equally important is that participants are encouraged to return to the group, time and time again. The creation of an interactive chat area in a Web site may, on its own, be insufficient encouragement for potential participants to join or for other participants to continue to contribute. If this situation should arise, participation may need to be encouraged by the posting of reminder emails on mailing lists and listservs. When participants are successfully encouraged to return to a non-real-time online focus group discussion, their repeated contributions will assist group bonding and rapport as well as keeping discussion dynamic and lively. When Horn (1998: 305) asked the participants of the Echo MU* why they stayed, more than half cited as the reason their co-participants and the resulting bond they had developed with them.

In non-real-time focus groups, while regular contributions from participants can serve to bind a group together, successive lots of 'new' participants may lead to discussion being disjointed, if not stymied altogether. A key question, however, is how, in publicly conducted, asynchronous focus groups, can superfluous participants be prevented from participating? When and how should an online focus group be closed? What are the consequences for the focus group when an overload of participants occurs?

Participant Dynamics

Morgan (1988) has noted that focus groups can often be dominated by one or more vocal members while other participants say little. Apart from suggesting strategies around this common problem he asks the further question: 'does this matter?' Does it matter that discussion can be dominated by some, while other members do not speak at all? Does it matter if the conversation is not evenly distributed or that contribution is not equal? These are issues for both FTF as well as online focus groups. In the online focus group, however, such issues can present unique challenges for the facilitator. See Chapter 6 for a more detailed discussion of the role and requirements of the online focus group facilitator.

Uneven Participation In any group situation, it is almost inevitable that some members will contribute more than others to a discussion. But does this matter in the specific context of focus groups? In FTF focus groups, the uneven contribution of group members may have little impact upon the quality of the data obtained. Those who are vocal may bring valuable insights to the discussion of the focus group topic. Rather, uneven participation may be undesirable because the participation of shy members is constrained. This is problematic because it is assumed that focus group participants will each bring a unique perspective to a discussion. In this line of thinking, this may mean that the opportunity to obtain data of substance and value risks being squandered. When introverted, shy or softly spoken participants are overridden by those more vocal, the researcher needs to be concerned not only about the nature of the data generated, but also about those which remain out of reach.

In the online focus group, shy or introverted group members may be less likely to be silenced. Of course, quiet participants may have their questions or comments ignored by others, but this is a different issue. Yet, in online groups, participants may get confused and be unsure of their participation, in finding out how the group is operating or what is expected of them. For example, in her online focus group about online research activities, Sweet (1999) discovered precisely this problem. Although some believe that: 'The online world is famous for its democracy - everyone has a voice! You gotta modem, you can talk' (Horn, 1998: 32), this is not always the case. The following example is taken from the opening stages of one of Sweet's online focus groups where the participant Edward was unsure of the process:

> 01:17:38 PM Casey: ALSO, I WOULD LIKE TO KNOW THE KINDS OF HOBBIES YOU PARTICIPATE IN? AND DO YOU EVER RESEARCH THEM ONLINE?
> 01:18:20 PM Sue: Hobbies: sports, investing and I research both online
> 01:18:36 PM Lisa: Biking, reading, collecting enchantica. I research all online
> 01:18:38 PM James: CART racing, football cards, wheat pennies; research racing daily
> 01:18:45 PM Edward:am I here now?
> 01:18:48 PM Jane: Craft projects, cooking, fishing, investing and fitness. I research most of them online
> 01:19:00 PM Ben: I love sports, writing, reading, cards, computing,investing, and I research them online
> 01:19:02 PM James: hey edmund
> 01:19:38 PM Edward: have things started yet?

After this exchange of dialogue, his pleas for information were quickly addressed by the skilled group moderator.

A further factor which can influence the nature of participation in both online chats and conference areas concerns the virtual environment of the focus group. Because fellow participants can be neither seen nor judged 'in the flesh', participant inhibitions may be loosened. In the online focus groups of the Young Women and Health Risk study, differences of ethnicity and nationality were experienced in a distinctly non-hierarchical manner. In contrast to an FTF focus group, which would have needed to have been held in a single location in one of the participating countries, the online focus groups can be understood to have been conducted in a 'neutral' space, which in turn engendered free and equal participation. Furthermore, the young women could not discriminate between one another on factors such as prettiness, body shape, fashion or makeup.

On the other hand, group rapport may be difficult to establish, precisely because of the distance which anonymity in participation may engender. There are no clear arguments in these respects. There are, however, issues about which online researchers need to be vigilant. Some of these concerns can be addressed via the intervention of the online focus group facilitator. Here, facilitator intervention can take the form of requests for further explanation, reminders about the topic at hand, questions to one or more particular participants as well as requests for adequate pauses to allow everyone to respond. These techniques are discussed in further detail in Chapter 6.

Pair Friendships Although online focus groups are not without their drawbacks, disadvantages long inherent in FTF focus groups can be, sometimes quite inadvertently, addressed in the online environment. For example, in the literature about participant numbers in FTF focus groups, Morgan (1988) and Krueger (1988) have identified 'pair friendships' and 'whispering', respectively, as problem areas for focus group facilitation. Yet, with focus group software such as Firstclass Conferencing, it is impossible for any two participants to have a private conversation, unless they resort to external email correspondence. This is because the chat room or conference area of both the real-time and non-real-time focus groups are public spaces. Fellow participants can automatically see what is typed in by any other group member. While one line of text may be addressed to a single co-participant, the text can be neither whispered nor hidden from view. With this software, the discussion will be heard and created by all participants. However, other software packages, such as Hotline, allow any participant to 'click' on anyone else and to invite them to chat privately. With this software, participants may 'whisper' even more effectively than in an FTF session, as no-one would realize what was happening.

Group Conflict Online Although conflict can arise in an FTF focus group, efficient group facilitation can usually prevent its open occurrence. For a range of reasons, conflict may be more likely in the online environment.

Conflict online is known as 'flaming' (see Technology Introduction for a more precise definition of this). Flaming can occur on the Internet in chat rooms, conferencing, Usenet and email, to name a few, and represents an on-going challenge for Internet users, regardless of whether they are conference hosts, facilitators or participants.

It is unrealistic for researchers to expect that online focus groups will be exempt from flaming as conflict may occur between participants themselves or between participant and facilitator/researcher. That said, researchers need to be aware of the possibility of flaming and ready with strategies for addressing it, should it occur.

Reasons for flaming are diverse. What is agreed upon, however, is that the narrow 'bandwidth' of online chat or conferencing can create situations of intense frustration for all involved. In communication terms, bandwidth refers to the range of elements involved in various communication styles (Kollock and Smith, 1996). For example, an FTF focus group would be considered as having a wide bandwidth as communication is not only oral and aural but also visual. It is informed by body language, eye contact, appearances, the environs of the room where the group is being held, as well as the appearance, demeanour and voice tone and intonation of the facilitator or researcher.

In contrast, online communication is usually only textual. The multiplicity of components which constitute a wide bandwidth of communication are not present in the online environment. 'In cyberspace we are what we talk about. The electronic dialogue is at the bottom of everything. This is how we communicate our personalities'. 'We are stripped of everything but our words' (Horn, 1998: 49 and 81).

This is not, however, to suggest that online words are without intonation, inflection or the support structure of a paralanguage, for these are all important features of CMC (see Chapter 8 for further discussion). The bandwidth does, however, remain narrow. The main point for researchers to consider here is that while participants in an FTF focus group may use their bodies, either consciously or subconsciously, to emphasize a point, make eye contact and support what they are saying, or object to what is said by others, in the online situation there is only words. The frustration that some participants may feel as a result of the limitations inherent in text-only communication highlights the need for the online focus group facilitator to be comfortable and capable of dealing with online personal relations. As Horn has again stated: 'You can't get away with having absolutely no social skills online. It's a social medium! You must possess some social artistry' (1998: 33).

Participant Disclosure

Krueger (1988: 23) and others have suggested that the success of a focus group depends, in part, upon the emotional disclosure of its members. It is assumed that these same feelings will not always emerge in other forms of interviewing. These authors argue that it is the permissive atmosphere of the focus group that maintains it as a valuable part of the qualitative toolkit. Focusing upon the nature of the high interactivity of FTF groups, Morgan states: 'the hallmark of focus groups is the explicit use of the group interaction to produce data and insights that would be less accessible without the interaction found in a group' (1988: 12). Interactivity follows disclosure – this is the core of the focus group method.

In all qualitative methodology, interviewee disclosure is reflected in the data. Data which are in-depth and rich in detail usually reflect a high level of personal disclosure by participants about a particular issue. In both FTF and virtual focus groups, participant disclosure can produce valuable data on a range of topics.

Given the broader debate about personal disclosure in the online environment, the benefits of conducting online focus groups may be multiple.

Disclosure Online In the context of the online focus group, self-disclosure can be influenced by a range of factors. This can include the rapport of the group, the permissive atmosphere which researchers aim to create as well as the nature of the topic under discussion. The degree of intimate or personal disclosure can be further influenced by whether online participants are using computers which are located in public laboratories, private homes, or whether they are members of small teams of participants, as occurred in the Young People and Health Risk study.

A further key issue which can influence online focus group disclosure is the assignment of usernames. Usernames can be used as a foil or mask by the participants concerned. When an online participant has a userid of this nature, they need not declare their real names, or who they 'really are'. Of course, this may be dependent upon whether a participant gets to choose their own online name.

While FTF focus group participants, too, can take part in focus groups without disclosing their (real) names, the embodied nature of FTF participation places obvious limits upon the extent to which this is possible. Even if focus group participants use pseudonyms during the FTF focus group, it is unlikely that they will feel anonymous in the group environment. The online environment may have clear advantages in allowing participants anonymity, one of which is the potential for greater personal disclosure.

Disclosure in Real-time and Non-real-time Focus Groups The timing of an online focus group can have repercussions for the degree of participant disclosure which may be achieved. For example, in a real-time focus group conducted over a single session, personal disclosure may be uninhibited as the likelihood of participants re-meeting is diminished. Similarly, if a series of real-time focus groups is conducted with the same set of participants, personal bonds may form between the members as discussion progresses. This may serve either to inhibit or disinhibit personal disclosure as participants need to 'face' one another at some moment again in the future. When a focus group is conducted in non-real time, the ongoing nature of the dialogue may also temper self-disclosure. This possible limitation, however, can be compensated by the more considered responses of participants (non-real-time interaction can give participants time to develop carefully formulated responses). The nature of these responses may then lead to the development of greater personal disclosure than the rapid fire of real-time chat room conversation.

Comparing FTF and Online Focus Groups At the current time, debate about whether or not the online environment promotes or hampers personal intimacy is wide open. Some, like Horn, suggest that cyberspace can only go so far as a substitute for FTF communication. In discussing the value of meeting someone

FTF *vis-à-vis* knowing them online, she argues: 'You can tolerate a wider range of behaviour once you look someone in the face. I don't think it's that you know them better once you've met them, necessarily, it's that when you get back online you project less' (Horn, 1998: 117). For others, the online environment provides a nirvana for self-expression – all from the anonymity and comfort of one's own home. For example, as one participant in Sweet's online market research focus group commented:

> Aside from my difficulties in finding the right room to be in ... this was easy ... a little hard to follow the conversation at times, but you get used to it ... and you can do it in your sweats without putting on makeup or combing your hair ... a big plus in my book. (Sweet, 1999)

The popularity of singles' dating rooms and online romance also attest clearly to this perception of openness and convenience.

The nature of disclosure by participants can reveal an important area of difference between FTF and online focus groups. For example, in the Young People and Health Risk study, in the separate online focus groups of both the young men and the young women there was considerably more disclosure about the topics of sexuality and alcohol than there had been in the FTF focus groups which were conducted immediately prior to the online link-ups. In the Australian young men's FTF focus group, when the scenario of sexuality was presented for discussion there was much head bowing and mumbled one-line answers. Furthermore, in the FTF discussion of the scenario for drinking, none of these boys admitted to having tried any sort of alcohol. In the online focus group, however, the same young men were keen to ask the Chinese young men a range of questions about sex. They were also keen to reveal their experiences of drinking. The example below reveals the degree of personal disclosure which took place online:

On sex and girlfriends:
Green Australia: Have you ever had sex before?
Green Beijing: Never!
Green Australia: Sorry' I accidentally sent that
Green Beijing: Sex? And you?
Green Australia: Have you got a girlfriend?
Green Australia: No' just 1 night stands
Green Beijing: We have girlfriend, but we think it just is normal relationship.
Green Australia: that was Jack that had the one night stand

On pornography:
Green Australia: what do you think about porn
Green Beijing: What meaning is "porn"?
Facilitator: GREEN beijing please ignore the last question, the australian boys want to talk only of sex...

On condoms:
Yellow Australia: do you have condoms in china
Yellow Beijing: Yes.
Yellow Australia: can you buy condoms at school
Yellow Beijing: No we can't buy, and you ?

On alcohol:
Yellow Australia: I have tried beer, wine, champaine, vodca and JIM BEAM [bourbon].
Yellow Beijing: Do you know how many ways to transmit AIDS?
Yellow Australia: By having a root
Yellow Beijing: We tried beer, wine, white alchol
Yellow Beijing: Any others?
Yellow Australia: Alchohol is alright as long as yo
Facilitator: as long as you what?
Yellow Australia: Sorry I accidently pressed enter
Yellow Australia: You dont drink it to get drunk
Yellow Beijing: Have you been drank?
Yellow Australia: I got pissed off my face

The second example shows the discussion which took place in the FTF focus group on some of the same issues:

On alcohol:
Facilitator: What is the risk of being drunk?
Participant A: Well you feel really bad in the morning and you get all these lectures from your mum and dad and you get grounded for a day.
Facilitator: How do you know?
All participants laugh
Participant who spoke is silent
Facilitator: Who's been really drunk here?
All participants laugh
Participant A: Um,
Participant B: He can't remember.

On sexuality:
Facilitator: Do you know any boys who act like Robert (a character in the scenario presented for group discussion) and get girls pregnant?
All participants laugh
Facilitator: Are there any older kids that you know?
No
No
No
Facilitator: Do you think it was a good thing what Robert did or a terrible thing?

> *Group silence and giggles (no comment forthcoming)*
> Facilitator: So you don't know any boys who would act like Robert?
> Facilitator: Do the older boys who you know, would they act like Robert or would they do it differently?
> *Silence and giggles (still no comment forthcoming)*

Online Discussion

By definition, focus groups depend upon, and are created by, the contributions of multiple participants. Following Krueger, a focus group discussion is unique because it represents 'a carefully planned discussion designed to obtain perceptions on a defined area of interest' (1988: 18). As discussed above, the process of group interaction serves to encourage participants both to challenge and respond to each other. As a result, focus group interviews can both clarify arguments as well as reveal a diversity of views and opinions (Denzin, 1989). Morgan states that the FTF focus group can be thought of usefully as a 'process [of discovery]' (1988: 17).

Topic Selection

Given that the focus group is commonly used to develop advertising strategies and obtain information about consumer products, as well as in the social sciences (see Frey and Fontana, 1995), it is not surprising that a wide range of topics can be explored. In the online environment, factors such as lack of a strict and/or enforceable privacy, however, may hamper some people's preparedness to discuss sensitive topics. In turn, any hesitance on the part of online participants to discuss a particular topic will also affect both the degree of disclosure and the group interactivity.

Topic Suitability Determining the suitability of a topic for an online focus group will be largely a result of trial and error. However, researchers may benefit from twisting and turning existing FTF focus group guidelines. While Morgan (1988: 40) has cautioned that it is not productive to ask people to talk about issues which they are not used to talking about in public, the anonymity of the online environment may render this tenet problematic. Rather, a more useful guideline for the online environment may read: 'it is not productive to ask people to talk about issues which they are not used to talking about'. Period!

Topics, Disclosure and Group Rapport While technology has been accused of creating distance between people (see discussion in Argyle and Shields, 1996), CMC is also thought to present a unique opportunity for the fostering of relationships, communication, community and co-operation (Spender, 1997; Hardey, 1998). Indeed, CMC may engender a greater degree of intimacy and a greater preparedness on the part of users to divulge personal views and attitudes. In the Young People and Health Risk study, the behaviour of the young women in Malaysia illustrates this point well. The nature of what these young women were willing to talk about in their FTF focus groups *vis-à-vis* the virtual link up revealed marked differences. In the FTF group, which was moderated by a female Malaysian health worker and Eckermann, these young women refused outright to discuss any aspect of sexuality. In the online focus group with the young women in the three remaining countries, they proceeded to disrupt the formal discussion with highly sexualized jokes.

The Questioning Route

Two defining features of FTF focus groups are the predetermined questioning route and the sequencing of questions (Krueger, 1988: 30). In contrast to the type of open-ended questions which characterize FTF focus group discussion, however, questioning for online focus groups may need to be altered. This is for several reasons and is irrespective of whether the focus groups are conducted in real or non-real time.

Whereas in FTF groups, the open-ended approach is relatively unproblematic from the point of view of allowing participants 'ample opportunity for comment' and to explain and share experiences (Krueger, 1988: 19), the high interactivity of real-time focus groups introduces the risk that the data will be superficial. Gaiser has noted that a principal danger with obtaining data online in either chat or conferencing is that they will provide few in-depth insights into the subject at hand (Gaiser, 1997). As Horn, too, has noted of real-time CMC, 'Chat is not the place for an in-depth conversation. It doesn't give you the opportunity to consider what you want to say' (1998: 64). 'In general [chat] does not attract the kind of people who might have had a more sophisticated exchange. Or, rather, chat is where you go when you don't want to think anymore' (Horn, 1998: 84).

In the non-real-time focus group, different problems can emerge. Although the questioning route can be established at the outset of the period of operation, the absence of a facilitator can cause its own dilemmas for the ways in which the questioning proceeds. For example, if facilitators are not present online they cannot respond to the comments of focus group participants, nor can they ensure that the discussion develops in a productive direction. If all questions are posted at once, as can be done for a non-real-time focus group, the entire issue of the questioning route becomes problematic. This is principally because the route becomes determined by the group participants themselves. In the non-real-time focus group, questions can be answered out of sequence and at the leisure of the individual group members. Discussion of these issues is continued in Chapter 6 where the range of strategies for online focus group facilitation is explored.

Rigour and Validity in Online Focus Groups

Background Detail

Krueger (1988: 41) has suggested that the validity of FTF focus group data depends not only on procedure but on context. By this he suggests that projection should be minimized and that adequate contextual detail should be provided both of the focus group participants and the actual focus group. He suggests that this context is central in order to support the direct statements of focus group participants.

In the online environment, however, the researcher may or may not have access to any background detail about group participants. The development of researcher knowledge about and analysis of a particular focus group context may need to take a qualitatively different format. For example, rather than compiling a demographic outline, the context of an online focus group may centre upon small snippets of information provided in the course of the interaction. In the Young People and Health Risk study, this information took the forms illustrated below. The following extracts are from the young women's various online focus groups.

Yellow Oz: Hello my name is Lisa. I like playing sport and talking to my friends on the phone

Green Oz: hi this is Helen from australia i enjoy doing drama. Hi this is Kim and i enjoy dancing and drama. We are both 13 years old.

Yellow Oz: what does a pretty girl look like in china, what would you call a pretty girl and a handsome boy?
Yellow Oz: (descriptions)
Yellow Beijing: we call a pretty girl is" white snowprincess" handsome boy is "white horse prince"

Blue Beijing: We are not smokers. But Tai's father is a smoker.

However, if the online focus group is conducted in non-real time and in a public forum (without userid access), contextual information, at least about the participants, can be collected in a more conventional manner. For example, an electronic proforma of a short, yet anonymous, demographic questionnaire could be attached to the Web site or conference areas concerned. Participants could then complete this questionnaire and email or mail it to the researchers' contact address. Although this is all technically feasible, the researcher would still be largely unable to enforce any 'true' identity of possible participants.

Defining Rigour Online

When highlighting the importance of procedure, Krueger (1993) reminds his readers of the scientific underpinnings of qualitative methodology. The online environment presents unique dilemmas for conventional discussions of methodological rigour. This is particularly the case when the online researcher may not even be able to verify the identity of the participants – that they really are who they say they are. At best, rigorous online focus group practice may be better served by a transparency of decision making at every phase (see Ratcliffe and Gonzalez-del-Valle, 1988). For example, if a researcher is unable to confirm the identity of participants, this should at least be acknowledged. If the questioning route is severely disrupted by participants or if the facilitator has needed to act more like a discussion leader than an unobtrusive focus group facilitator, then this too needs to be explicit.

Online qualitative methodology is a newly emerging area of academic scholarship and requires an openness in debate of what can and should constitute acceptable practice. That the environment of cyberspace, itself, is the subject of ongoing and highly complex debates highlights the need for researchers to be clear in what they are doing and able to justify the design of their studies.

Conclusion

David Morgan (1988: 17) suggests that you can never trade off what you did not have in the first place. While the data which a focus group generates may not be perfectly detailed, fully explained or sufficiently indepth, is it better to have imperfect data than no data and no insights at all? While there are certainly disadvantages with the focus group method, without them we are no doubt poorer. This is especially so when the extra dimensions of online focus group practice are considered.

First, despite the numerous drawbacks of the online environment in terms of participant verification, the problematic nature of the data and language, and the cultural and gender biases arguably inherent in the online environment, cyberspace allows researchers to gather data on issues which would previously not have been possible. In this respect, the online environment creates new space for new discussions. Second, and like the telephone focus group before it, the online focus group also allows researchers access to populations in disparate places. Cyberspace can invite the focus group participation of people who may never, otherwise, have been contacted, let alone involved in a focus group discussion.

A third point to consider in the broad argument for the online focus group is the issue of interactivity. It is now widely agreed that the group interaction of an FTF focus group interview can generate data which are uniquely different to those generated by either participant observation or the individual interview.

The ability of the focus group to reveal the process of decision making and flux in value formation maintains it as a central qualitative tool. The online environment can furnish new levels and types of group interactivity, highlighting its potential as a legitimate addition to qualitative methodologies. Finally, and as outlined in Chapter 2, the online focus group is an efficient and highly cost-effective mechanism for gathering detailed data, in large quantities.

6 The Online Interviewer

In qualitative research the interviewer is commonly considered the 'human instrument' of the research process. Ideally, 'the human interviewer can be a marvellously smart, adaptable, flexible instrument who can respond to situations with skill, tact, and understanding' (Seidman, 1991: 16). Working FTF, such an interviewer would seek to be a careful listener, non-judgemental, perceptive, focused and able to engage with interviewee(s) on both a personal and professional level.

Is it possible to transfer these skills online? Will researchers be able to conduct unstructured in-depth one-to-one interviews or to deal with the interpersonal dynamics of group discussions in a virtual venue? Will they be able to match personal skills with sufficient technical knowledge to navigate the electronic medium? In this chapter we shall consider the limitations and possibilities of interviewing online. We shall focus on interaction established by the researcher, although many of the skills will be transferable to open access settings.

Is CMC a Suitable Medium for Interviewing?

Generating data in qualitative interviews depends upon developing rapport with participants (Fontana and Frey, 1994). Traditionally this has been associated with a mutual reading of presentation of self. In any social situation there is a swift appraisal of age, gender and ethnicity; of accent, dress and personal grooming; of conventionality, eccentricity and subcultural markers; of confidence levels, physical attractiveness, friendliness or restraint. In addition, oral dimensions of language (pitch, tone and so on) might identify whether what was said was spoken from a position of confidence, doubt, irony and so forth.

The sense of the other attained by such means allows each person to assess (a) how others are interpreting what they say and (b) the genuineness of intent in a query or a response. If, as a result of this delicate interaction, participants come to trust in the sincerity and the motivation of the interviewer, they may be prepared to share in-depth insight into their private and social worlds. At the same time, the interviewer will increasingly be able to sense the appropriateness of questions and the meaningfulness of answers.

Reading signs of the other is a human characteristic which many FTF qualitative researchers develop to the level of a skill. But is it possible to 'connect' at these emotional and mental levels when communicating online? Is it possible to develop rapport with participants whom you may never have seen or heard?

The authors posed these questions to two researchers who had conducted qualitative email interviews. They responded differently:

> Generating an atmosphere of rapport online can be a problem, and given the lack of tone or gesture and the length of time between exchanges it can lead to something of a formal, structured interview. This is in contrast to the spontaneous speeding up, slowing down, getting louder, getting quieter, getting excited, laughing together, spontaneous thoughts, irrelevant asides etc. etc. which I have experienced in off-line interviews. The best words I can think of to separate off-line from E-mail interviews then, are FLOW, and DYNAMICS, both of which, in my view are liable to contribute to greater depth and quality of information in an off-line interview than over e-mail. (Hodkinson, 1999: *personal email*)

> Is rapport online possible? Absolutely!!!! Rapport comes from being very up front with what you are doing and responding as you would with anyone. Laughing, listening and connecting are the key. (Smith-Stoner, 1999: *personal email*)

These perspectives reflect current debates about in-depth communication online. In one view, CMC cannot achieve the highly interactive, rich and spontaneous communication that can be achieved FTF. Communication differences between media are often conceptualized in terms of bandwidth; that is, the 'volume of information per unit time that a computer, person, or transmission medium can handle' (Raymond cited in Kollock and Smith, 1996). CMC communication is said by some to have a narrow or lean bandwidth, in contrast to the 'rich' bandwidth of FTF interaction (see Sala, 1998). As there are insufficient social cues transmitted to establish the human 'presence' of the other, CMC is impersonal and distancing (Hewson *et al.*, 1996; Kiesler *et al.*, 1984; Short *et al.*, 1976). Particularly in groups (see Chapter 5), psychological distance between participants, and the depersonalization of 'the other' which can result, can lead to various kinds of unsociable behaviour such as flaming (Dubrovsky *et al.*, 1991; Kiesler and Sproull, 1992). When seen as an 'impoverished' communication environment (Giese, 1998), it is not surprising that CMC is mainly considered appropriate for tasks requiring little social interaction or intimacy (Rice and Case, 1983). Walther's review of this literature summed up the implications for research if CMC is viewed in this way. If investigations seek 'information that is ambiguous, emphatic, or emotional ... a richer medium should be used' (Walther, 1992: 57).

If CMC is indeed a 'lean' communication medium which is neither conducive to establishing good interpersonal relationships nor capable of addressing delicate information, then it is clear that the work of the online qualitative interviewer will be challenging if not doomed to failure from the beginning. However, relational development theorists have challenged these findings. Lea and Spears (1995) point out that most assumptions about interpersonal relationships (such as the need for physical proximity) predate CMC and may not be fully applicable in online settings (see also Parks and Floyd, 1996). Walther's review of non-experimental studies of CMC found evidence that warm relationships can and do develop online. He points out that the same motives that drive people in other contexts drive them in CMC. People want to interact, they seek social reward, they want to be liked. Thus research interactants, just as communicators in any context, will 'desire to transact personal, rewarding, complex relationships and ... they will communicate to do so' (Walther, 1992: 68).

This chimes with the view that people can convey their personalities as well as their points of view in a wide range of technological environments which have different strengths in terms of conveying personality (Galegher *et al.*, 1998). CMC is itself a cluster of different technological environments. For instance, in synchronous forms of CMC there may be a chatty, dynamic, 'produced on the fly' quality (Murray, 1995: 81), an interactivity which may give research interactants an immediate sense of the other (Colomb and Simutis, 1996; Yates, 1996). It is argued that the awareness that there really are people on the other side of the computer screen (Ruedenberg *et al.*, 1995) makes communication 'psychologically real to many users' (Werry, 1996: 50) and there is a heightened sense of mutual involvement (Aoki, 1995; Murphy and Collins, 1997) which leads to a rapid increase in intimacy between previous strangers.

In contrast, email and asynchronous conferencing are considered less 'immediate' but more personal and thoughtful forms of CMC. Email, in particular, is 'where two people go when they want to continue a conversation in private' (Horn, 1998: 258). The intensity of single person-to-person interaction, combined with the potential liberation from being judged, can foster particularly intimate relationships (Boshier, 1990: 50–53). These forms of CMC may also benefit from repeated interactions over time. In Walther's view, this enhances the possibility of users gaining heightened positive impressions of each other. A combination of 'over-interpreting' the positive points gleaned about the other from any available data, while simultaneously controlling their *own* presentation of self, seems to foster mutually reinforcing positive 'feedback loops' between users. As a result, research interactants may be propelled into even greater feelings of intimacy than FTF, the communication becoming not only personal but 'hyperpersonal' (Walther, 1996).

The distinction between different forms of CMC is an important one. It is one issue raised by an influential critique of 'media deterministic' theories (Baym, 1995a), a critique which may go some way towards elucidating the contextual differences which might affect the quality of interviews online. Baym argues that too much work on CMC assumes that the computer 'is the sole influence on communicative outcomes' (1995a: 139). She draws on an extensive literature to identify five factors (including the temporal differences just discussed) which might affect CMC interaction. Her work provides a detailed conceptual framework which could be adopted as a mental check list by online interviewers, helping them them to understand, and to prepare for, the factors which might impede or enhance their interview strategies in a 'cueless' environment.

Preparing Interviewing Strategies

Baym's five factors can be presented as this check list for considering the possibilities and limitations of online interaction:

1. What is the purpose of the interaction?
    How might the specific purpose and focus of a study influence the extent to which participants are prepared to become involved and to invest in the interaction?

2. What is the temporal structure of the research?
    Are synchronous or asynchronous methods used?
    Is there a single interaction or a series of interactions with an individual or group?

3. What possibilities and limitations for interaction are built into the software used?

4. What are the characteristics of the interviewer and participant(s)?
    (a) What is their experience of, and attitude to, using technology? What is their knowledge of the topics under discussion? What is the level or range of their writing skills, wit and insight?
    (b) What is the size and composition of the interactive unit? Is it one-to-one (researcher and participant) or many-to-many (large numbers of group members interacting)?
    (c) Have the researcher and participant(s) interacted before – either FTF or online?
    (d) Is there a balance, or a monopoly, of (for instance) age, gender, ethnicity, or socio-economic status in larger groups? Are larger groups hierarchically structured, either overtly (as in some organizations) or in terms of social status or difference?

5. What is the external context of the research?
    What national (and/or international) cultures and/or communities of meaning are involved?
    What might be the impact of their communicative practices outside CMC?
    What impact might subcultural 'field' factors, such as the general socio-economic environment, have on the research?

What are the relevant details about the immediate context of the interaction, such as where computers and the Internet are accessed?

These factors are complex and require considerable reflection. We shall look in depth at issues which relate to group composition and the external context of the research in later chapters. In this chapter we shall focus on the following areas:

- Purpose and focus of the interview
- Aspects of technological expertise
- Interpersonal expertise
- Relational expertise in group discussions
- Asking questions one-to-one
- Asking questions in groups
- Finishing interviews

Purpose and Focus of the Interview

For researchers the interview process may have many 'purposes' but, at base, there is just one aim: to generate data. In her analysis of group interactions using CMC, Baym (1995a: 147) showed that the purposes of participants were diverse and extended beyond the ostensible purposes of the group. Does the same apply to individual participants in CMC interviews? In short, why do participants agree, and continue, to take part? And how can the researcher encourage them to do so?

Some participants may become involved with an interview-based project (either FTF or online) because they are deeply committed to the research process for personal and/or social reasons. However, for others the purposes of the research may be neither clear nor personally significant and their reasons for getting involved will vary. They may participate for material reward (as in much market research), or for fun, out of curiosity, or as displacement activity.

Whether online or FTF, the interviewer who seeks data must be responsive to the participant's agenda. This may involve offering payment, making interview sessions lively and stimulating and/or personally fulfilling, or convincing participants that a study is intrinsically valuable and worth their attention. The often unspoken 'contract' between researcher and participant, implying that the research should address the concerns of both, has implications for the time and energy participants will be prepared to invest in the study and, hence, the depth of data obtained.

Participants with a superficial interest in the research topic may be initially intrigued and attracted by the option of interacting online, but this might not be enough to sustain their ongoing interest without the impetus of enthusiasm and focus that can be injected in the FTF setting by a skilled interviewer working 'on all cylinders'. Online, interviewers may not be able to offer enough verbal 'dazzle' to compensate for the charm or charisma that can be so effective FTF.

Hodkinson has hypothesized that online interviewers might generate more data from participants who have no particular vested interest in a study, or a low boredom threshold, if they were to use highly interactive 'real-time' forms of CMC. For, as he experienced, when using asynchronous methods there may be a tendency for less involved participants to drop away:

> The longest of my e-mail interviews has been a few weeks ... usually I found that people lost interest before I am able to get to the same degree of detail as a face to face interview. (1999: *personal email*)

However, other evidence suggests that a shared research agenda and/or being given an opportunity to be 'heard' in a meaningful way can 'lead virtual relationships to become very personal very quickly' (Smith-Stoner and Weber, 2000). In these circumstances interest in the interaction is sustained.

> Respondents often spoke of the value of our dialogues for helping them to make sense of their lives. They remarked on the time they had taken in thinking through their responses (some taking several hours) and messages were usually very long. (Dunne, 1999: 3)

Smith-Stoner and Weber, who reported excellent rapport with their participants, pointed out that the women they interviewed were very enthusiastic about the research topic: it did not 'require any selling at all'. Not only did these women with multiple home responsibilities want to tell their story, they also 'expressed deep satisfaction with the process and were grateful to be able to do it online' (Smith-Stoner and Weber, 2000). A similar overlap of appreciating methodological and personal factors ensured the effectiveness of O'Connor's real-time group discussion with new parents.

> The interviews all provided high levels of self-consciousness, reflexivity and interactivity. Whether it was owing to the nature of the interviewees (self-selected, motivated, frequent on-line users), or owing to the nature of the subject matter, clearly very close to the hearts of the women involved, it is difficult to judge. (O'Connor and Madge, 2000)

Students in Mann's study participated for a variety of reasons (not least as displacement activity), but once again the method and the focus of the research seemed to be jointly attractive to participants.

Example: GOTM students
It's 2:45 am and it's beginning to dawn on me that this is just a delaying-tactic akin to, but (fatally) more justifiable and so more insidious than, making multiple cups of tea or searching the college library for a quotation by someone in some book somewhere that you know you don't really truly need and will never re-find anyway, but saves you actually WORKING or anything.

Telling a complete stranger the hassles of Cambridge life is rather cathartic and extremely easy to do via the email.

I am really enthusiastic about being involved in thsi study because i think that there is definitely room for change and this sort of study seems to me the best possible way to achieve it

I find it intriguing that you come to me personally for viewpoints. I am not at all worrid about it, mind, I just find it amusing to think of you compiling studies in which my thoughts are written

The continuing participation of so many Cambridge University students may well have been a result of the study's potential to tap into different levels of interest: both shared research aims and enjoyment of the process.

Perhaps the final word on 'purpose' should come from Smith-Stoner who saw the research 'contract' in these terms: 'participants had the choice to answer or not. I had the job of making the research interesting and relevant enough for them to want to answer' (1999: *personal email*).

What skills might an interviewer need to do this? According to Myers (1987) there are two kinds of expert online: the technologically astute and the 'relationally' astute (that is, the 'social experts' who nurture and direct online relationships and create interpersonal bonds). We shall now consider to what extent – and in what ways – the interviewer may need to develop these skills

Aspects of Technical Expertise

Adapting to a Technological Mode

Because CMC requires researchers and participants to have access to computers and a measure of technological expertise, there is a danger that experience with the technology, rather than qualitative research skills, will drive the research.

Some techies promote themselves as being able to conduct focus groups because they have conducted chat rooms. Sort of like letting a professional gardener operate on your heart. Sure they know how to open the ground -- but do they know how to open chests? Techies are comfortable and familiar with the technology, but they will not have the background to expertly develop a project based on sound objectives and then analyze it in a professional manner. (Sweet, 1999: *personal email*)

In all the studies discussed in this chapter, researchers with established interviewing skills set out to add technology to their repertoire. This could involve a steep learning curve, and some false starts. For example, when contacting different groups of students (such as lawyers or engineers), Mann initially inserted one email address from each group in the 'To:' section of the email header and added the rest to the 'Cc:' (copy to) section. This inadvertently exposed the addresses of everyone in a group to all individuals within it. Students who arrived at the university as computer novices did not seem to register this breach of confidentiality. However, one highly computer-literate chemist wrote back tactfully:

> There is a better way to do this. In the 'To:' field put something like 'chemists@university' (can be anything). In the 'Cc:' field put nothing. But in the 'Bcc:' field put all our email addresses plus your own so you can see if the mail works. Since 'chemists@university' doesn't exist you will get an 'error' but the mail should be delivered to everyone else in the Bcc list and no one will see anyone else's email address.

(This works because the contents of the 'Bcc:' (blind copy to) field are used by the email system in deciding where to send messages but, unlike the 'Cc:' field, are not included in the transmitted message.)

While Mann immediately started to act on this excellent advice, some damage had already been done. The mathematicians in the study had seen the mistake at once and seized on the opportunity to 'crack the system'. A flurry of excited emails (most of which were also posted to the crestfallen interviewer) soon ascertained 'who' in the maths department was involved. The cohort mathematicians eventually set up their own private spamlist, called Gradz. This (a) led to two students leaving the project because they were being swamped with Gradz mail, (b) changed the very perceptions of fresher experience that Mann was investigating and (c) probably siphoned off much of the energy she had hoped to draw on in the study! ('Thanks for setting this up, we're now e-mailing each other regularly, and holding parties. In fact we're having one tonight, so thanks, it's been fun!' (Cambridge Gradz list student: *email message*)

Interviewers hoping to use real-time focus group software have an additional challenge. They need to understand the technology themselves and also to present it in a user-friendly way to participants. Interviewers who are developing their own technological skills may be fortunate enough to have technical staff on hand to give advice (in a university, for instance). However, even without this, software manuals set out to be accessible and researchers report a gratifying sense of achievement when they co-ordinate hardware and software for the first time.

> Overall we were happy with the technical side of this project and we have benefitted from other people's technical expertise. We have carried out the research successfully without technical experience. (O'Connor and Madge, 2000)

Presenting the software to participants varies in form depending on the situation. At the most sophisticated level there are tailor-made interviewing rooms (see 'Facilities' in the Technology Introduction) where participants are talked through the technological side. In Stewart and Eckermann's study (described in depth in Chapter 5) informed adults were on hand in each country to help the young teenagers who were assembled to use the software. In contrast, O'Connor and Madge sent the software directly to adult participants who would work from home.

> We sent them a disk containing the software and a set of guidelines on installing and working the programme along with a covering letter. Once the user had installed the package and she/he had posted successfully to a newsboard on-line, we were able to check our server to see if participants had been able to log on successfully. When there were problems the interviewees emailed us and we were able to advise via this medium until they succeeded in logging on. (2000: 4)

As Baym (1995a) has noted, the technological experience of participants can be crucial to the success of CMC research. Yet it is often difficult for interviewers to anticipate, and to prepare for, technical glitches. O'Connor and Madge had to hope that the Web users they interviewed would have sufficient interest in the technology to motivate them to install the software at home. In contrast, Smith-Stoner and Weber, whose study required a lower level of technical skill (email), were surprised to find, in their pilot study, that computer skills varied widely between participants. As some did not know how to 'cut and paste the consent and demographic form from an email' the researchers began to include separate sections for how to do this in the initial interview preparation (2000).

The experiences described in this section suggest that the good practice of conducting a pilot study may contribute to the success of research where either interviewers or participants are technological novices.

Using Electronic Paralanguage

Apart from absorbing information about specific software, interviewers need to be aware of linguistic conventions that are available in text-based CMC. Electronic paralanguage consists of repetitions, abbreviations and verbal descriptions of feelings and sounds which help to convey the mood of the communication and make social and emotional connections:

> 'hehehe' for laughter
> 'lol' for 'lots of laughs' or 'LJATD' for 'let's just agree to disagree' (discussion going nowhere)
> '[smiles ruefully]' (added after a statement)

Further clues to projection of personality are found in personalized signatures:

> 'I think animal testing is a terrible idea; they get all nervous and give the wrong answers'.

'It's difficult to work in a group when you're omnipotent'.
"'Let's toss as men do" Bathsheba Everdeen, Far from the Madding Crowd'.
(GOTM students)

Underlining and capitalization can be used for emphasis (read as SHOUTING).
As Hodkinson has noted (1999: *personal email*), an exclamation mark on its
own is often a very effective conveyer of amusement. The following examples
from the Young People and Health Risk study show this language in action:

> Yellow Australia: Alchohol is alright as long as yo
> Fiona Stewart: as long as you what???? (
>
> Green Beijing: We think Chinese food is more healthy.
> Green Australia: THATS BULL SHIT

Emoticons (see Technology Introduction) offer interviewers another textual
means to show feelings (:-) for smiling/happy; :-o for surprise/shock) and to
soften the potentially distancing abruptness of some CMC messages by adding
humour or whimsicality (Murphy and Collins, 1997). One survey found that, out
of 3000 posts examined, 13.4% of users included an emoticon at least once as a
way of enhancing the socio-emotional content of their messages (Witmer and
Katzman, 1997). However, the use of emoticons is not transparent in
communicative terms. They may indicate a friendly but rather impersonal
approach (Aycock and Buchignani, 1995). They can also be seen as lazy and
unimaginative, possibly alienating some members of sophisticated online
communities. As Horn has warned, it is possible that 'people will assume that
you are without language, or conversation and suggest that you go back to
America Online (a place known for its liberal use of emoticons)' (1998: 63).

Use of emoticons may also be responsive to the social and communicative
practices of the subculture (see Baym, 1995b). In Stewart and Eckermann's
study, young teenagers were experimenting with the technology as much as
transmitting information and they used paralanguage freely. In contrast, working
with highly literate undergraduates, Mann rarely used emoticons and neither did
the students who wrote to her, although strength of feeling sometimes evoked a
rash of exclamation marks and capital letters. One student revising a Physics of
Materials course wrote:

> I'm taking a break from 'displacive phase transitions in perovskites' today. I
> don't even care about perovskites! I loathe and detest perovskites with every fibre
> of my body! I HATE MATERIALS! (GOTM student)

In addition, emoticons may not always work cross-nationally. In Japan, where
signs of respect are finely graduated and where relationships develop in indirect
ways, a highly complex system of emoticons attempts to parallel some of the
delicacy of FTF interaction. However, these emoticons are not familiar to most

western interviewers. (Such emoticons are read in a traditional horizontal format rather than side-on: (-o-) I'm sorry; (^o^;) excuse me!; (^o^) happy; (^-^;;) awkward (see Aoki, 1994).)

Finally, as with varying responses to such friendship gestures as hand shakes and open body language in FTF research, participants may not always see an interviewer's use of symbols like emoticons as an appropriate way of 'doing research'. This can be intensely frustrating for interviewers who have found them a useful means of transmitting affect: 'Very few participants wanted to do it! Darn it!!!!!!' (Smith-Stoner, 1999: *personal email*). It would seem that electronic paralanguage should be used judiciously. However, in the opinion of one student in the Graduates of the Millennium study, it will never be subtle enough to compare to FTF interaction:

> You'll see people annotate their mails using smilies, HTML-style tags, capital letters, etc., but even so there is no reliable way of conveying tone. How you say something is often more important than what you say - and email doesn't have this dimension. (GOTM student)

Setting the tone of an interaction is the first step towards achieving rapport. It is important from the time of making first contact with participants (see Chapters 4 and 5) and it is further established within the interview. Because electronic language can be rather clumsy and/or specialized in its use, interviewers need to be alert to the potential of the written word for establishing tone – as we shall see in the discussion of online interpersonal skills that follows.

Interpersonal Expertise Online

We are assuming that most researchers will bring FTF interviewing expertise to the online environment. In our experience, the virtual venue offers interviewers new methods of working, but core methodological issues remain. In this section we discuss some of the generic factors which relate to establishing rapport in all kinds of interviews. Then in the following section we discuss additional factors associated with facilitating group discussion online.

Establishing Trust

Being Open About the Research We have already mentioned the 'atmosphere of suspicion' which can exist when faceless researchers contact participants (Chapter 4). One way to dispel feelings of caution and to work towards the levels of trust which allow rapport to develop is to be as open as possible about the purposes and processes of the research. For facilitators of focus groups this can be done formally by making an interview schedule available well before the interview and inviting clarifying questions (see below). However, many asynchronous studies are incremental in the ways they gather data (Seymour *et al*., 1999) and the process can stretch over a considerable period of time. Here, one aspect of 'openness' would be to fully inform participants about the time frame of the interaction as well as substantive issues relating to the research.

Mutual Self-disclosure Some researchers may conclude that in-depth research, particularly of sensitive topics, would benefit if participant(s) and researcher met FTF before attempting to conduct an online relationship. However, there are precedents for conducting deeply personal research without ever meeting participants in person. One means of establishing trust, and bridging the geographical and perhaps personal distance that may characterize online interviews (Moore, 1993), is self-exposure. This does not always mean 'revealing intimate details of your past life' but rather 'revealing how you are reacting to the present situation' (Johnson, 1972: 10). However, interviewers and participants may also share information about themselves (Murphy and Collins, 1997). Cutler (1995) and Parks and Floyd (1996) suggest that the more one discloses personal information online, the more others are likely to reciprocate, and the more individuals know about each other, the more likely it is that trust, satisfaction and the sense of being in a safe communication environment ensue.

This strategy poses methodological and practical problems for the virtual interviewer. Choices have to be made about whether it would be desirable to disclose details of gender, ethnicity and age (see Chapter 7). Smith-Stoner stated her gender as a point of principle seeing it as 'authentic' behaviour. In contrast, early emails in Mann's study had both her name and that of her co-researcher attached, giving a degree of ambiguity. And even if the interviewer wants to transmit personal information, it may be difficult to do online. As we saw in Chapter 4, Hodkinson had to 'gently get across' his insider knowledge and enthusiasm for the Goth scene:

> The trick was to try and get it across to people in as 'natural' a way as possible - I didn't want to just go straight in and say 'by the way, I'm a Goth you know' ... indeed such a statement might even indicate to some, that the individual concerned is something of a wannabe! (Hodkinson, 1999: *personal email*)

Hodkinson's recourse to a Web site displaying his photo as a cultural 'pointer' raises the possibility that, in the future, interviewers may choose to make their appearance available on Web sites as a matter of course – and participants might also direct interviewers to their own Web sites, as part of the process of mutual self-disclosure.

In some research contexts, interviewers seek reciprocity at deeper levels. For Bennett, 'the key to developing rapport is to see yourself, not as a researcher, but as a friend, confidant and above all a person wishing to listen and learn from participants' (1999, *personal email*). In her in-depth email interviews, she sought to establish relationships which 'would "nurse" equal degrees of self-disclosure, between myself and my co-investigators' (1998: 38). She made initial disclosures about herself to encourage this pattern of discourse and her efforts were rewarded. The men involved came to see her as someone who was both open and genuinely interested in what they had to say. They also began to self-disclose:

> it's like you opened up a tap and my thoughts are so much easier to put on paper for which I will always be beholden to you (Marv, 72, 12 March 1998). (Bennett, 1998: 39)

Ryen set out to bridge the cultural gap between herself in Norway and 'Sachin', her respondent in Africa, by sharing information about her job and her family. As with Bennett, it was preliminary self-exposure by the interviewer which evoked intimate confidences. When she told Sachin about the death of her uncle he responded by describing his own helplessness in the face of his dying grandmother:

> my grandmother has been our pillar of support and encouragement for several decades and for someone to fade away underneath our eyes is quite sorrowful...all we can do is just pray for her ...and the almighty help her from her misery... (12.02.99) (Ryen, 1999: *personal email*)

These extracts suggest that mutual sharing online can increase trust and emotional connection and may even allow interviewers to tap into areas which might be difficult to address FTF. It should be noted that researchers themselves may also find it easier to be relaxed and to open up online than FTF.

Developing Trust in Repeated Interactions Technical ease of contact in CMC gives the option of repeating interview interactions over time. There is evidence that trust and warmth in CMC relationships increases over extended interactions (Walther, 1992; Walther *et al.*, 1994). As Baym has also noted, 'In CMC, as in real life, relationships take time to build' (1995a: 158).

This has been the experience of qualitative researchers who have used sequential one-to-one email interviews (Bennett, 1998; Dunne, 1999; Anders, 2000; Mann, in Leman and Mann, 1999). Similar patterns have also been found in email discussion forums set up specifically for research purposes (Daws, 1999) and regular newsgroups (Baym, 1995a). Kendall's research into the MUD BlueSky suggested that a history of online interactions may also compensate for the loss of embodied relational cues in groups which 'chat' regularly (1999), findings confirmed by research into some virtual worlds (Horn, 1998; Rheingold, 1994; Parks and Floyd, 1996). However, interviewers who plan to set up longitudinal interviews with groups may reflect that here, perhaps more acutely than one-to-one, commitment to the research agenda is necessary for extended communication. Online groups which have developed deep relationships over time have invariably shared a common purpose, such as social interaction or the discussion of mutual interests, which was very close to the hearts of participants.

Even if research interests are shared, findings from sequential interviews using email suggest that the outcome in terms of intimacy is not predictable. Partly this reflects differences in the research design. With Dunne's (1999) study of gay fathers it was the participants' strong desire to be 'heard' which led spontaneously to interviewer–participant closeness. This continued after the formal closure of the research and, in some cases, led to FTF meetings. Anders (2000) began her research as a 'reluctant interviewer' who used to dread FTF interviews. The level of intimacy that was to develop between herself and the women to whom she talked from all over the world came as 'a huge revelation' (1999, *personal email*). The cross-national home visits and the practical and personal support offered to her by her participants suggested that the global reach of the Internet had drawn together individuals with a great deal in common who may never have met otherwise. In other studies (Mann, in Leman and Mann, 1999; Ryen, in Ryen and Silverman, 2000; Bennett, 1998) the development of long-term relationships was part of the research design. Both Bennett and Ryen sought to strengthen relational bonds through online disclosure (see above), phone calls, exchange of photographs and, in Ryen's case, some FTF meetings. In Mann's study, extended relationships were the inevitable result of contacting students regularly over the course of their degree. Here, the aim was to establish mutual trust rather than intimacy. Mann talked freely about the research and her commitment to it, as we see in this early response to a student questioning the agenda of the study:

> Help me out here. The point of this project is to see if the Cambridge system is failing some students - and, if it is, in which ways. We pick up clues from talking to students and try to recognise patterns of experience which we then (tentatively) explore further. We have no axe to grind - if we're completely off track we're happy to be told so.

However, Mann did not initiate talk about herself nor did she see students FTF. This was not a misguided attempt to claim research 'neutrality'; rather, she accepted that she was a very minor part of the students' lives, and preferred to keep the focus of the interaction on the issues and students' perspectives on the issues.

In all these studies the interviewers may be presumed to have different agendas. It is perhaps unsurprising that this should lead interviewers to different conclusions about whether electronic communication can sustain personal relationships over time. For Bennett and Ryen, the intensity of the relationship with participants seemed to peak and then falter somewhat, leading Bennett to admit that 'maintaining long-term relationships is much more difficult than it appears'. In Bennett's study the frequency of online interaction over a seven-month period might explain a participant's disengagement due to pressures of time and a (sometimes reluctant) need to prioritize other commitments. Another possibility might have been a sense (from the participant's point of view) that all that could be said, had been said.

Ryen suggested that, as the novelty of the research project wears off, a participant might use the interaction for more instrumental purposes. In her case study, Sachin, her correspondent, had initially been intrigued and challenged by the research process.

> AR: "How is it to be at the other end of my e-mails?"
> S: (pause) "Your questions are very new to me. I have never thought of them before. It takes a long time for me to answer them. I have to sort myself out before I can write my answers to you. They help me to think of these matters. I hope you will continue sending me questions." (face to face, in the car, April 1999) (Ryen, 1999: *personal email*)

However, as time went by, Sachin changed from enthusiastically responding and apologizing when 'late' to becoming what Ryen called 'the director of the communication'. As Ryen was anxious for the communication to continue, and Sachin became increasingly casual in his approach, the communication turned from 'starting with "interviewing down" to "interviewing up" where he has climbed the "power-ladder" or turned the balance' (Ryen and Silverman, 2000). Finally, Ryen began to wonder if Sachin's own 'purpose' had changed from commitment to the research process to a general desire to keep in touch because she might prove a useful contact in his business world. In Mann's study a 'slow and steady' approach to developing relationships within a time-limited, albeit extensive (3–4 year) period was required. The interviewer–student relationships lacked the intensity of the previous studies but, perhaps for this very reason, most relationships were sustained for the duration of the research.

Considering these differing research patterns, it seems likely that human relationships have similar variability online as in real life (see Parks and Floyd, 1996; Parks, 1997). Some remain at the constant level of good neighbourliness while others reach deeper levels of intimacy which must increase (which would alter the research relationship), change in nature, or diminish. While the ease and availability of CMC allows for extended communication, it does not follow that the technology can circumvent those life patterns.

Interactive Skills

Listening An attentive pause to listen is a key feature in FTF interviewing skills. However, this may be a luxury in some CMC contexts. For instance, the characteristic rapid fire of chat can preclude pausing, whether it be for thought, or for effect. As Horn has noted, real time rarely 'gives you the opportunity to consider what you want to say' (1998: 63–64). In addition, for participants, an interviewer's pause to listen may be experienced not as attentiveness but as indifference, as absence. Listening too much (read as being absent from the screen) may cause participants to feel 'leaderless and uncomfortable' (Gaiser, 1997)

It is clear that online listening needs to be expressed as words, not silence. Listening with interest may be expressed by 'responding promptly to questions, overtly expressing interest in particular points made, asking follow up questions, or perhaps enthusiastically sharing similar experiences to that described by the interviewee' (Hodkinson, 1999: *personal email*). Meanwhile the interviewer is also 'listening' to the written script of participants. The researcher needs to be alert to changes in the tone of the conversation, to any fracture in the flow of a response which might point to a reluctance to speak or a failure to understand language or concepts, and to verbal 'cues' which might suggest that participants would be happy to talk more about something if asked (see 'Probes' below). As relationships develop, 'listening' may also point to the possibility of mixing focused work with interaction at more relaxed levels:

Example: GOTM student

S. ... Decided not to get invloved with any blokes until May week [exam week], because they are bound to mess with my emotions and fuck everything up.

C. ... Good luck with the (bloke free) revision.

One week later:

S. Just to let you know... and my revision didn't stay bloke free

C. ... Good luck!

Reassurance Co-operating in research in general, and online research in particular, may be a new and challenging experience for many people. Yet, in a situation where participants may need regular confirmation that they are communicating in an appropriate way, that their contributions are valued and that the faceless researcher is trustworthy, interviewers have only words to offer them. As a wider range of ways to reassure participants is unavailable, the main option for online interviewers is to send frequent and explicit verbal assurances. Smith-Stoner and Weber discovered this at the start of their study:

> People all had different ideas about research and so many myths had to be dispelled. The most common one was that they couldn't talk to me, they couldn't know anything about the study for fear of "messing up" the results. It was interesting, most of the women made one comment or another about hoping they were answering the questions "right" - the way I wanted them. I had to constantly reassure them that their answers were perfect the way they were. (Smith-Stoner, 1999, *personal email*)

Similarly, in Mann's study, some students needed to be assured that research did not need the finished quality of essays: 'I'm really grateful that you've spent time explaining things. It is always hard to pinpoint the nuances of personal experience - you were definitely NOT waffling'. While, Sweet (1999) was vigilant in praising and thanking participants for their contributions in her real-time focus group:

> 01:23:04 PM Casey:CHERYL -- YOU'RE DOING FINE. LOVE THE SENSE OF HUMOR!

Finally, as with FTF research, self-disclosure needs to be acknowledged. 'People often wish to talk about very sensitive and private issues but they need constant assurance that what they have to say is as important to you as it is to them'. (Bennett, 1999: *personal email*)

Sensitivity Sustaining rapport depends upon an interviewer's skill in dealing with sensitive issues and/or potentially embarrassing or conflictual interaction. How can researchers negotiate delicate interaction online? As with reassurance, language has to be explicit. Nuance in tone of voice, facial expression and subtlety of gesture are unavailable. However, as noted in Galegher *et al.* (1998: 517), the use of mild imperatives (for example, 'you may want to check out') and mitigation ('if you'd like...') shows how skilful choice of words can avoid making presumptions about the reader. However, in real-time interaction, rapid choices have to be made about the ways sensitive issues are handled. O'Connor and Madge, who interviewed together, found the interaction felt abstracted from real life and online language use often seemed inadequate:

> There were occasions when we were 'lost for words', taking some time to decide on what to send as a message, because we felt like our written comments sounded banal or our questions too direct and leading. We 'policed' each other on this and feel that we very much benefited from working on-line together simultaneously. (2000: 4)

Talking with a new mother they wanted to show empathy for a previous experience but realized that real-time chat was an awkward medium for this:

> Hen and Clare: What do you mean dubious?!!
> Sarah: When I had a miscarriage but got no reply
> Hen and Clare: Sorry to hear about the miscarriage - it must have been hard for you
> Hen and Clare: Who did you write to?

Email allows more time for interviewers to choose their words in one-to-one or asynchronous group interactions. For instance, in Seymour's asynchronous long-term conferencing study, the participants had disabilities.

> Sometimes an exacerbation of the disability interrupted the process of some interviews. These events required gentle and sensitive communication to ensure

that participants did not feel pressured to continue, so that they felt valued, and so that they would feel welcome to continue with the project once the episode had passed. (Seymour *et al.*, 1999: 3)

Ryen was afraid that sensitive issues might arise when 'performing "long-time interviewing" with someone from another continent that you do not know (Tanzania/Kenya versus Norway) and culture (Asian versus Norwegian)'. Her approach was to try and clear the ground at an early stage in the interaction:

AR: "Well, I am very happy indeed that you will go on with the interview. If there are questions you find odd, or that you do not "appreciate", please do not hesitate to tell me" That is the only way to make me learn or to avoid repeating the mistake..." (e-mail 10.12.98)
S: " Anne, theres one thing which i'll tell you frankly is that i'm a pretty cool person and any sort of questions and comments will be welcomed by me...i really enjoy your emails..." (e-mail 12.12.98) (Ryen and Silverman, 2000)

This direct approach, where the interviewer makes no attempt to disguise the possibility that questions might come across as crass or impertinent, may also be a way to negotiate the questions themselves: 'I should like to ask you more about something you said, but if you feel my question is too intrusive please do not bother to reply to this - I shall not bring it up again' (Mann)

Finally, there is the difficulty of dealing with an emotional outburst online. We discuss strategies for real-time group interviews below. In one-to-one interaction, Smith-Stoner suggested writing 'PRC' (pause, reflect and contemplate) on screen as a sign that the interviewer saw what was online and was trying to become composed before speaking. Later the interviewer would try to see 'if it was something factual that needed to be addressed, a simple misunderstanding or, if it was something else, to try to address that too' (Smith-Stoner, 1999: *personal email*)

Explaining Absences Non-response in a virtual venue can undermine a developing sense of rapport. As we saw above, participants in real-time chat who lack visual cues that an interviewer is 'listening' may need verbal substitutes to reassure them of continuing interest. Absence, in terms of long gaps in communication in asynchronous studies, can be deeply unsettling for both interviewers and participants. Committed participants may take time to explain irregular messages. In Ryen's study, the laptop of her correspondent broke down while he was travelling. However, he phoned to inform her of this. In Mann's study, students frequently emailed to explain that work had taken over: 'I haven't written for a while because the tide of work that I was plunged into at the beginning of term has only just abated - although I think that's temporary'. Similarly, Mann alerted students when she would be away at conferences, or indeed preoccupied in writing this book. Interviewers have greater responsibility than participants to explain absences but, as Bennett discovered, this can be a taxing process:

> For example, when I was ill in bed I still had to check in with my co-investigators; write replies, explain that I was ill and that my conversations would only be short, but thus maintaining the link between us. Whilst this may seem to make online interaction appear both tenuous and transient, I would argue that it is simply the nature of the environment that makes it so, and not the people who are involved. (Bennett, 1998: 39)

Relational Expertise in Group Discussions

In one-to-one investigations qualitative researchers who question are usually referred to as interviewers. However, asking questions in groups requires additional skills, as suggested by such titles as moderator or facilitator. Morgan (1988: 15) has argued that the key role of the focus group moderator is 'to control the assembly and the running of the session'. This is a task with multiple strands and it is clearly a challenge to transfer these skills online. In another view, a moderator is a 'person who reminds, tracks, clarifies, prompts, reviews, distils, negotiates, mitigates, mediates, arbitrates' (Davis and Brewer, 1997: 70). In the fast-paced and hectic environment of real-time chat, flexibility and patience (with everyone involved) are definite virtues (Sweet, 1999).

From a human relations perspective the task of moderating/facilitating groups has two principal aspects: (a) developing rapport between all interactants and (b) providing a non-contentious atmosphere for all – even at the cost of exerting control over the few. We discuss these next.

Developing Rapport Between Participants

Many of the participants who are prepared to join online group discussions already have experience in chat rooms so they are adept at creating online relationships quickly. However, as Sweet reports, the guided group discussion 'draws participants out and personalities begin to emerge, thereby creating a dynamic that develops during the group and varies just like in-person groups ... The amount of interaction between online participants can vary and may be influenced by the topic and moderator' (1999: *online*).

The initial moments of an online focus group are perhaps the most crucial as this is when introductions are made and group rapport first attempted. The facilitator needs to be forthcoming, if not explicit, in requesting that participants introduce themselves. In the Young People and Health Risk study, rapport was encouraged in two ways. First, the facilitator posted a welcome message in a non-real-time conference centre ahead of time. This message sought to set the tone and atmosphere of the online groups to follow. Second, as the group facilitator, Stewart entered the young women's real-time focus group with the following lines:

> Fiona Stewart: Welcome Yellow Beijing - I am fiona the controller, please introduce yourselves and tell the other girls about your hobbies, your subjects at school and then we can proceed. Have you read the welcoming message?

It was anticipated that messages such as this would create a sense of personal connection between the young people in the four participating countries.

Another effective approach to encourage group rapport is to ask all participants about their immediate, physical environment (Sweet, 1999):

> 01:46:20 PM Casey:WHAT HAS BEEN GOING ON AROUND YOU SINCE WE SIGNED ON TODAY, THAT IS, RADIO, TV, CHILDREN, ETC.
> 01:46:43 PM Sue:tv and occasional talking with my friend
> 01:46:50 PM Lisa:My husband is surfing realtor.com at his desk
> behind me and interrupting me to look at houses.
> 01:46:55 PM Jackie:I have been throwing logs in the fire place,
> and sewing in between questions.
> 01:47:07 PM Ben:I have on netradio using real audio on the net
> 01:47:08 PM James:ate lunch, put shoes on
> 01:47:16 PM Lisa:My dog occasionally rolls over, growls and licks
> my ankle.

The running dialogue that followed this opening became increasingly informal and established a strongly felt sense of rapport and group solidarity:

> 02:01:43 PM Lisa:asking hubby to refil my drink
> 02:01:50 PM Liz:Stop that I'm hungry! :-)
> 02:02:03 PM Lisa:Anyone want to split a pizza?
> 02:02:06 PM Edward:I just changed radio stations
> 02:02:11 PM Casey:DO YOU INTENTIONALLY GO ONLINE TO PURCHASE OR DO YOU PURCHASE ON IMPULSE?
> 02:02:11 PM Ben:Anyone ever hear of Krispy Kream or Trader Joe's?>
> 02:02:13 PM Lisa:Hubby just left room to refill my drink
> 02:02:27 PM Jane:sounds good laura
> 02:02:29 PM Steve:IS IT A VIRTUAL PIZZA?

Creating a Non-contentious Atmosphere In an FTF focus group a facilitator may choose to be passive, exercising 'mild, unobtrusive control over the group' (Krueger, 1988: 73), but in the online focus group this is rarely possible. Here, establishing researcher expectations can minimize participant confusion and enhance adherence to both subject matter and protocol. This can avoid inhibiting 'the freeflow of discussion', a common criticism of the FTF focus group method (see Stewart and Shamdasani, 1990: 35).

Rule Setting The setting of rules is appropriate for most online groups. Arguments and disagreements in cyberspace 'can erupt with little warning' (Horn, 1998: 56) and facilitators do not have the option of ignoring outrageous, patently false or volatile comments. Rules are one means by which the potential for conflict can be managed, although rarely eliminated. Drawing upon her experience as Listowner for 'Echo', Horn (1998) developed the following 'mission statement' as the baseline rule of conduct. It proved an effective mechanism for facilitating discussion and containing conflict, although its on-going implementation remained problematic (see Horn, 1998).

> "The management of Echo believes in freedom of expression. However, personal attacks are not acceptable behaviour on Echo. Remember: Attack the idea, not the person. Repeated attacks may lead to being placed on read-only status, or, in extreme cases, the closure of your account" (Horn, 1998: 56).

Rule setting is important for managing the volatility of real-time groups. It acts as a means to encourage effective group self-management, which is particularly important in asynchronous groups (see below). Rules make explicit the ways in which participants may engage in the online discussion and can set a positive tone for the interaction. However, there is also a risk that a hostile and unwelcoming environment may be inadvertently created, by seeking to establish behavioural guidelines. The facilitator's challenge is to introduce rules in a positive and acceptable way.

Maintaining Behavioural Control Facilitators rely on text to maintain order in online groups. Because a facilitator cannot use body language such as shuffling papers or turning away (Krueger, 1988: 84), the style of the textual communication must be clear and precise. Such facilitation can range from subtle to more assertive and formal approaches. In Sweet's experience, subtle approaches can sometimes be more successful online than FTF.

> I find in FTF groups that some dominators can push a position over and over and over again even after I, as moderator, have repeated it to them and asked them to indicate if I have heard correctly. Online, I find they can fizzle out, or if I put it in print that, 'I understand your point of view to be ...' , or 'you dislike the idea because...' , they seem to back off. They don't seem to have the same impact on the group as FTF. (Sweet, 1999: *personal email*)

At other times facilitator intervention may seem overbearing compared to FTF conventions, but it is sometimes the only response to a fast-moving situation. Real-time groups are characterized by high interactivity and a facilitator may not be able to intervene quickly enough to prevent an outburst of flaming. Even if the facilitator steps in promptly there is no guarantee that intervention will be successful.

The example below is taken from the Young People and Health Risk study. In this extract, while flaming did not occur, the young male participants did need to be reprimanded. As facilitator, however, Stewart was not sure that her request for an apology would be adhered to. She was thankful when it was.

Facilitator: Does anyone know what the health pyramid is?

Red Beijing: We know many good jokes

Facilitator: Red oz why don't you explain what the health pyramid is?

Red Australia: i don't like fiona

Facilitator: I beg your parden red oz

Facilitator: you should apologise for saying that

Red Australia: can you tell me a joke?

Red Australia: sorry

Red Beijing: the health pyramid is the meaning of different food. for example,

Red Beijing: bread meat milk

Red Australia: yours is pretty much the same as ours

As we see, the need to reprimand participants can detract from the quality of the discussion. In the online environment there is no such thing as a quiet word in the ear of an individual participant. What is more, in the middle of attempting to obtain a public apology, the facilitator may need to repeat a particular question, even if this means spending more time than anticipated on a particular subject.

In the above example, it was only after the facilitator pursued a line of questioning about the health pyramid that the participants contributed meaningfully to the dialogue. This was despite the fact that discussion and the flow of the dialogue had been disrupted for only a moment. It can be noted that it was only after Stewart received her apology that the Beijing participants continued the discussion.

Asking Questions

The core skill for any interviewer is asking questions that elicit the desired information while maintaining the interest and co-operation of the interviewee. In this section we look at how questioning strategies need to be adapted when interviewing individuals using email. In the following section we consider online interviewing with groups.

Email Software The asynchronous nature of most email communication can be advantageous to an interviewer because it enables participants to send considered responses to questions at their leisure, and to keep a textual record of questions (and their responses) for future reference. On the other hand, this flexibility means participants may 'decline to answer altogether or forget to respond until half way through the interview' (Hodkinson, 1999: *personal email*).

Preparation for Questioning Interviewers working FTF are able to set boundaries between the organization of interviews (often conducted by letter or phone) and the personal meeting at which, after a few pleasantries, the interview proper may be flagged, 'Well, shall we begin ...'. Online, the organization and execution of the interview are conducted in the same medium, which can blur boundaries between them. Three studies showed various ways in which an interviewer could avoid this.

Smith-Stoner and Weber (2000) sent a preliminary introductory email which carefully and rather formally described how the interview would approach the participants' experiences of online education: 'The interview process will include several email exchanges where the researchers ask questions and will explore one example of a time in class where you felt really alive and excited by what you were learning'. The interviewers were then free to focus on interview questions in subsequent emails.

Ryen, conducting a longitudinal case study of a single individual, realized that her professional and personal interaction with Sachin might become hopelessly intermingled. It was finally agreed that Sachin's messages would be in two parts: a research section with numbered questions/topics, and an informal section which would allow him to 'differentiate my research questions from regular inquisitive questions on family relationships, religion, gender etc. (though they probably often look the same)' (Ryen, 1999: *personal email*).

Hodkinson was working in a subcultural environment (Goths) where perceived pretentiousness could alienate participants. His challenge was to move directly into the interview exchange with as few off-putting preliminaries as possible:

> Pre-interview "light conversation" seems difficult - I don't think the interviewee would see the point. You might as well try to create rapport in the introduction to a postal questionnaire. (1999: *personal email*)

Hodkinson's strategy was to present the interview questions as soon as possible and hope to develop rapport from that point. 'I try to open it up into a conversation and make things more informal after things have got going, rather than beforehand'.

Question Schedule A key debate in email interviewing is whether to send questions or 'cues' for themal areas all at once, or whether to stagger them. As the software allows for a textual 'script' of the questions to be retained the former option is certainly viable in practical terms. Methodologically, as with FTF research, the decision will depend to a large extent upon the level of 'structure' in the interview. As discussed in Chapter 4, extended in-depth narrative interviews may begin with, and branch from, a single 'narrative generative question' (see Flick, 1998) while more structured interviews might have a worked-through question schedule which could be sent ahead.

However, there are extra factors in online research which have a bearing on interview approaches. One of these is the ease with which participants can 'withdraw' from the interview.

> If the respondent is actually there with you in person, there is little chance of them simply walking off mid-interview. This is partly due to the perceived social rudeness of such behaviour, and partly because it is simply easier for them to continue to talk, having turned up in the first place and become interested, rather than returning to an e-mail conversation possibly weeks after it began. (Hodkinson, 1999: *personal email*)

An interviewer's confidence in a participant's commitment may well have an impact on the initial organization of questions. Interviewers who fear that participants will drop out of a study may choose to present all areas of interest immediately in order to get 'at least a brief response to all questions' (Hodkinson, 1999: *personal email*). The problem here is that participants tend to 'go to the questions they have the most to say about and skip the others' (Smith-Stoner, 1999: *personal email*). This can also happen if a cluster of linked questions are asked at one time. The conversational nature of the medium can tempt the interviewer to 'think aloud' in a stream of consciousness, but participants may only address one aspect of a multi-dimensional query. As Hodkinson notes, 'this creates something of a difficulty, because I then have to repeat the other parts of the question with the risk of sounding patronising' (Hodkinson, 1999: *personal email.*).

A second, related factor is the flexibility given by the time-scale of the research. In Mann's study, students agreed to take part in the research over the full course of their degree. This allowed the interviewer to send out a 'seed' question to all students at the beginning and end of every term, regardless of whether individual students had responded infrequently or briefly on previous occasions. If an individual student responded in depth to a seed question, Mann could pursue that 'thread' of discussion. If not, there was always the opportunity to interact with the student again at a later date. The further option of sending spontaneous diary entries, if and when they felt moved to do so, gave students another opportunity to reflect on interview motifs in their own time. While the success of short-term email interviews might depend upon developing rapport with participants quickly, with the concomitant fear that this may be unsuccessful and they will drop out, sequential interviews offer more possibilities. Participants with their own lives to lead may have reasons for being more 'chatty', or indeed reflective, at some times than others. In Mann's study students might reply regularly or irregularly, crisply or at length, methodically question by question or in a flow of answers, and in other permutations besides, but the 'open door' of the research design still allowed the interviewer to pace questions rather than rushing into presenting them.

However, as noted earlier, the success of a longitudinal research design depends upon gaining participants' allegiance in the first place.

Probes Asking for clarification of points or further, deeper, information is a key feature of qualitative research. In a text-based environment where ambiguity can arise from faulty sentence structure ('The message was the unfortunate victim of bad phrasing', GOTM student), poor choice of words ('In your final comment was it illusive you meant - like you wrote - or elusive?', GOTM student) and/or misunderstanding of connotation ('I had better tell you what i am talking about as you can't - as far as i know anyway - read my mind', GOTM student), probing becomes increasingly necessary. Email software facilitates this by enabling interviewers (and participants) to cut and paste the sender's obscure or evocative comments into a return mail for further elucidation. However, unlike FTF interaction and real-time chat, this is a delayed process because the reader is unable to interrupt someone who is in full flow. This can have advantages and disadvantages:

> I have found myself frustrated at not being able to interrupt - for example, if the respondent has completely misunderstood a question. However, it is undoubtedly useful (not to mention polite?) to allow people to finish what they are trying to say. It means, amongst other things, that it is less likely that any issues will be forgotten as a result of becoming side-tracked - as has happened in some face to face interviews. (Hodkinson, 1999: *personal email*)

Within a shorter-term email interview, probes may be a means of developing issues raised in open-ended questions or a detailed personal narrative. In longer sequential interviews, the possibilities for looking deeper into participants' perceptions and experiences increase:

> Respondents and myself had time to reflect in the exchange of questions and answers, enabling clarification and elaboration ... As I was viewing these men as experts on their own lives, I was able to feed back ideas and insights as they crystalized to see if they held broader relevance. (Dunne, 1999: *personal email*)

Mann found that, as her participants were used to deconstructing texts, they were able to expand their words/thoughts quite readily. In addition, should she get a sense of conscious half-exposure from students (cautiously inviting further exploration), she was able to ask more searching questions.

> **Examples: GOTM students**
>
> C. I was rather bemused when you said you wasted time 'experimenting' - is one allowed to ask for clarification here?
> S. Errm! I think I may have given TOTALLY the wrong impression here.....

C. You may not want to add anything to what you last wrote - so please ignore this next bit if that is the case. I was just wondering - this feeling you describe of sometimes feeling like 'a fraud' here - did you ever feel like that before coming to Cambridge - or is it just to do with being here?

Smith-Stoner has also noted ways in which participants flag that they are prepared to talk in more detail:

Often they put a tag line at the end of the phrase-"let me know if you want to know more" or they bring the subject up more than once. I think many people need to be invited to expound on a topic, they are courteous about people's time and don't want to abuse it. (1999: *personal email*)

However, it would be wrong to assume that all participants will be prepared to talk in depth or that all interviewers will decide to follow up every lead. As with FTF research, the context of the interaction might have implications for the questioning. Some queries might be deemed 'impolite' for reasons of cultural difference (Ryen and Silverman, 2000). Others might be considered slightly exploitative. 'The women in my studies were very short on time ... I felt that I had a responsibility to ask follow-up questions that were very relevant to the topic and not go "fishing" without good cause' (Smith-Stoner, 1999: *personal email*).

In one area, the online environment seemed to offer an additional constraint for interviewers. For, as we have noted throughout this chapter, studies in which participants are not personally committed to the research agenda seem to present more difficulties online than they might FTF. If the interviewer is afraid that participants will drop out, probes will be used with care:

I do find myself constantly thinking, in my various follow up questions, or probes, about the risk of the participant declining to participate further. Hence, I try to limit the risks of confusing, boring or offending the interviewee. (Hodkinson, 1999: *personal email*).

And some participants can remain resistant to any requests for information. In this extended quote Hodkinson describes the frustration which may meet any interviewer whose attempts to conduct interviews online are blocked by the recalcitrance of participants who are beyond the persuasiveness of the FTF 'personal touch'.

People simply not responding to particular issues or questions, or, as has commonly occurred, giving relatively uninformative one line answers has been a much greater problem for me than rambling off topic. At least in the latter case, there is something of a conversation going on!! My response to failure to answer questions often depends upon my assessment of the individual's enthusiasm throughout the interview. If they have generally responded enthusiastically and in detail to my questions, then I will repeat the question, perhaps blaming my wording for their failure to address it and including some kind of example to make it more clear. In some cases, however, interviewees respond to the first set of questions with a series of one line and sometimes dismissive answers, giving me the impression that they don't have the time or can't be bothered to give much detail. I have usually tried to encourage further detail by probing and expressing interest, but this is usually in vain. It is also very difficult, because their very limited initial responses give very little of interest for me to pick up on - and simply repeating the original questions seems likely only to cause irritation. In general, I have found that those who give highly limited responses to start with tend not to reply at all a second time, regardless of the style of my probing. (Hodkinson, 1999: *personal email.*)

Non-response With email, mailing lists and Usenet services, interviewers may wait for responses which never come. 'A possible ethical advantage AND practical disadvantage of e-mail, is the ease with which respondents can completely ignore questions!' (Hodkinson, 1999: *personal email*). This can happen at the beginning of the research:

Some participants responded, some didn't - some responded immediately, some took weeks. I usually sent polite E-mail reminders (usually blaming the possibility of lost e-mails) at least once, but after that I usually let them drop out. (Hodkinson, 1999: *personal email*)

Later in the research gaps in communication might lengthen to permanent silence and interviewers may have no sure way of knowing whether or why participants have left the research. Interviewers may prepare for this eventuality by establishing a range of ways to make contact with participants (Seymour *et al.*, 1999). Otherwise the only option is the follow-up mail sent 'in "casual" language, but with a reminder at the end. "By the way..." ' (Ryen, 1999: *personal email*).

Asking Questions in Groups

When working with groups, interviewers may plan to ask fewer direct questions (because they hope that questioning will develop among the group members), but they may have to work harder to keep the conversation on track. In this section we discuss the questioning strategies that are appropriate when facilitating real-time and non-real-time (asynchronous) discussions.

Facilitating Real-time Groups

Software Possibilities and Limitations Real-time IRC software usually gives the interviewer the option of taking a high degree of control over the interview process, or allowing participants to converse amongst themselves with little direct intervention. 'The technology can therefore be applied in varying ways according to the remit of the research project and its chosen methodology' (O'Connor and Madge, 2000). With much real-time focus group software researchers are alerted to the arrival (and the exit) of participants, which excludes the possibility of lurkers and allows the interviewer to invite everyone to participate by name. Real-time chat is a fast and furious environment. Multiple answers come in very quickly and in a fragmented and disjointed way. As comments from interviewers and participants can only be made as fast as someone can type, interviewers may prepare questions in advance and cut and paste them into the interview (O'Connor and Madge, 2000). Limiting participants to six or eight can avoid excessive delays between questions and responses.

Form of Control Facilitating focus groups often needs to be a delicate balance between leadership, direction and interviewer bias (Gaiser, 1997). In view of the high levels of interactivity, real-time facilitators may do well to take an active role in stimulating conversation, asking for clarification, responding to what is said and changing topics. Krueger (1988) has suggested that an FTF focus group is likely to be damaged by too many questions and too many areas of interest. In order to avoid the strong possibility that the conversation will diverge to inappropriate or irrelevant topics, the online interviewer may choose to be highly directive (see Chapter 5).

Question Schedule Giving out a question schedule in the first few minutes of a group discussion will help ensure that the allotted time is well used. For example, if participants are made aware that they have six issues to discuss with a time limit of fifteen minutes for each, they are alerted to what is expected of them in terms of both time keeping and recognizing the 'defined area of interest' (Krueger, 1988: 18). However, interview guidelines can also make clear that participants are free to contribute topics to the discussion:

Example: Guidelines

As this is an 'interview' we do have some topics that we would like to cover and we will probably use these to guide the discussion. However, please feel free to ask questions yourselves and to raise any topics that you think are relevant that we have not mentioned - but do try and stick as much as possible to the theme of the Internet and parenting. (O'Connor and Madge, 2000: 2)

Identifying questions from the outset has another benefit. Unlike its FTF counterpart, online chat offers no non-verbal cues to suggest that it is time to change a subject or to cut a description short. Without clear warning of the interview schedule, participants may completely 'hijack' the conversation, thereby disrupting the online researcher's 'carefully planned discussion'. Alternatively, queries following probes can become exhausted or move too far from the original research concerns (O'Connor and Madge, 2000: 3). By referring participants back to an interview schedule the facilitator can politely shift the discussion to a new topic. Such intervention is more likely to be interpreted as a legitimate task than unwarranted interference, allowing the 'positive tone' of the interaction to be retained.

Keeping to the Schedule Textbooks suggest that focus group questions should be arranged in a 'sequenced manner' (see Krueger, 1988: 66). Thus, an online interview schedule might begin with a general question linked to a questionnaire and then the following questions might link to themes raised in the questionnaire (O'Connor and Madge, 2000). When time is short and there is a range of issues to cover, facilitators may need to actively direct the research agenda throughout the interview. Some facilitators (O'Connor and Madge, 2000) have found that the 'abstraction' of the dialogue from the rich texture of FTF life can ease the process of keeping the interview flowing along key themes and avoid being side-tracked too much. 'Interrupting a conversation about the price of nappies felt somehow more acceptable in the written word than in the spoken face-to-face context'.

Example: Interrupting a Conversation

Hen and Clare: Rowena - do you do much shopping on-line?
Hen and Clare: and Barbara - have you ever shopped on-line?
Rowena: not much - usually books and nappies!
Hen and Clare: I didn't even knmow you could get nappies on-line!
Barbara: I can't say I have. It is useful to see what is available but I'm paranoid about security!
Rowena: from canada - they are cheaper - reusables
Hen and Clare: that's useful info
Rowena: most credit card payments are through a secure server
Hen and Clare: Do you find that you use the discussions for info. or for support from other parents?

Probes Even when time is limited, qualitative focus group facilitators are usually prepared to depart from the interview schedule in order to probe for more information or to follow up some points in depth. One problem for interviewers is the timing of their probes. As O'Connor and Madge (2000: 3) commented, in a real-time interview:

'Silences' take on an added poignancy as one needs to consider whether the silence is owing to the fact that the participant is thinking, is typing in a response and has not yet hit the return button, or has, in fact, declined to answer the question. No subtle visual clues are available and so direct questioning replaces the subtle:

> Hen and Clare: Rachel - do you mind us asking if your friend from BW lives near you or is it an email based thing?
> Hen and Clare: ..and Sarah is your penfriend an email one or a paper based one?

In the FTF context, probes may be elicited through the body of the researcher (leaning forward, a smile, a hand movement), but working online, probes must be textual. This can raise new issues for the facilitator. First, while a probe may be directed to a single participant, all group members may respond. (The use of first names can help to signal that an individual response is called for. In addition, some specially dedicated servers such as 'Hotline Client' offer private chat rooms which can be accessed immediately if researchers wish to develop issues privately with individuals.) Second, textual probes in fast-moving online chat may not have the flexibility of the spontaneous spoken word. As O'Connor and Madge (2000) discovered, there may be a tendency to cut and paste 'snippets of conversation/questions' to use as probes rather than deleting the original material and retyping it. As a result, when the researchers traced 'the genealogy of the interview', they found that this shortcut sometimes impeded the flow of the conversation. Consequently,

> both the interviewers and the participants followed the main thread of conversation and ignored conversational side-tracks probably more effectively than would have been the case in a face-to-face encounter.

Third, facilitators might probe using 'follow-up or 'think back' questions of the kind that have proved so effective in FTF group research (Krueger, 1988: 65). However, while such questions are generally used to open out discussion FTF, they may work in the opposite way online. As Stewart found, the liberal use of follow-up questions online was an effective mechanism to prevent her participants from straying to unrelated issues.

In the boys section of the Young People and Health Risk study, the interaction was rapid. One of the consequences of this was that questions were left unanswered. The extract below reveals the interjection of the facilitator to draw further information from the Australian blue team.

> **Example**
>
> Blue Beijing: where do you have lunch?, we both have lunch in schools
> Blue Beijing: do you smoke and drink?

Blue Australia: why do you talk about food so munch
Blue Beijing: How old are you?
Blue Australia: 11 12
Blue Beijing: we are both 12
Blue Beijing: are you worried about your test scores?
Blue Beijing: Do you know AIDS?
Blue Australia: NO
Facilitator: What blue australia - you have heard of aids havenn't you?????
Blue Beijing: are we welcome if we come to Australia?
Blue Beijing: we learn HIV/AIDS in our health education.
Blue Australia: we did not

We have assumed so far that facilitators are actively seeking ways to move a topic on as part of a decision to direct the research agenda. However, other facilitators might seek to increase the interventions of participants. In this case, the skill of 'listening' for an online facilitator is perhaps knowing when, and for how long, to be quiet. The experience of O'Connor and Madge was that, as their series of group interviews proceeded, they tended to intervene less. They felt that this resulted from, 'a combination of our increased reliance in our ability to handle the technology, our increased confidence in the research process, and thus a reduced necessity to "control" the interview and to allow greater flexibility' (2000). It was also in response to an increase in the size of the group which led the other participants to engage with each other more.

Facilitating Asynchronous Focus Groups

Software Possibilities and Limitations: Non-real-time discussion group software offers benefits and drawbacks for the facilitator. With asynchronous 'threaded interview' software, participants may enter a discussion site as often as they want, whenever they want. Their messages can then be logged allowing the researcher to map the whole course of the interaction (Seymour *et al.*, 1999). However, the unlimited availability of access for participants takes the group out of a facilitator's control. As a result, the effectiveness of an asynchronous group may depend on 'its ability to achieve some degree of self-management, due to the fact that a moderator is unable to function 24 hours per day' (Gaiser, 1997: 140). Asynchronous interviewing may take place 'in small instalments over many months' so participants may have to find a balance between the project and 'other life activities, such as work place pressures, access to computer technology, and family holidays' (Seymour *et al.*, 1999). Many of the possibilities and limitations of email interviewing discussed above apply to this section

Form of Control In asynchronous discussion groups facilitators are a largely passive presence. Because of the decrease in interactivity between researcher and participants, there may be little guarantee that all individuals will participate. Their participation is one step removed from the facilitator's control. An effective option for interviewers is to explain the situation and to ask for the co-operation of the group. 'Indicate that the medium limits certain types of ... feedback and that you are relying on the group to have a "discussion" in which you will interact and provide guidance' (Gaiser, 1997: 141). The aim is to 'get the group to function as a group and respond to one another's questions and comments' (ibid.). However, if groups have to generate data in a short time period, the need to develop self-management quickly may act as a barrier to their successful operation.

Question Schedule There are a range of ways in which a question schedule may be transmitted to participants. The group could benefit from having all questions posted ahead of time: if all messages are posted at the start, participants can browse the questions and participate in the group at their leisure. They can post a reply to a discussion of any one of the questions, or post replies to several or all questions at the one sitting. What is more, this approach may provide the members of the focus group with valuable information about the study (because the line of questioning is known to all participants), which may increase interest and hence participation. However, if the group is to be conducted over weeks or months, another approach might be to send an overview of the research, and then to post individual questions at weekly or monthly intervals. This may help ensure that participant interest is maintained throughout the process and help to refocus the discussion.

Finishing Interviews

Inevitably the conclusion of an online interview will reflect the nature of the interaction that took place. Some email interaction will simply die away. Some will finish with mutual good wishes. However, if the interaction is deep and extended there may be difficulties of closure:

> To me this is and has been a "research-relationship". However, communication "line-to line" over time, may change that. ...a long lasting e-mail communication resembles long lasting field studies where it is difficult/problematic to find out how to end the relationship... And there is no waving "good bye" because one never stayed there, so one cannot leave something one never has entered (by car, plane etc.). E-mail is just a question of a keyboard and a line, there is no "natural" end to it compared to leaving the jungle (Africa). (Ryen, 1999: *personal email*)

In an FTF focus group the moderator can close books, shuffle papers, turn off a tape recorder, or get up from a chair to signal the end of a group interview, but the online group facilitator has to focus on the style and tone of the discussion.

It was clear from the following exchange that an ideal point for departure had been reached.

Example: O'Connor and Madge

Hen and Clare: did the fact that we were both new mums influence your
decision to take part? or were there other reasons?
Kerry: I like doing anything that involves parenting although it was
nice to know that you would understand my experiences
Hen and Clare: kerry - we have some more info. on teh project in a minute
Kerry: thanks
Amy T.: It did help - talking to people who haven't experienced it
themselves is never satisfactory really. Also, I wanted to do my bit to
help, as other people have helped me in this new experience.
Kerry: Me too
Hen and Clare: yes - thanks very much for that, we have really appreciated
your help
Hen and Clare: and we enjoy it too
Kerry: That's ok any time
Amy T.: Ditto

On the other hand, in the Young People and Health Risk study, it was decided to end the young men's real-time focus group once the tone and content of the discussion changed from being educative to entertainment.

Example

Blue Beijing: does your country have any drug sellers?
Blue Australia: Millions!
Blue Beijing: oh, my god
Blue Beijing: is it true, we cann't believe it
Blue Australia: YEAH!!!!!
Facilitator: there are many drug dealers but millions is an exageration
Blue Beijing: hi, blue Australia, is this John and Cain?
Blue Australia: NO Its Bobby and Bruce
Facilitator: heroin is a very big problem in melbourne at the moment, isn't it
boys?
Blue Australia: NO not nececeraly
Blue Beijing: hello Bobby and Bruce,my name is Xian.What is you address?
Facilitator: yes it is, there were 10 deaths from heroin overdoses in a one week
period

Blue Beijing: what is your city' s name
Blue Australia: hong kong
Blue Beijing: is it kidding
Blue Beijing has left the chat.
Blue Australia has left the chat.

Conclusion

This chapter has not attempted to make definitive judgements about CMC as an interviewing medium, although it would hope to contribute to earlier insights about the processes involved (see Markham, 1998). Further research will ascertain whether it is a suitable method of, for example, conducting research on sensitive topics (Lee, 1993). Rather, we have tried to alert qualitative researchers to the possibilities and limitations of CMC as an interviewing method, drawing on theoretical insights from previous studies (Baym, 1995a) and the practical experience of 'pioneer' online interviewers. As we have seen, the jury is still out with regard to the effectiveness of online *vis-à-vis* FTF interviewing. One view is that the former is inferior for in-depth work. However, another deeply held conviction is that, once participants are committed to the research, in-depth interviewers and focus group facilitators can gather data online as effectively as when working FTF, and often more efficiently.

The quality of the data will depend in part on the factors discussed in this chapter. However, only certain aspects of the check list derived from Baym have been touched on here, and in the following chapters we shall discuss other key factors which have implications for the online interviewer.

7 Power Issues in Internet Research

Power relations between researchers and participants are an important aspect of qualitative research (Denzin and Lincoln, 1994; Weiss, 1997). In this chapter, we consider the claim that CMC may foster a 'democratization of exchange'; that is, a non-coercive and anti-hierarchical dialogue (Bashier, 1990), which would establish CMC as an ideal medium for conducting unbiased research.

Certainly, the early Netizen community hoped that online interaction would have democratizing characteristics. Idealized visions of Net culture stressed the importance of information sharing between individuals who would be part of 'a grand intellectual and social commune' (Licklider's Vision, see Licklider and Taylor, 1968). People online would be helpful, answer queries, follow up on discussions, and 'put their opinions into the pot of opinions' (ibid.). This would be an inclusive environment where 'people who have been overlooked or have felt unable to contribute to the world, now can'. Everyone would be seen as 'special and useful', for 'brainstorming among different types of people produces robust thinking' (ibid.).

Such visions held out the hope that CMC would allow new forms of social interaction with wider participation and openness, a 'potentially egalitarian network' (Spender, 1995: 227). Most importantly, barriers common to FTF communication would disappear. The lack of visual information would eliminate the often 'irrational biases and prejudices that disadvantage "outsider" or low-status groups' (Lee, 1996: *online*). In the disembodied environment of textual CMC, participants would be free from judgement or retribution, social hierarchies would be dissolved, and flatter and more democratic ways of communication would emerge (Kollock and Smith, 1996) As one commentator stated, 'only when all participants are on an equal footing and anonymity is the rule is fully honest, unfiltered, open, unbiased discussion possible' (Whittle, 1997: 124).

However, the optimistic view that CMC would be marked by universal altruism, equality, honesty and mutual respect is not shared by everyone, and there are reservations about '[u]topian visions of class- and gender-free societies' (Herring, 1996b: 1). An alternative view is that, 'as with earlier technologies that promised freedom and power, the central problems of social relationships remain, although in new and possibly challenging forms' (Kollock and Smith, 1996: 110). The electronic 'social commune' would have insiders and outsiders both in terms of access (see Chapter 2) and usage (Anderson *et al.*, 1994; Anderson, 1997).

Some commentators argue that virtual spaces are so constrained by powerful structural forces of class, race and gender that they cannot be equally friendly environments for everyone (Kramarae, 1995: 53–54). For instance, social interaction online is seen to be steeped in a racial context determined by dominant white users, the majority of whom are (young) men. In some online contexts, 'anonymous participants are assumed to be white and male until proven otherwise' (Kendall, 1999: 66; see also Kendall, 1998) and 'racist and homophobic outbreaks are regular events' (Rheingold, 1994: 185). In addition, classes traditionally given low status are more 'excluded from participation, privilege, and responsibility in the information society than they have been from the dominant groups in the past' (Turkle, 1984: 244).

Nor can we assume that anonymity will fulfil its egalitarian promise. In contrast, it may allow 'predatory mayhem' (Whittle, 1997: 123). Cushing (1996), for example, drawing on Fraser (1994), has claimed that Habermas's conception of a fully participatory public sphere is not possible, even in cybersociety. Power relations remain because, even online, we are incapable of 'bracketing-off' (Fraser, 1994: 83) differences in status and culture. In other words, we find new ways to discriminate between individuals. This is the conclusion of the Virtual Society? programme[1], which is co-ordinating research about the power structures of cyberspace at a number of European universities. The programme suggests that power relations online are not that different from the elitist social structures of the real world.

These conflicting views about the egalitarian potential of CMC suggest that researchers need to look more closely into the ways that power issues are actually manifested and experienced online. Feminists argue that any discussion about power relations online needs to acknowledge that science itself, and consequently computer and Internet usage, has been dominated by, and still reflects the needs of, white, wealthy, western men (Kramarae, 1995; Penny, 1994). In her review of the literature relating to gender dynamics online, Rodino (1997) points to findings suggesting that users who 'present' maleness online (whether or not they are actually men in real life) have more power than those who present femaleness (Herring, 1993; Kramarae and Taylor, 1993; Selfe and Meyer, 1991). There is little doubt that gendered power relations within conventional research (Reinharz, 1992), as well as online, present an ongoing challenge to the qualitative researcher. In this chapter we shall draw upon studies which have examined gender and CMC as a means to focus discussion about the potential of the Internet as a democratic medium for research. However, many of the issues discussed will also throw light on the interaction of participants who are differentiated in ways other than by gender.

Responding to Fraser's claim that it is impossible to 'bracket off' status we begin by looking at the literature related to the impact of social cues in FTF and online research, with particular reference to gender. Following Spears and Lea (1992: 45), we distinguish social cues from interpersonal cues which give information about mood, levels of intimacy and affect (we discussed the last in Chapter 6). Here, we discuss what Spears and Lea have called social categorical information: the social cues which inform power dynamics between individuals. In a text-based environment the two main areas for discussion are (a) the loss of visual cues and (b) the increased importance of language use as a social category cue. In the second part of the chapter, we shall consider evidence from a range of empirical studies which have grappled with issues of social status power, and in particular gender, in online research. These studies suggest that researchers can anticipate and prepare for many of the factors which may inhibit or enhance democratic possibilities online.

Visual Social Cues and Power Relations

Why are visual social cues relevant to power relations in qualitative research? There is considerable evidence to show that, in FTF research, participants ascribe beliefs and opinions to a researcher on the basis of social status cues. This can affect researcher–participant dynamics, so that interviewers who are 'seen' differently will receive different replies to the same questions (Wilson, 1996: 97).

Qualitative researchers adopt different methodological approaches to deal with this phenomenon (see discussion in Sudman and Bradburn, 1982). For instance, Wilson suggested that an effective way to minimize the social cue effect in conventional research is to match people with ascribed characteristics – so that 'blacks interview blacks, women interview women, and middle- or working-class people interview their class equals' (1996: 98). Similar methodological issues are raised in focus groups where the power relations are more complex as they also involve participant–participant interaction. In FTF focus groups 'a heavy accent, cultural bias, or socially mixed participants can very much influence the dynamic of the group' (Sweet, 1999: *personal email*).

Losing Visual Social Cues Online

> Unless you choose to disclose it, no one knows whether you are male, female, tall, short, a redhead or blond, black, white, Asian, Latino, in a wheelchair or not. (Kane, 1994: 204)

> You can't excuse or dismiss someone because you see that they are short and 'everyone knows that people who are short have certain kinds of complexes'. (Smith-Stoner, 1999: *personal email*)

As these quotes confirm, CMC eliminates visual social cues which may inform power relations FTF. The Internet has been called a 'level playing field with respect to physical attributes' (Wallace, 1999: 138). Wallace suggests that text-based CMC offers a possibly 'fleeting moment in history [when] beauty's power is restrained' and people can interact without suffering from physical attractiveness stereotypes. There are also suggestions that the lack of physical cues frees participants from status-based prejudices and the fear of being judged by any criteria other than what an individual has to say (Bashier, 1990: 54). Claims that the 'filtering out' of such cues in CMC helps promote egalitarian behaviour and wider participation in groups have been reported by studies such as Short *et al.* (1976), Kiesler *et al.* (1984) and Sproull and Kiesler (1986, 1991). In a wide-ranging study of several CMC systems, Kerr and Hiltz (1982) reported that factors such as race, gender or organizational status were not as likely to inhibit free communication as with FTF groups. Experimental studies of electronic discussions confirmed that online groups were less dominated by those with high status (Dubrovsky *et al.*, 1991) as they were able to bypass the hierarchical barriers found in organizations (Sproull and Kiesler, 1991).

These 'cues-filtered-out' approaches point to the possibility of freedom of expression, egalitarian behaviour and the dropping of social barriers in one-to-one and group research. However, these theories have been challenged by the findings of other studies which examined more naturalistic and less experimental online communities (see Baym, 1995a, 1995b; Herring, 1993; Lea and Spears, 1995; Mantovani, 1994; Myers, 1987; Spears and Lea, 1992). This body of opinion suggests that awareness of social cues remains active online and, in addition, that there are new social processes of domination and marginalization with which qualitative researchers may have to contend.

For example, Matheson (1992) has suggested that working in a medium where visual social cues are removed increases the focus on the restricted material that *is* available (rather as people who are visually impaired increase their aural and tactile awareness). Participants take a few descriptive cues and try to create a whole picture of what an individual is like (Turkle, 1995: 207). In this situation, textual clues to role, status and category membership become more important and influential rather than less so (Spears and Lea 1994: 452). For instance, as with gender and age, physical cues provided by the body have been pivotal clues to racial identity (Burkhalter, 1999). However, online, users are seen to examine 'an individual's perspectives, beliefs and attitudes to make assumptions about the individual's racial identity' (*ibid.* 1999: 63).

How are text-based social cues manifested? Paccagnella (1997: *online*) suggests that the medium of CMC may have 'new strategies of visibility'. For instance, cues exchanged or made available in the ancillary part of a message may have a strong impact (Matheson, 1992) with 'category information' found in names, message headers, usercodes and signatures. Like real-world addresses, email addresses carry connotations of culture or status. For example, the domain name can give clues about someone's organization. Familiar examples might include: .edu (for an educational institution in the USA or Australia); .com (for commercial); .gov (for a government department); and .ac (for an academic institution in the UK). Those with accounts at prestigious research universities are likely to be accorded more status (Lawley, 1994). Thus, the format of the electronic text may explicitly or inadvertently give clues about real life status. However, opportunities to self-name, as described by Myers (1987) and Reid (1991), or to use an anonymous remailer to disguise addresses (see Technology Introduction) can protect a CMC user from this.

There are other pointers to an individual's status in the online world. Many commentators (see discussions in Jones, 1995) point out that CMC environments are themselves structured by in-house boundaries and hierarchies. There are *new* forms of visible cultural capital and both obvious and subtle controls over the interaction (Lawley, 1992, 1994). As discussed in Chapter 5, typing skills in real-time chat can increase participation, improve status and allow domination of the interaction. Such problems may be compounded when English (the most common language for interaction) is a second language, as Stewart and Eckermann discovered in their multi-national health risk study. An international student mentioned in Murphy and Collins' report of online education using IRC remarked, 'Well, chat is never my friend. I cannot keep on with the speed of information coming in. Instead of pitching in at the wrong time, I prefer to read and contribute when necessary' (1997, quote: S8, 2-22-97).

Longevity of Internet use may also increase one's cultural capital online. According to Lawley the dominant cultural class in CMC is defined in terms of expertise and experience with CMC, and through affiliation with particular CMC environments (such as established systems like WELL[2]). Lawley points out that, 'having a "history" on the network places individuals in positions of authority, from which they often then feel they can dictate how current practices of communication should operate' (1994: *online*). These users display their technological power in ways that give clues (to the initiated) that they are system administrators, possess better programming skills, or have access to advanced forms of the technology.

While CMC systems tend to reward seniority and celebrity, new users of CMC systems are regularly ridiculed or attacked for shows of ignorance or inexperience (Lawley, 1994). In some circles use of emoticons is considered unsophisticated (see chapter 6) which might inadvertently work against women who tend to use these 'graphic accents' more frequently than men (Penkoff, 1994). As with real-life societies, insider/outsider status boundaries are created, by the use of in-group jokes, invitation-only mailing lists, discussion groups which can only be accessed by a password, private virtual 'rooms', and 'absences' (such as any acknowledgement of race or ethnicity). In special interest groups, members may need to demonstrate their legitimacy within the context of the group (Galegher *et al.*, 1998). Displays of 'belongingness' increase 'the likelihood that the individual will be granted some airtime during which others will pay attention and respond when he or she speaks' (ibid.: 499). As Wallace points out, it is frequently women who are categorized as newbies, 'particularly in the less settled psychological spaces' (1999: 225).

Other scholars focus on the particular ways societal differences are experienced in 'MU*' environments (Bruckman, 1992; Meyer and Thomas, 1990; Myers, 1987; Reid, 1991). As Paccagnella (1997: *online*) has noted, 'newcomers to a computer conference or a MOO are immediately recognized as such and the same holds true for the leaders. Both acquire and use symbols that make them different one from the other ... Such a status differentiation, of course, may not match a pre-existing differentiation in the off-line life, if any'.

(See Chapter 9 for further discussion of social boundaries in virtual communities.)

Gender and Social Cues Online

A survey of *Systers*, a women-only forum of computer scientists (see Winter and Huff, 1996; Camp, 1996), provides excellent insights into the ways in which some users might respond prejudicially to social cues online. Winter and Huff asked about the group's perception of the largely male culture of computing and CMC. Quotes from this study describe the ways in which ancillary data (see above) can first identify a woman writer, and then evoke particular responses from male users. For instance, when posting a message to a computer newsgroup, some women found they were ignored if they were identified as a woman in their signature:

> If I post something to a newsgroup like comp.sys.transputers and use my name (in my sig), I usually don't get a response to a query. If I post using my initials, I get a response. (Response no. 284)

Others reported being both harassed and patronized.

> Posting to any group is always an experience - regular "wanna-fucks" and other such annoying email come just due to having a female name in many groups. Often I've had to argue my points more strongly and then been put down merely due to being female. (Response no. 369)

The login ID, another possible gender identifier, also evoked responses:

> If you have an obviously female login name and you login to IRC, you will almost immediately be hit on by some jerk with a sexually suggestive login name. I found this very disorienting. It's like being groped in a dark bar or an elevator. (Response no.135)

Apart from receiving sexist or insulting responses to their own identifications, some of the women experienced the social cues in the men's ancillary details as sexual harassment: 'Sometimes the signatures of men are misogynist and/or violent ... It implicitly devalues me or makes a more hostile environment for me' (Response no. 476). Findings from Winter and Huff's study confirm other reports that 'marking oneself feminine' online (Rodino, 1997) can entail vulnerability to harassment and oppressive practices (Bruckman, 1993; Cherney and Weise, 1995; Kramarae and Kramer, 1995; Spender, 1995; Korenman and Wyatt, 1996), a situation which would seriously compromise a research study.

We shall now turn to another arena where power relations are exercised online. As Cushing points out, the 'minimal paralinguistic cues immediately present on-line, such as body language, status, age and intonation of voice, create an environment where language becomes particularly influential' (Cushing, 1996: 57).

Language as Social Cue

Language in any context is a very powerful social cue. Burgoon and Miller (1987: 199) have concluded that 'by evaluating our language choices, others make attributions about social and professional status, background and education and even the intent of communication' (see also discussions about recognizing restricted language codes in Bernstein, 1971, 1975). However, the following quote from Horn suggests that, once reduced to words, men and women can be stripped of the non-voluntary signs of gender.

> The only gender differences online are the ones that are expressed with words. You can't see anyone. There's no scent of perfume, no sweat. Nothing soft, nothing hard. We are stripped of everything but our words. And if you take everything away from us but our words, what are the differences between men and women? (Horn, 1998: 81)

The implication here is that language use is neutral rather than gendered. This view would not be accepted by early feminist linguists such as Fishman (1983) and Lakoff (1975), who have argued that women's language use is clearly marked by patriarchy. These authors suggested that women's language transmits powerlessness (women ask questions, are apologetic, make attenuated assertions) while also seeking a response from listeners. In contrast, men are seen to make strong, 'powerful' self-promoting assertions characterized by flat, unequivocal statements that do little to encourage further talk.

More recently Cameron (1996) and Tannen (1991) have attributed these apparent discrepancies in male and female speech patterns to differences in acculturation. Women are brought up to see the world as a network of connections and men to see it as a hierarchical social order (Tannen, 1991: 24–25). Consequently, women use conversation to connect with others and to negotiate relationships. Men sustain hierarchy by challenging and criticizing others. They use language to attract attention to themselves and, 'engage in "contests" as a result of which they gain or lose in status' (Tannen, 1991). Tannen concludes that women's conversation can be characterized as 'rapport-talk' while men more frequently use 'report-talk'.

Gendered Language Online

There is considerable evidence that these perceptions of basic patterns of gender-based communication are 'at least replicated, if not magnified, in electronic communication' (Winter and Huff, 1996: 30). According to Hall (1996), studies on gender in CMC (see, for example, Herring, 1993; Sutton, 1994; Tannen, 1994) parallel the earlier findings of feminist linguists. For instance, '[t]he male style is characterized by adversariality, put-downs, strong often contentious assertions, lengthy and/or frequent postings, self-promotion, and sarcasm. ... The female-gendered style, in contrast, has two aspects which typically co-occur: supportiveness and attenuation' (Herring, 1994: 3–4).

As with visual social cues, qualitative researchers need to be alert to the possible impact of a researcher's or participant's use of language on the responses of other interactants in a research study. Daws (1999) conducted research with what was ostensibly a woman's list connecting rural communities in Australia. She reported that the only time that participants expressed discomfort was when the few men in the list took a stance on an issue which was different from the rest of the group and maintained their position aggressively. As almost all of the men seemed 'more topic focused, more self interested, more status conscious, and less willing to engage in the general conversation of the group' there were times when the rhythms of the women's communication were challenged,

> The classic example was the man who asked the women to confine themselves to a single topic per message and to make sure the topic was clearly identified in the subject header as he was too busy to wade through messages with multiple topics. (Daws, 1999: *personal email*)

In a qualitative research interview a tendency for men to use 'report' talk can undermine the whole momentum of the interaction, as this frustrated comment from a woman researcher conducting an asynchronous group discussion suggests: 'despite repeated requests for more discursive responses some male participants maintained what could be described as an instrumental highly quantitative style of language' (Seymour *et al.*, 1999). In addition, the evidence from the literature discussed above suggests that some men would 'silence their female conversational partners by employing electronic versions of the same techniques they have been shown to employ in everyday face-to-face interaction' (Hall, 1996: 154–156). On the Internet, as in real life, some men will dominate discussions as they ignore topics introduced by women, favour a hierarchical, rather than collaborative, style and dismiss women's responses as irrelevant (Hall, 1996).

Reconsidering the Online Environment

How is it possible that the hopes of the 'cues-filtered-out' theorists are so dashed by the experiences of many women online? In answering this question, Matheson (1992) claims that, although anonymity or pseudonyms may *cut down* social status cues (such as gender), some status differences will still be registered. In this situation, internalized and frequently stereotyped responses to signs of social status will be activated. For instance, in one literature review, Rodino (1997) found that when users are assumed to be female they tend to be perceived stereotypically as too talkative (see also Herring *et al.*, 1992), more co-operative (Matheson, 1992) and in need of technical assistance (Bruckman, 1993). The assumption that a user is female is also seen to lead to an increase in self-exposure from men (Kiesler *et al.*, 1985) as well as an increase in openness and intimacy in (assumed) woman-to-woman discussions (Van Gelder, 1991).

Conversely, when women have 'swapped' genders online many are shocked to find that other 'male' characters seem considerably less helpful and polite (Serpentelli, 1993). As Matheson has concluded, there seems no reason to believe that, using CMC, 'the salience and importance of gender as a social category would be any less important than in other contexts' (1992: 79). We would further surmise that patterns of stereotyping activated by textual and language cues online might characterize other forms of power relations apart from gender. Qualitative researchers may have to accept that, 'this supposedly egalitarian, socially neutral and objective environment may not be neutral at all, and responses on this medium do involve an awareness of the other communicator (including expectations, stereotypes, etc.)' (Matheson, 1992: 79).

When we reflect on the evidence presented so far we may conclude that, should research participants be identified as women, they would indeed be (a) treated in stereotypical ways and (b) silenced by a dominant male style of communication. This suggests that Internet interaction may actually exacerbate, rather than diminish, the biases associated with gender and, by extension, other social status differences.

However, the danger for researchers is to look at the Internet as 'a single entity, with a single "culture", a single set of interaction rules, and a single style' (Winter and Huff, 1996: 52). Not only does the history of different CMC systems affect their use (Lea, 1992: 15–17), but also, as the CMC field develops, it becomes evident that findings for one context of CMC will not necessarily apply to others (Savicki and Lingenfelter, 1996).

For instance, Cushing (1996) has conceptualized CMC as a collection of 'sub-environments' with different socio-linguistic styles that lean to a greater or lesser extent towards the male conversational patterns described above. In addition, as Baym (1995a) pointed out (see Chapter 6) the emergent social dynamics of any form of CMC are linked to the general context, purpose and makeup of each interacting group within any of the CMC systems.

A variety of empirical research studies suggest that qualitative researchers can negotiate most sub-environments of CMC and secure democratic processes which can at least match, and may in some instances improve on, FTF alternatives. We shall now consider the main CMC systems under the general classification of either (a) semi-private or (b) public communication.

Semi-private Interaction Using CMC

CMC systems offer several main areas of semi-private communication: email; one-to-one discussions using 'chat' software; conferences/fora (asynchronous discussion groups) and real-time chat groups (such as IRC). These systems allow the researcher (and participants) different levels of control with regard to the power relations that may be evoked during discussions. For preference, a one-to-one email or chat connection between researcher and participant would be a voluntary and mutual association. Bennett (1998) found that setting up voluntary one-to-one chatting (using ICQ) allowed high levels of equitable interactivity and diminished researcher and interviewer hierarchies. However, as we shall discuss below, some one-to-one email interaction can be an intrusion by one person into the 'private space' of another.

Group interaction between a researcher and multiple participants might involve asynchronous conferencing software (see Chapter 5). Researchers have some control over power relations in this form of conferencing in so far as they can set up, or join, groups with particular membership characteristics (for example, all women, all black, all young). However, once established, the groups become self-governing. Although researchers may take steps to encourage participants to exercise appropriate netiquette, some of the power dynamics associated with public CMC may still pertain.

In contrast to asynchronous conferencing, IRC and real-time chat can be 'controlled' by a group facilitator who can give structure, focus and fairness to interactive dialogue (see Chapters 5 and 6). The experience of focus group facilitators is that power imbalances can be effectively minimized in virtual venues because (a) the moderator can decide on the social makeup of the group beforehand, (b) participants benefit from a 'neutral' environment, (c) visible social cues are missing, (d) the stated purpose of the group is clear and – for either altruistic or reward reasons – will be generally adhered to, and (e) the moderator can be prepared to deal with likely power dynamics which may be evoked by different combinations of individuals. In this situation, a skilled facilitator can encourage strong opinions to be voiced while limiting inappropriate behaviour. 'I encourage online groups to express opinions that represent them regardless of whether they are in agreement with other participants. On the other hand, I rarely see rudeness and am quick to manage it' (Sweet, 1999: *personal email*). Apart from the personal skills of the facilitator (see Chapter 6), some focus group software also has the capability to 'quickly bump someone out of the group' if things get out of hand (Sweet, 1999: *personal email*).

As power relations in the semi-private area of focus groups have already been examined in some detail (Chapters 5 and 6), we shall now consider email as an example of a semi-private system where researchers might hope to establish egalitarian research relationships. We shall refer to a variety of studies which have used email, identifying the ways that the general context, purpose and makeup of email interaction might affect researcher and participant perceptions of its democratizing possibilities with particular reference to gender dynamics.

Email as Mutual Exchange

Differences in email usage are broadly connected to the levels of mutuality established between correspondents. Used as a means to connect family, friends and colleagues, it can be a relaxed, private and often intimate form of one-to-one communication in which participants are consensually engaged. However, as we shall see below, this is not always the case. As discussed in Chapter 6, the norms which develop in different CMC systems are also directly related to the specific *purposes* of the communication established between different individuals and groups.

Let us consider some of the gendered uses of email. Email, as a mutual, highly personal mode of communication, is frequently associated with woman-to-woman communication. One view, which is shared by a number of commentators, is that email *between* women is used for social purposes, almost as an extension of women's historical connection to the telephone, in order to make and maintain friendships and contacts (Spender, 1995). CMC offers communicating women a 'network of lines on which to chatter, natter, work and play' (Plant, 1996: 170). It can be a form of 'high tech note passing by girls' (Herring, 1996a: 81) and a new lifeline for women in their fifties and sixties (Derkley, 1998). However, the level of intimacy which is freely achieved in a mutual exchange of email messages is not an automatic characteristic of the medium.

For instance, email may also be used as a means of following up public interactions in Usenet or IRC. Here, the purpose for making contact may be instrumental, antagonistic or exploitative, rather than beneficial and egalitarian. Efforts to set up a subsequent private email conversation may falter if mutuality of interest between individuals is not established. In some cases, this may be because the norms familiar to many public sites (see below) are transferred to one-to-one email interaction where they can be experienced as alienating and offensive. In the following quotes, email was used by men to follow up women who had made Usenet postings:

> I have been contacted several times in the past year by men who didn't know me, but just 'saw that I was logged in,' and because I am a woman, they sent me mail and 'talk'ed to me in personal and inappropriate ways. (Response no. 331)

> On a fairly regular basis, I get unsolicited email from men who say they saw my address somewhere and who want to 'get acquainted'. I used to get unsolicited 'talk' messages on my terminal from strange men, but I put a stop to that by permanently setting a flag to deny write access. Just last week, I received an unsolicited and anonymous email message that consisted of our online

encyclopaedia's article on sperm. (Response no. 68) (quoted in Winter and Huff, 1996)

As we see, in some situations writer and receiver are not equally committed to the email conversation. Although the examples given here reflect the experience of some women relative to men, the point to be made is that email is not by definition egalitarian. Efforts to impose an unwelcome intimacy can make email a highly intrusive communicative medium which can be used to harass and oppress individuals.

This kind of intervention has a different quality to that experienced should people be importuned by others using regular mail or the telephone. Letters and phone calls have established patterns of formality which regulate early encounters. If these social norms are flouted recipients quickly recognize that evasive action may be called for. In contrast, CMC conventions give 'permission' to make contact in a direct way using a relaxed conversational style. It may take time for the recipient to assess whether 'friendly' messages have a subtext and, by that time, a spurious intimacy may have been established. Within research settings, unsolicited overtures and even inadvertently 'inappropriate' comments may be experienced as power moves by some participants.

The Context of Email Use

The impact of the *context* of communication on CMC practice (Lea, 1992) cannot be neglected. It is therefore important to consider the ways in which the purpose of a research design may have an impact on power relations. The following discussion draws upon three studies which have used email as an interview technique. As we shall see, an interesting aspect of all these studies is the potential for gender anonymity in CMC and the ways that virtual spaces *may* allow power dynamics between genders to be diffused.

First, the Graduates of the Millennium study. At the beginning of this study, participating male and female students would not have been aware whether replies to their email messages came from a man or a woman (both researchers' names were appended to all messages). Furthermore, the *purposes* of the interaction seemed to make this information almost irrelevant. It was certainly never mentioned by participants. Even when Chris Mann took over sole responsibility for the research, the few comments referring to gender seemed to be stimulated more by curiosity over her non-gender-specific name: 'I think you're a woman but I can't be sure'. Only one message connected that assessment with a value judgement: 'I think you're a woman because you seem to care'.

Clearly, there may have been differences in the participants' responses if only one researcher with an unequivocally gendered name had conducted all the research from the beginning. It may also be the case that other freely available social status cues relating to the researcher (such as level of affiliation with the university) could have been a more significant categorizing element than gender. However, Mann's own view is that a shared focus on the research agenda served to override responses which may have reflected expectations and stereotypes linked to projections of her gender.

The second study is Hodkinson's (2000) analysis of Goth culture, both on- and offline. Hodkinson reported that, as far as he could tell, his male and female participants did not respond differently to his email interviewing. He argues that, in this particular context, his gender was of less relevance to participants than the cultural affiliation he shared with them. 'The characteristic about myself which has made a difference to my interviewing is my insider status in relation to the Goth scene'. Nor was Hodkinson disconcerted by the few clues given about gender in some of his participants' online names. For, in his experience, there is 'a greater proximity of the genders' in Goth culture than mainstream life. Thus, research focusing on the Goths would lend itself to in-depth, email interviewing of (frequently) textually androgynous fellow enthusiasts in which there would be little place for gendered power relations.

Finally, in Dunne's (1999) study, which used email to interview gay fathers, there appeared (as with Hodkinson) a similar flexibility about gender boundaries and (as with Mann) a commitment to the research agenda which was apparently unmarked by power play. Given that Dunne's participants had already challenged conventional meanings of masculinity (through being gay) it is, perhaps, not surprising that, '[n]one of the sample appeared to be surprised that a woman had initiated and was conducting this research'. However, although Dunne made no attempt to conceal her female gender, she admitted wryly that she suspected that some of the North American respondents originally thought she was a man, because 'Gil' is a man's name in the USA.

These studies all make the point that a research technique may be more or less effective – and may attain greater or lesser levels of democratization – depending upon its suitability for the investigations a researcher is pursuing. We develop this point further in the following section.

Email as Rapport Talk

With every CMC sub-environment, the question for researchers intending to use the medium will be, why might individuals (researchers and participants) choose this particular form of CMC and how might their purposes affect the nature of the communication that ensues? (Baym, 1995a). Patterns of women's email usage (such as 'nattering') suggest that qualitative researchers might use the medium as a means of tapping particular forms of female interactivity and that the communication may have particular linguistic characteristics.

Typically, basic e-mail is exchanged directly between people who know each other (from the virtual or physical world) and thus most closely resembles

"Rapport Talk" in a "Private" environment - both female conversational preferences. The user can express ideas in any preferred conversational style and expect to be "heard" because the understanding is that writer and receiver are committed to the conversation ... The user can also adjust his or her content and style based on what is already known about the receiver and on how the receiver responds to each message. This also fits the female syndrome. (Cushing, 1996: 59)

This description of language use seems to suggest that email is an ideal communication medium for qualitative interviewing which seeks to establish rapport with participants. But should we assume that because 'rapport talk' has been traditionally associated with women, it is limited to all-women interaction? Will communication between genders inevitably reach a linguistic impasse between rapport talk and report talk? Studies which have used email in mixed-gender settings have demonstrated that, in situations where participants greatly desire to 'be heard', email evokes 'rapport talk' in men as well as women.

We have already mentioned Dunne's (1999) study. Here, gay fathers who were 'extremely keen to have their voices heard', developed in-depth and 'truly interactive' email relationships with the woman researcher over a considerable period of time. When Bennett (1998) set up email interviews (and one-to-one chat software) to discuss emotional issues with heterosexual men she was unsure that a similar rapport would develop. She experimented with email as a possible way to communicate with a group of six men, who ranged in age from 21 years to 72 years, as she assumed that they would be unwilling to discuss personal experiences in 'normal' conversation. Speaking about emotions FTF could threaten to break conventional codes of masculinity, particularly in discussions between men and women where social barriers to communication are often 'ideologically entrenched' (Bennett, 1998: 10).

Bennett was concerned with whether power or binary oppositions still apply in cyberspace, and specifically when the interviewer is a female and the interviewee a male. She points out that the interviewer, under conventional conditions, 'is seen as being the one with power and the interviewee the "other"'(ibid.: 41) and quotes Townsend who found that, in her FTF research, people actually challenged her right as a woman to write about men:

They didn't believe I would get the truth from men. Men, I was told, would clam up, tell lies, divulge less than the whole truth, or engage in good old-fashioned male confabulation. (Townsend, 1994: 5–6)

At the close of her study, Bennett made a point of asking her participants how they actually felt about this issue. One replied that:

The fact that information was going to be obtained via an email exchange rather than a face to face interview made personal information easier to divulge ... The fact that you were a female made it easier when you consider my views of man as an entity in today's society. I felt confident that I would not be judged and be able to offer what would be a different perspective (Victor, aged 41, 7 July 1998). (Bennett, 1998: 43)

Townsend also points out that the act of sharing emotions is much more complicated than just opening up. It involves 'dropping the masculine façade of knowing, of being right' (Townsend, 1994: 93). This is an important consideration in research studies such as this, where men are actively encouraged to drop this façade, and more specifically risk being seen as something other than the perceived masculine norm.

In Bennett's view, her online dialogue with all six men became a fully reciprocal and equal relationship between a female researcher and her male participants. Electronic interviews allowed the voices of her participants to be '"heard" and understood'. There was also an openness of interpersonal communication.

> Midori, one of my co-investigators (aged 43) voiced this spirit, saying that: 'you know I'm very happy with the way things are progressing, and I know we get sidelined sometimes into talking about other things. But the important fact is that I'm telling you things about myself which I've given very little, if any, thought to, let alone spoken to anyone close to me, not even my wife' (2 March 1998). (Bennett, 1998: 36)

Bennett concluded that the electronic environment presented a neutral, and hence egalitarian, space in which participants could communicate without fear of undermining their 'masculinity'.

In the Graduates of the Millennium study, Mann also found that male as well as female students wanted their voices to be heard. In this study, young men were prepared to discuss their undergraduate experience, in all its light and shade, because they wanted future students to benefit from their insights, strategies and suggestions. Mann found that both men and women used email as a flexible, sensitive, responsive and informative communication medium.

> I didn't make enough effort (or any at all really) in Fresher's week and the time following: I know SO few people in college and this grieves me greatly. I feel as if i have really messed up the social side of things. (Male GOTM student)

It was the students' commitment to the purposes of the research, rather than gender factors, which increased their responsiveness to the researcher, informing their desire to understand and to be understood, to transmit ideas and experiences faithfully, to seek and offer clarification.

These findings suggest that when email is used as a mutually responsive medium it may evoke 'rapport talk' not only between women, but also between men and women (and presumably other individuals who may be divided by social status differences) whose priority is to understand each other. As such, it offers an invaluable communicative tool to qualitative researchers.

Negotiating Power Relations in Email

Finally, we consider a closely observed account of email interaction. This provides an excellent example of the way that power relations can be negotiated in an email context. Ryen and Silverman's (2000) study involved longitudinal email interviews with a male Asian entrepreneur from Tanzania. Ryen acknowledged that this interview may have been made possible because 'Sachin' was intrigued by the idea of communicating with a western researcher who was also a woman. This combination of factors alerted her to the fact that she might have to negotiate cross-cultural as well as gendered power relations. In the following account, Ryen describes how she and Sachin 'achieve mutual understanding on a turn by turn basis'.

> Take the case of how AR and Sachin work at achieving agreed forms of 'sign-off' greetings at the end of their mutual e-mails. Sachin's first message ends as follows: 'tell me more about yourself in your next email ... love Sachin'. [ending of first message 26.10.98]
>
> AR replies among other things: 'I am married and have two small children'. [30.10.98]
>
> Presumably, even if she were married, AR might not have mentioned it. Note how in categorising yourself, you categorise the other person (e.g. in this case as a 'friend' or something 'more').
>
> Moreover, AR doesn't use 'love' as a greeting but Hilsen (Norwegian for 'greetings'). Sachin monitors the category-bound implications here. His next message now ends: 'regards Sachin'. [05.11.98]
>
> In his later messages, 'love' is again not used by Sachin but: 'Well regards' [17.11.98], 'well cherio' [10.12.98] and 'cheeeers' [26.12.98].
>
> In her later correspondence [23.11.98], AR modifies her somewhat impersonal 'hilsen' to 'Beste hilsen' and then: 'Kjaere (=dear) Sachin!'. [22.12.98]
>
> Despite her self-identification as 'non-available', AR responds to Sachin's information that he intends to get married soon by writing: 'Lucky woman to marry you, - tell me more!'. [10.11.98] (Ryen and Silverman, 2000)

Ryen explains that such banter is intentionally used to maintain a 'friendly' relationship with a respondent who is, after all, giving his time freely to help her. She notes that the use of flattery ('lucky woman') is another reward that can be offered to research subjects. Ryen has described how she and Sachin 'negotiate the parameters of their relationship, invoking a range of paired identities: researcher-researched; female-male; married woman-single man; friend-friend'. She begins by implying her sexual unavailability and this is recognized by Sachin's modification of his sign-off greetings. However, 'conscious of the rewards that research subjects rightly may expect', she later uses what Sacks (1992) calls a 'category-modifier', 'to show her respondent that just because she is "unavailable" does not mean that she cannot treat him as a friend or that, indeed, she is unaware of his attractiveness to other women'.

In the next section, we examine CMC systems which rarely allow such fine-tuning in research relationships – those systems which are public.

Public Interaction Using CMC

The main public arenas using CMC are facilities offered by Usenet, and undirected real-time 'chat' systems such as those found in most IRC and MU* environments. These areas of CMC remain beyond the direct control of the researcher and the power relations in these areas may be extremely volatile (McLaughlin *et al*., 1996).

Purposes of Usenet

Usenet incorporates various public forums such as BBSs, mailing lists and newsgroups. Before pursuing a research objective with a Usenet group, researchers would need to consider *why* particular individuals have chosen to communicate through a particular facility (either spontaneously – or as part of a research project) and how their purposes might affect the democratizing potential of the communication, and hence the research findings that might ensue.

Usenet groups have a wide range of purposes. Some groups are recreational and have the aim of enhancing the online social life of everyone involved. Discussion topics in such groups have a personal rather than a professional focus (Baym, 1995a: 147). Other general interest newsgroups exist to exchange information, to act as a support system, or to enjoy discussions and debate.

'Report' Language in Usenet

Cushing (1996: 60) sees many Usenet services as 'clearly male in structure'. She suggests that, in many instances, this form of CMC is an environment of public utterances meant to convey facts and opinions in the male 'report talk' style identified by Tannen (see discussion above). In this sub-environment, 'the dominant male-style of discourse acts to enforce a single default style for how to communicate effectively' (Cushing, 1996: 61).

Cushing argues that female discomfort with Usenet is borne out by usage patterns, and the evidence that she and other commentators present suggests that Usenet remains a male-dominated CMC system. BBSs and newsgroups are generally concerned with male issues, there are a disproportionate number of male postings relative to female postings, and postings by men also tend to be longer than women's (Selfe and Meyer, 1991; Herring, 1993; Winter and Huff, 1996). Furthermore, men tend to monopolize discussions, even of academic lists (Herring, 1993) and women-related and women-only lists (Kramarae and Taylor, 1993; Kramarae and Kramer, 1995; Spender, 1995). They do this in a highly assertive, challenging and patronizing way (Herring, 1993; Winter and Huff, 1996), often ignoring messages using forms of attenuated language associated with women (Cushing, 1996). If women do increase the frequency and assertiveness of their contributions, they may be accused of 'going too far!' (Herring *et al.*, 1995). With these online groups, norms and patterns of behaviour can be experienced as unfamiliar, even hostile, territory by women (Kendall, 1999). Winter and Huff's (1996) study, discussed above, confirms that some unregulated Usenet environments do alienate women.

These findings raise serious concerns for qualitative researchers who hope to utilize Usenet to generate substantive data from or about women. A central concern is that women who have experienced or witnessed negative male–female power relations in Usenet may withdraw from this CMC system. Women who are 'afraid to be belittled and laughed at as I have seen other women treated on the net' (Response no. 155; Winter and Huff, 1996) may become simply unavailable for research initiatives. Researchers report that some women go off-line completely after unsolicited attention or abuse (Cushing, 1996; Kramarae and Taylor, 1993). Research would also be restricted when women decide to post self-censored messages for fear of harassment of some sort (Winter and Huff, 1996); or 'retreat into silence' (Herring in Spender, 1995: 196–197), choosing to lurk rather than posting anything in an open forum or participating in discussions. Other women may leave mixed-sex lists in favour of women-only lists. In response to the question, 'do you feel that women-only forums are necessary?', one of the subscribers to *Systers* stressed that it was prejudice present in Usenet environments, even more than that experienced FTF, which made women-only lists necessary:

> YES, YES, YES, YES, … for us who live in the middle of a well-entrenched GOOD-OLE-BOY system. This is the ONLY place that I can talk to other professionals as an equal. (well, not quite, my colleagues in my field treat me as an equal, but, the situation here is unreal!) (Response no. 441)

However, the previous experiences of some women may make them reluctant to contribute even in these segregated fora (Winter and Huff, 1996).

Hearing Women's Voices in Usenet

Cushing (1996) has noted that a male approach to discussion groups using CMC can be highly effective in terms of transmitting certain kinds of information. Certainly, much qualitative research enquiry could capitalize on the accessibility and articulacy of male participants in Usenet fora. However, it presents a problem for researchers if women's voices are silenced in public for which are made up of both men and women.

One alternative for qualitative researchers may be to pursue woman–woman dialogue threads within groups. For example, in Denzin's (1999) study of a mixed support group focusing on the implications of alcoholism, discourse analysis identified the ways that conversational threads within the newsgroup might have a very different tone depending on the gender balance of contributors. One of the valued aims of the group was to 'create a supportive, loving and safe environment' for discussion. However, this 'purpose' did not impact on all contributors equally. One conversational thread, involving two women, was indeed warm and supportive. Each woman was apparently sincerely interested in the other, there was no flaming, and power was not an issue (Denzin, 1999: 117). In another thread, involving a man and a woman, the man was challenging, aggressive and controlling – positioning himself not as an equal participant but as a spokesperson for the group (Denzin, 1999: 119).

Another alternative for those who seek women's opinions and experiences through Usenet is to turn to groups monopolized by women. Baym (1995a), for example, studied the mainly female participants who were involved in the television soap opera newsgroup r.a.t.s. The purpose of r.a.t.s was to enhance enjoyment of soap operas through talk and this, 'whether computer mediated or not, involves practices of collaborative interpretation and distributing information' (Baym, 1995a: 147). However, Baym noted that the gender balance of the group (mostly women) did affect both the subject matter and the interaction. There were no signs of the 'locker room environment' (Spertus, 1991) described by women in other contexts. In r.a.t.s, participants preferred to use real names rather than pseudonyms because personal topics were broached and there was much private 'socio-emotional' self disclosure. There was also a taboo against flaming, 'a consideration that, in the light of other Usenet interaction, seems gendered' (Baym, 1995a: 148).

A final option is for researchers to work with women-only groups[3] All-women groups formed specifically to resist male-initiated harassment on Usenet tend to be open with each other regardless of the general interests the group might discuss. Hall (1996), for example, found one women-only mailing list that she examined 'aggressively collaborative' while women in *Systers* welcomed the opportunity to express opinions and to ask questions without needing to feel 'on guard' or 'on the defensive' (Winter and Huff, 1996).

If qualitative researchers choose to investigate men and women separately online, they may need to take account of the arguments, described by Herring (1996a), which suggest that men transmit information using computers while women focus on interpersonal relationships to such a degree that they have nothing of informative value to say. In order to evaluate that stereotype Herring analysed two Usenet mailing lists, one mostly male and one mostly female. Her results suggest that, 'both men and women participate in discussions on electronic mailing lists to exchange opinions, beliefs, understandings, and judgements in social interaction with other human beings, with the pure exchange of information taking second place' (Herring, 1996a: 104). Although Herring found significant gender differences in language use in posted electronic messages (differences already touched on above), she concluded that such differences were, 'not the same as claiming that men are not interactive, nor women interested in the exchange of information. Rather men and women present different styles of interaction and information exchange' (ibid.: 104).

Research on Usenet interaction suggests that many mixed-sex fora may be characterized by power relations detrimental to qualitative research. However, depending on the nature of the research interests, a careful choice of group would seem to allow a wide variety of research options to be pursued. In addition, Usenet is clearly a fascinating research site for studying various kinds of group interaction in virtual settings (including gendered interaction).

Real-time Chat

Undirected real-time chat can have a variety of purposes ranging from supplying fun and excitement to providing information and exchanging views. In one manifestation, chat worlds or MU*s allow participants to act in novel, creative and imaginative ways which may have little association with their 'real-life' selves. As we discuss in Chapters 4 and 9, qualitative researchers have already turned their attention to virtual interaction and communities, with participant observation and content and discussion analysis offering rich sources of data *about* virtual power relations. As with Usenet studies, some commentators have focused on gender dynamics in chat. Their observations, however, are not encouraging in terms of using some established chat groups as research venues.

In a study of communication in MUDs, Bruckman (1993) found that female characters received more sexual attention (wanted or unwanted) and offers of technical assistance than male characters. Offers of technical assistance were often accompanied by requests for sexual favours. It has also been noted that, in chat, sexual harassment may have the additional characteristics of language marked by physically violent or sexually suggestive imagery (Cherney, 1994).

However, other commentators suggest that gendered power relations are not a feature of some chat worlds – suggesting, once again, that the context of CMC is a crucial factor which will impact on both the language and the interaction of research projects. When Horn wrote about the New York based portal 'Echo', she was describing a 'place' where some participants not only developed deep online relationships over time, but would also often meet FTF. This is clearly a different context to chat in virtual spaces where users meet briefly and anonymously and never FTF, and may have completely different agendas for communication. The following quote suggests that Echo users set out to establish rapport, in which case (as with the email studies discused above) language is not used as a vehicle of power relations:

> Quite frankly, the online voice has become so gender neutral in these past couple of years that I can't tell someone's gender like I used to. Over time you learn, but that's only because gender is one of the things you find out about a person when you get to know them. (Horn, 1998: 103)

Qualitative researchers will, no doubt, continue to observe how gender and other social relations are negotiated in IRC interaction. Their observations will offer a practical and theoretical frame for studies in which researchers use IRC with the express purpose of generating data about substantive issues.

Conclusion

As Paccagnella (1997: *online*) points out, online relationships 'can be altogether more or less democratic, uninhibited or egalitarian than in real life, depending on an intricate pattern of elements'. Cultural variation in public and private CMC environments does much to explain different perceptions of power relations online. In addition, as we flagged in Chapter 6, such factors as the purposes of the research, the social makeup and longevity of the group and differing levels of technical expertise will have an impact on the democratization of interaction. One consideration which is relevant here is the change that has taken place in the gender balance of Internet users. Spender, who was at the forefront of reconceptualizing the Internet from information superhighway to communication network, continues to map CMC usage over time. In her view CMC culture is changing. For instance, as the numbers of women online increase they no longer feel like interlopers, rather they see the Net as the safest place to interact (Spender, 1999: *personal email*). It is to be hoped that the increasingly mainstream usage of CMC will contribute to establishing a power equilibrium between future participants whatever their sex, age or ethnicity. However, as we shall see in the next chapter, differences of power on the Internet do not only apply between those, for instance, who adopt 'rapport' or 'report' talk; they also exist between those who relish and those who struggle with the written word. For, as noted briefly earlier in this chapter, qualitative researchers who seek to democratize the social relations of research may also need to acknowledge that not everyone will thrive when the research medium is a form of writing.

Notes

1   More details about the Virtual Society? programme can be found at www.brunel.ac.uk/research/virtsoc.
2   WELL is a California-based portal. The acronym refers to Whole Earth 'Lectronic Link.
3   A range of different interests and approaches are demonstrated at the following locations: www.women.com; Femina: femina.cybergrrl.com; FeminaMail: listserv@lists.cgim.com; WomensNet: www.igc.org/igc/womensnet/; Virtual Woman: www.WWWomen.com. New sites are starting all the time.

8 Language Mode and Analysis

In previous chapters we have discussed practical and procedural advantages and disadvantages of using CMC. We now turn to questions about the nature and quality of the data produced via CMC.

Qualitative data are textual data. In most conventional qualitative research, text is obtained via FTF interaction in a real-world social context. Typically, data from interviews and observations are transformed into texts and methods of interpretation start from those texts (Flick, 1998). Because CMC research bypasses the FTF stage of this process it seems to offer a shortcut to text, with digital data literally at the fingertips. But we have to consider what is won and what is lost when data are produced in this way. As Jones asked: 'what does it mean for scholars and their scholarship when a particular technology with distinctive and peculiar modes of address, identity, behaviour, and responsibility becomes a pre-eminent medium of information exchange?' (1999b: 13).

In this chapter we consider the status of 'CMC as language'. This is a matter of key importance. Language in qualitative research needs to allow 'thick description' of the 'webs of significance' that people spin (Geertz, 1973: 5). It needs to have the power to display a picture of the world in which we can discover something about ourselves and each other. We address these challenges by considering the implications for qualitative data of the following queries: (a) Are we talking about a new mode of communication? (b) How does CMC compare with traditional data sources such as oral and written language? And (c) what are the implications for data analysis?

CMC as a 'Hybrid' Mode of Communication

Qualitative researchers cannot overlook the possibility that technology has produced, and is continuing to develop, new ways of transmitting meaning through language. Features like interaction, rapid feedback and, in some cases, co-present users suggest that CMC, and particularly synchronous CMC, may be a completely new form of communication. In the past communication by the written word involved a considerable delay in the communication loop. With CMC, reduction in response time is dramatic and has led to various attempts to classify this particular type of text-based communication. Various analogies have been suggested to place CMC in a linguistic pantheon:

Conversation Both synchronous and asynchronous CMC have been seen as conversational, with claims that people do not 'write' to their friends on the Internet, they 'talk' (Giese, 1998: *online*).

Writing Asynchronous email, the least interactive type of CMC, has been associated with positive characteristics found in traditional writing forms (Morrisett, 1996). These include having the time to study, analyse and reflect on incoming messages and being able to compose responses carefully.

Telephoning Other studies challenge the assessment of CMC as a writing mode. For instance, Treitler (1996: *online*) suggests another analogy, the telephone. Here, people 'grab' a keyboard for quick transmission of thoughts.

Note taking The simultaneous terminal-to-terminal dialogue usually referred to as chat has linguistic qualities (such as typing errors, abbreviations) associated with saving time and minimizing effort, features which generally characterize notetaking (Ferrara *et al.*, 1991: 21).

However, the most exciting suggestion is that CMC is a new kind of discourse. Some communication theorists claim that CMC is unlike any genre previously studied; that it is 'a language that never existed before' (Ferrara *et al.*, 1991: 26). The most common claim is that CMC produces text which is historically unique because it is a hybrid showing features of both spoken and written language (see, for example, Reid, 1991; Ferrara *et al.*, 1991; Murray, 1995; Yates, 1996; Davis and Brewer, 1997).

CMC as a Hybrid Language

Why should it matter to qualitative researchers that CMC might combine characteristics of both oral and written language? It is important because it offers a new dimension to longstanding debates about the quality of data that can be collected using FTF *oral* interaction as opposed to drawing on various kinds of solicited and unsolicited *written* materials. Such debates are informed by communications theory. For instance, Good draws on a variety of sources to identify the less benign consequences of the ways in which writing transforms interaction:

> Spontaneity is lost; the communication is impoverished in terms of its social and emotional content; and the precision of the written page can exert its own form of pedantic tyranny as the prospects for negotiating meaning are reduced. (1996: 82)

Above all, in written conversation, the nature of the relationship between participants changes as 'neither need pay the same kind of real-time, moment by moment attention to the other, and there is no compulsion to orient to a collaborative [conversational] enterprise in the same way' (Good, 1996: 82).

For these reasons, many qualitative researchers believe that it is oral interaction in an FTF context which allows the greatest degree of mutually enlightening dialogue to take place between researcher and participant(s). The oral account is seen to be 'lively and responsive to the questioner', while written accounts are 'pallid, literary conventions', the loss of oral qualities rendering the text 'less personal and unique' (Bornat, 1993). Finnegan, for instance, claims that inner feelings, narrative characteristics such as atmosphere, emotion, tension and irony and, finally, the capacity to reflect on one's own narration, are more successfully transmitted in an oral 'performance' than through written words (1992: 191–192). In her view, it is almost impossible to translate the whole range of performance characteristics into the 'narrow channel' of print.

However, Temple, drawing on her research comparing oral and written accounts of the same historic moment (a journey from Poland to England at the outbreak of World War II), concluded that the extent to which such a range of narrative elements can be transmitted in any medium is open to debate and 'anyway cannot be tied unproblematically to the medium the account is presented in' (1994: 38). Temple's research suggested that: 'The written account is an interaction between author and reader just as the oral is an interaction between speaker and listener. Moreover the written account can also serve to evoke emotion, tension, and irony by its interactive qualities' (1994: 38).

A slightly different point is made in Havelock's (1998) discussion of the oral and written characteristics of language. Havelock claims that when we speak orally we often express a kind of common sense which can actually be *obscured* by the abstractions and logical processes of the written word. However, this view would not accord with that of commentators who classify writing as an even more effective means of ordering and communicating thought than speech. Here, writing is seen as an empowering and intellectually engaging process because it favours 'deliberative response over immediate response, and active thought over passive reception' (Morrissett, 1996) resulting in rich and informative data.

For qualitative researchers, these debates centre around the claim that oral narrations produce data with greater personal and interpersonal accuracy than written accounts (Thompson, 1988: 150). For methodological reasons, researchers need to be aware that such debates now look beyond the oral-writing dichotomy. For the first time, we have the suggestion that the 'electronic word' should be considered a stand-alone conceptual category distinct from, but sharing qualities with, the spoken *and* the written word (Lanham, 1993).

How do commentators characterize the 'electronic word'? In one view, CMC (a) is typed and therefore like writing and (b) contains exchanges which are 'often rapid and informal' and therefore like talk (Collot and Belmore, 1996). Similarly, Murray drew attention to the possibility of CMC showing speech characteristics seen in 'emotive and informal diction; hedging and vagueness' and written qualities of formality, technical language, definiteness (1991: 36). Authors stress the overlap of the two traditional modes. According to Davis and Brewer 'electronic discourse is writing that very often reads as if it were being spoken - that is, as if the sender were writing talking' (1997: 2). The written text is 'laden with conversation-like conventions' (1997: 156). In similar vein, Spitzer has conceptualized CMC as 'talking in writing', or as 'writing letters which are mailed over the telephone', where participants 'use language as if they were having conversation, yet their message must be written' (1986: 19). Ferrara *et al.* (1991) argue that CMC shows involvement (such as asking direct questions) in ways traditionally associated with FTF interaction. But CMC is also like written language because it is elaborated, expanded, and thus edited.

If we accept that CMC is a hybrid language, the following questions are salient in terms of the quality of data that might be collected: Does CMC include the best of both talking and writing? Does it suffer from the disadvantages of both? Does it offer qualities that are different from both?

Negative Aspects of the Hybrid Inheritance

Some commentators who discuss CMC emphasize negative aspects of its links to either speech or writing. The spontaneity of speech may be valued by some, but for others it is associated with superficiality. In Treitler's (1996: *online*) analogy of email as a casual phone call, 'People "grab" a keyboard for quick transmission of thoughts, often to unburden themselves and go on with other activities without "wasting" time or mental energy'. As a consequence, she claimed, data collected could be unfocused, trite and 'faulty' information. As Sproull and Kiesler noted, 'it is so easy to send a message, people may be tempted to speak before they think' (1992: 33).

A superficial exchange may be even more likely when using synchronous forms of CMC (Gaiser, 1997; Giese, 1998). In situations where short postings and extreme brevity are valued, or where participants are constrained by minimal response times and competition for attention, there may be a 'low signal to noise rate' (Herring, 1996a: 105). In other words, we cannot count on the verbal flurry of electronic 'chat' to transmit a great deal of useful information. In addition, as with speech, some synchronous programmes leave no physical traces: 'there is no record of the message on the screen or in a file' (Murray, 1991: 39) which might aid reflection. The ephemeral nature of verbal exchange in speech and in synchronous CMC means participants may forget questions or lose focus in their responses: a problem that is increased when online interaction is brief, rapid-fire interjections, consisting only of short lines of text.

Other commentators discuss literature which suggests that the written aspects of CMC might limit its use as a method for collecting useful data. Davis and Brewer review studies pointing to speech as 'natural language': the 'unprompted, unselfconscious, uninterrupted, untainted language which can be seen as characteristic of the speaker's habits and the speaker's largely unconscious conventions of or preferences for expression' (1997: 24). In contrast, in Denzin's discussion of 'cybernarratives' (1999) the text of 'screen talk' is characterized as 'deliberative, stilted, formal'.

Apart from losing the spontaneous qualities of speech, CMC text is also seen to hinder the exploration of meaning allowed by 'the give-and-take of ordinary conversation in which persons may debate what was spoken or what was meant by what was spoken' (Denzin, 1999). Some studies suggest that the ambiguity of the written word online can slow down discussion about 'what was spoken'. Hodkinson noted that it was common for participants to misunderstand what he was trying to ask. Perhaps from feelings of frustration, bewilderment or embarrassment they 'were more liable to ignore things or answer the question as best they could understand it, rather than ask for clarification' (1999: *personal email*). When Smith-Stoner and Weber set out specifically to explore participants' ideas 'word-for-word' they could be met by incomprehension. It was as if the formality of writing gave words a new resonance which left participants feeling 'stumped' and slightly defensive:

> It was a continual issue. Participants often asked what we meant by terms such as meaningful. They would use phrases such as, 'I am not sure what you mean', or 'You should talk with someone who knows more than I do, I am not sure what you mean by memorable'. (Smith-Stoner and Weber, 2000: 9)

These views suggest that CMC data might share the drawbacks of some oral communication in terms of being casual and superficial, and the drawbacks of some written communication in terms of distancing the thought from the speaker, and increasing misunderstanding rather then deepening understanding between speaker and listener.

Positive Aspects of the Hybrid Inheritance

In contrast, other commentators focus on the ways in which hybrid CMC assimilates positive features of spoken and written language. One perspective is that the new technology (particularly asynchronous versions of CMC such as email and conferencing) allows thoughtful, organized and detailed communication (Morrisett, 1996). This is combined with a challenge to earlier claims that 'involvement with one's audience ... is lacking in any kind of writing' (Chafe and Danielewicz, 1987: 110). In the positive view of asynchronous CMC there is an emphasis on interaction (as found in FTF conversation) but with the additional bonus that responses to comments are produced at a 'pace set by the writer alone and can be consumed at any speed the reader chooses' (Yates, 1996: 33). The software allows for an extended and deliberative sequence of events: writing a reply remembering personal experience or previous texts, constructing and planning forthcoming writing, doing the writing, choosing to save the writing and so forth (Davis and Brewer, 1997: 44–45). This gives time to digest even 'extended messages' (Murray, 1995: 71). Such reflexivity is seen to increase the accuracy of data:

> When you're writing an email, there's time to think about what you're saying and revise it if you feel it doesn't quite sound the way you think it should, which gives a better reflection of the student's opinion than a note scribbled in five minutes between lectures would do. (GOTM student).

At the same time characteristics of orality are not lost. One view, based on perceptions of conferencing behaviour, is that when participants are really concentrating on the content of their messages, the manner of communication may be 'fairly close to being characteristic of the writer's habits and preferences in oral discourse' (Davis and Brewer, 1997: 24). That is, the writing has conversation-like characteristics, as we see in the following quote:

> Excuse me - I need to go get my washing out of the tumbledrier right now before someone gets impatient and hauls it onto the floor. I haven't figured out the 'postpone' bit of this thing yet so I'll continue in the next bit • Maybe I'll even come to the point, who can tell? ... OK - washing all safe and dumped in large pile on bed. Sorry about that. The point ... [continues narrative]. (GOTM student)

In addition, as with written materials, many forms of CMC produce a 'space-bound, static and permanent' script (Davis and Brewer, 1997: 2). This can increase the range and focus of data in various ways. In the experience of one researcher (Hodkinson, 1999: *personal email*) the script partly compensated for difficulties found in conveying information in written form online. The researcher could attend to the ordering and format of questions, and participants had the opportunity to read through the questions several times to make sure they understood them. Participants were also able to reread, and to reflect on, their own messages before sending them: 'reading this back, it sounds like sexism is a majorly obvious problem. But it's not that obvious and the people who react in this way would never be consciously sexist' (GOTM student).

The visible presence of a script may also ensure that the conversation stays on track, as participants can scan the interviewer's text for multiple prompts or questions. This minimizes demands on participant memory and attention (Colomb and Simutis, 1996). As a result it is possible for researchers to present more material for discussion than is possible FTF. In newsgroups participants can handle multiple 'threads of discourse'. Yet such complex levels of conversational stimuli would stretch their cognitive resources if they were presented in FTF interaction (Black, 1983). For instance, in a context like asynchronous conferencing, scripts allow participants to deal with one or more aspects of a topic. Contributions, which are typically longer than a comment but shorter than an essay, may be clustered into several general themes or distinct narrative patterns (Davis and Brewer, 1997). The presentation of written material in this way can be very helpful for researchers organizing data.

Most importantly, a script allows previous interactions to be relived and they become a point of reference for future communication (Giese, 1998). 'Thank you for your message. I was in a bit of a bad mood when I wrote [my last message] so although I still stand by it I'm sorry if it turned into a bit of a tyrade! I do think ... [message continues]'. Scripts can also be archived over time not only by the researcher but also by participants. 'Looking over my previous messages my file must be quite a fun (and disturbing) read!' (GOTM students). When researcher and participants build up a communication 'history' this tends to increase the reflectivity of both.

Some online researchers point out that the written script is also the means by which researcher and participant(s) can emulate oral debates about 'what was spoken or what was meant by what was spoken'. Unlike much conventional 'writing' the reader *is* able to ask for clarification and elaboration of the writer's script. In Dunne's study of gay fathers, the possibility of reflecting on written answers increased her 'knowledge' and enriched her data. Following a period of deliberation she was able to 'ask new questions, touch on difficult topics, feed back themes as they emerged and test out ideas' (Dunne, 1999: 2).

Unprecedented Aspects of the Hybrid Inheritance

The possibility of simultaneously communicating many-to-many is one of the innovations of CMC and it presents opportunities and constraints unknown in other language modes. Let us look at this in more detail. Synchronous CMC is constrained by computer screen size, average typing speed and skill, minimal response times and by participant competition for attention (Werry, 1996). As a result, this highly interactive medium has occasioned an 'incessant drive to reduce the number of required keystrokes to the absolute minimum' (Werry, 1996: 55). In order to maintain rapid interaction, participant postings are rarely more than a sentence or two long. There are also short gaps between conversational turns. These unique characteristics of synchronous CMC have led to a mode of communication where a minimum of words is used to convey meaning in the text and little attention is paid to the formalities of spelling and punctuation. The example below, from one of the online focus groups conducted as part of the Young Women and Health Risk study, illustrates many of the characteristics found in synchronous CMC:

Yellow Oz: what did you talk about on the subject of alchol?
Yellow Oz: ni shi Beijingren ma?
Yellow Beijing: we think excessive alcohol can be harme
Yellow Oz: So does our group. Does anyone in your group watch what they eat. Is anyone anorexic or bulemic?
Yellow Beijing: we are beijing ,you speak chinese very well, can you speak o lot?
Yellow Oz: No, I just started this year.
Yellow Oz: In China do girls worry about being fat?
Yellow Beijing: may we talk about breakfirst? we think breadfirst is very important for our health ,but many of our classmates don't have.

> Yellow Oz: We also think that we should have breakfast, but some of us don't
> have time to eat it in the morning.
> Yellow Oz: Is the teenage pregnansies percentage high in china, do chinese boys
> pressure girls to have sex with them.

As we see from this example, the script has many typographical and spelling errors (some of which were also a result of speaking in a second language). With the speed of the conversational exchange, conventional communication patterns such as turn-taking and adjacency pairs (question–answer couplets) are largely absent (see Murray, 1995; Davis and Brewer, 1997). Although the dialogue is sequenced chronologically, the 'written conversation' is non-linear.

The design of (most forms of) real-time chat software allows these multiple and disjointed conversational threads to occur. Rather than one developing theme, there are rapid shifts in conversational topic. As the discussion continues, a number of separate conversational threads intertwine through the ever-scrolling lines of text (Murray, 1995: 15). These characteristics seem able to produce a new form of 'hybrid' group interaction:

> From the oral side, it is as if everyone who is interested in talking can all jump in at once, but still their individual voices can be clearly heard. From the written side, it is as if someone had started writing a piece, but before he/she gets too far, people are there magically in print to add to, connect, challenge, or extend the piece. Therefore, what we have is a written quasi-discussion. (Shank and Cunningham, 1996: 30)

As Sudweeks and Simoff point out (1999), each communication environment requires specific knowledge. Real-time chat requires both knowledge of language and, for instance, management of turn-taking; it needs technical proficiency and the ability to respond rapidly to multiple comments from others. Some authors suggest that inexperienced participants and non-native speakers of English may feel uncomfortable with, even alienated by, this form of interaction (Aoki , 1995). There are also fears that the non-linear 'flow' of the conversation, and loss of turn-taking, may create conversational chaos in some contexts (reported by Murphy and Collins, 1997). However, the evidence suggests that the online community has defined communication norms and conventions somewhat differently from FTF conversations (Murphy and Collins, 1997). The absence of unnecessary linguistic material is seen to be an efficient way to get meaning across to others (Condon and Cech, 1996). In addition, experienced CMC users have developed conversational strategies, such as addressing someone directly by name, which allow for new ways of turn-taking and maintaining focus on a discussion topic, even in multi-thread real-time conversations (Wilkins, 1991; Werry, 1996).

Communication theorists who have investigated the ways users adapt to real-time interaction draw attention to the importance of contextual factors such as the task in hand (Murray, 1991: 53). Murphy and Collins used content analysis to identify the communication conventions and protocols that real-time, interactive electronic chat users developed in *instructional* settings. In this context, students recognized a need to communicate clearly and minimize misunderstandings in their online transactions with others. They used the names of individuals, gave non-verbal cues in the text and, where necessary, asked questions and sought clarification. In another study which also drew on the experience of online teaching, Colomb and Simutis claimed that 'students learn how to conduct a successful CMC discussion, just as they once had to learn how to conduct a successful oral discussion' (1996: 206).

In addition, once participants have a certain level of skill, the charge of superficiality in all rapid multi-person interaction is not supported by the evidence. Ferrara *et al.* (1991) point out that synchronous CMC in any setting demands 'clarity and comprehensibility' from participants. Users are very aware that their 'efforts' are instantly exposed to others and there is the potential for immediate (and possibly less than complimentary) feedback. Rather than encouraging a careless indifferent approach to an ephemeral speech-like act, this may actually increase self-awareness – increasing spontaneity but *also* having 'undoubted effects on the composing process and the ability of writers to revise or edit' (Ferrara *et al.*, 1991: 14).

Is CMC an Effective Research Mode?

CMC seems to be a language mode which shares some of the advantages which can characterize oral *and* written forms of data collection. It could be argued that qualitative researchers would benefit from data which can access meaning through both a level of interpersonal involvement traditionally associated with oral interaction and the elaboration and expansion of thought associated with writing. Some commentators conclude that this double-pronged mode of communication makes CMC an excellent medium through which to 'exchange opinions, beliefs, understandings and judgements in social interaction' (Herring, 1996a: 104).

However, there are other factors to consider. The electronic word, just as the spoken and written word, will vary according to individual expertise and usage. Some participants may have less confidence or experience when it comes to making an immediate, spontaneous response to a discussion thread in a real-time focus group. Unless the researcher has excellent moderating skills, some data will be lost. Second, there are general literacy skills. As MacKinnon notes, command of written language, eloquence, the ability to write a 'potent or even vehement statement' can empower individuals online beyond their relative strength in real life (1995: 118–122). Of course, the opposite may be the case. Not everyone will choose, or will be able, to adopt highly 'literate practices' (Yates, 1996: 39). One of the reasons given by Cole for using email to canvass and to screen but *not* to interview participants in his study of the American men's movement, the Promise Keepers, was that 'many of the interviewees were skilled at oral discourse, hence able to articulate their experiences in richer ways than when constrained by writing' (1999: *personal email*).

In addition, as Murray (1991) pointed out, it is context of use (combined with content) which gives meaning to texts. Murray alerts us to that fact that CMC language use in qualitative interviews (as with other kinds of language use) will depend on one person's power and status *vis-à-vis* the other; the purposes that have brought them together; the topics they are discussing; the history of earlier conversations they have had; and the degree of intimacy between them. She also notes that the contexts which evoke such different genres as business correspondence, letters to friends, journal articles and so on make an indelible impression on the tone and mode of expression. (See Biber (1998) for extensive discussion of these issues.) Now, technology has introduced new ways to interact and new contexts for interaction.

Within this new cultural framework, assimilating both real and virtual worlds, people may use technology to relate to each other in novel ways. Thus, it is not enough simply to categorize CMC as a written conversation. We cannot assume that all CMC interaction capitalizes on oral–written hybridity to the same degree, or in the same kind of way. For individual computer conversations, like ordinary conversations, create a mode of discourse appropriate for particular tasks and topics and particular interpersonal relations (Murray, 1991).

This becomes clear when we consider the impact on communication of participants' different perceptions of what is an appropriate mode for conducting research. In the Graduates of the Millennium study, email conveyed the verbal virtuosity and dexterity of students who were very much at home with the written word and applied these advanced linguistic skills to their contributions as participants. The students moved easily, often in the same message, between a chatty engaging letter style and more discursive styles which exercized their fluency with words and syntax. Such multi-layered literacy skills allowed them to interact in ways which projected a convincing sense of personality, individuality and intellectual range:

> For followers of a discipline that's supposed to place emphasis on explanation and analysis of exactly HOW and WHY things are good/bad/ugly [English faculty staff] will rhapsodize about individual syllables in whoever-it-may-be they adore (who are by and large long dead and literally couldn't give a toss whether or not their synedoche are attracting admiration back in this strange place) yet they are little help for the living, content to scrawl "good [underlined twice]" or "avoid this" or whatever on what as far as I can tell - I'm sure it's not, but it may as well be - a blithely random basis.

> I come from a covertly-strong socialist background. There has been a bit of a questioning of how loyal I have been to this - it's not a tension between my old life and my Cambridge life, just a questioning, which is healthy and regenerative.

Are you telling me there's SUPPOSED to be a link between lectures and supervisions? [small group teaching] Every so often i do get the eerie feeling there may be some mysterious holistic interconnectedness of what I need to know, what I have just found out, and what I am in the process of finding out - for instance, no sooner have I heard of John Foxe's Actes and Monuments for the first time in reading list, than it starts cropping up in every damn lecture I go to - but I've always put phenomena like this down to luck.

Sure - I think I could improve departments. I'd start with some redundancies and some promotions. Also some new lecturing guidelines: be inspiring, show enthusiasm, tell jokes. Give decent handouts, don't dim lights and expect students to take notes, hang around after the lecture to answer queries. Don't be confused by a microphone or a pointer. And absolutely do not assume that students all love you when they do not.

I've got a list of about a dozen words various supervisors have told me NEVER to use - this list includes "use" (and any synonyms, especially "employ"), "personality" and "character" (which makes writing about plays hard), "image" and "theme" (which renders anything by chance I did learn at A-level useless), and "although", and"surely" (which rules out hedging your bets). They all have different pet hates - at this rate, I'm not going to have any words left to use at all by the time they let me out of here.

In a different research context, a participant might consciously choose an informal approach to demonstrate that they are a member of a cultural elite familiar with computer use.

This was the experience of Ryen in her email interaction with an Asian Tanzanian businessman: 'Sachin employs the casual email style by dropping most capital letters, using a rather oral style indicated by use of dots (...) and by ignoring mistakes or slightly wrong manoeuvres at the keyboard' (Ryen and Silverman, 2000). Comparing his 'electronic' voice with that of his FTF communication, Ryen noted that Sachin was more formal in real life and that 'his e-mail written style is "more" oral than his oral speech' (ibid.).

In contrast, Hodkinson was frustrated to find that some of his interviewees participated expressively in newsgroups but were more constrained in their email interviews. Some wrote in a formal written style as opposed to 'chat', as though they thought they should 'sound more official or intellectual in the context of interviews than if conversing with friends online' (Hodkinson, 1999: *personal email*). As Davis and Brewer have noted, 'writing talking' is as complex, as varied, and as individual as the people who engage in its exchange (1997: 165).

The Way Forward

The important issue for qualitative researchers is to find a mode of communication which suits the purposes of an enquiry and the questions to be addressed. What considerations might researchers keep in mind, in order to generate the data they seek online?

Some thought must clearly be given to the strengths and weaknesses of different CMC options. For instance, if research is to focus on the complex inner life and in-depth subjective experiences of selected participants, it is probably unlikely that the verbal rough and tumble of much many-many real-time chat would be the first choice for communication. Yet, in other contexts, the dynamic, playful and performative aspects of synchronous CMC are positively beneficial. Researchers have a new opportunity to generate data from virtual or real communities that are known to dismiss or shy away from overly formal or 'academic' overtures. For instance, in the Young People and Health Risk study, synchronous CMC provided an innovative and relaxed mode of communication for excited young teenagers trying to find a common language cross-culturally. In such contexts the stylized 'illiteracy' of much synchronous chat, characterized by careless attention to grammar and uncorrected typographical errors, might offer a non-threatening mode of interaction for participants whose literacy level varies, or for those for whom English is not a first language. 'Try not to make your messages so letter-perfect that the recipient will think you spend all your time carefully writing and editing messages. Let typos sneak in. The recipient feels less threatened that way' (Windt, cited in Murray, 1995: 89).

At the other extreme, asynchronous CMC has the capacity to transmit a wide range of creative, analytical, reflective and highly literate exposition. In reflective mode the immediacy of the process might encourage 'what the novelist Samuel Richardson called "writing to the moment" – a kind of instantaneousness that catches the present-tense thoughts, and changes of mind, of the writer'[1]. When Ruth Picardie used email to keep in contact with a small group of friends in the last stages of her terminal illness, she valued qualities of this 'new and subtly different form of communication' because 'it was a way of expressing thoughts and feelings more spontaneously than in a letter, yet more reflectively than in a telephone conversation. It had a quality of being simultaneously intimate and serious, yet transient and disposable' (1998: viii). In documents that might be considered a combination of journal and letter writing, email transmitted Picardie's 'disarming candour and mordant wit, a crisply vernacular style and an unerring instinct for the emotional truth of a situation' (1998: 97).

A final point is that researchers themselves have an impact on the tenor of the communication. For instance, while some chat environments are relatively unfocused, a researcher using focus group software may establish a particular manner of interaction for real-time discussions. Virtual focus groups, like email interviews and asynchronous conferencing, are contexts where researchers set both the research task (for instance, the exploration of group and/or individual meanings, opinions, experiences) and research topics (the areas of interest to be discussed). These foci help structure both the content of messages *and* the mode of discourse between individuals and groups. Participants who are committed to expressing their opinions or sharing experiences usually aspire to communicate detailed information with clarity and conviction. Once the investigative tone of the research is established, there is the potential for both synchronous and asynchronous modes of CMC to elicit well-considered data.

Further Implications for Data Analysis

There is a final factor to consider when we reflect on what is won and what is lost using CMC as a 'shortcut' to data. In conventional qualitative research, moving from data to theory usually involves a preliminary process of reconstituting field notes and oral data as text. However, there is often a debate about ways in which spoken language, and non-verbal cues and paralinguistic behaviour, are transcribed and translated into texts. As we discussed in Chapter 2, CMC avoids the processes and the pitfalls of transcription. Nor does the method provide non-verbal data to translate into text. But what is lost here? Although non-verbal information has the potential to be of great value, the translation process involves the researcher making assessments of participants' mood or intention in ways which might well be incorrect. In addition, although some FTF researchers are scrupulous about including non-verbal behaviour in reports, it is fairly common for transcripts to omit this material. Even when complexities of focus group behaviour are involved non-verbal behaviour is only seldom reported (Morgan, 1988). Given this limitation, we might ask, with Korenman and Wyatt (1996), whether such transcripts are merely 'records' of spoken communication rather than the interview interaction in its entirety.

In contrast, these authors suggest that CMC scripts should be considered 'actual' communication because non-verbal aspects of interaction are explicitly presented within the body of the electronic text (using emoticons, descriptions of movement and expression and so on). Similarly, Kollock and Smith (1996: 114) point out that, like audio recordings or telephone conversations, CMC texts have 'the advantage of capturing everything that was publicly available to the participants in that setting'.

The implication for studies using CMC is that the researcher is no longer responsible for transforming 'reality' into text. Analysis can begin from data which are not already coloured by the researcher's theoretical and methodological choices – choices which can construct 'a different version of events' (Flick, 1998: 176).

Conclusion

It is hard to dispute Murray's (1991) claim that texts generated in CMC will depend as much on the way the technology is used as on qualities of the technology itself. However, once technological options are associated with the tasks, topics and purposes of research, it does seem possible that CMC will prove a mode that is capable of generating data which are more open, reactive and spontaneous than many traditional written accounts and more detailed, edited and reflective than many spoken conversations. This would mean that CMC would become an established tool for furthering what Denzin calls the interpretative project in the human disciplines. For investigations into how 'men and women live and give meaning to their lives and capture these meanings in written, narrative and oral forms' (Denzin and Lincoln, 1994: 10) may now have the option of including electronic forms.

Note

1   Mullan, J., *Guardian* newspaper, UK, 7 September 1998.

9 Virtuality and Data

A major challenge for the online researcher is to move from meeting people 'in the flesh' in the real world to working in the insubstantiality of the virtual venue. As we discussed in previous chapters, participants communicating online have only text to convey personality and mood (Chapter 6), social status (Chapter 7) and emotional and intellectual linguistic range (Chapter 8). However, in qualitative studies, researchers are attempting to 'make sense of or interpret phenomena in terms of the meanings people bring to them' (Denzin and Lincoln, 1994: 2). Using CMC, such meanings are transmitted in text which is detached from both the phenomenon and the participant. In some CMC studies researchers no longer enter the physical field and disembodied participants may have no cultural markers beyond those their language reveals. But if we lose so much of the context which gives meaning to language, are CMC texts second-rate or even meaningless data? What can such data tell us about the real world or, indeed, the new field of virtual worlds? And can we consider data from disembodied participants reliable?

Entering the Field Using CMC

Qualitative research takes an interpretative, naturalistic approach, studying phenomena in natural settings often referred to as 'field'. Field has been defined as 'a place or situation where some particular social action transpires whether or not the enquirer is present' (Schwandt, 1997: 51). Field is the social context and the 'local knowledge' through which experiences are made sense of (Geertz, 1973). Field is also the physical and cultural site where language takes place. Thus, field is both a physical locality with material objects, and the social processes and activities within which language is embedded. It provides 'the languages, emotions, ideologies, taken-for-granted understandings, and shared experiences from which the [participants'] stories flow' (Denzin, 1989: 73).

These issues are important because, in qualitative research, textual data are considered to be inextricably linked to the social contexts in which they were produced (Miller, 1997). Such contexts are diverse. Within a single country, there may be historical differences of region and district, dominant and minority ethnicities, urban and rural lifestyles and different forms of status classification. Norms of bonding, mating, raising children and caring for the elderly may vary. In addition, there may be specialized sites for subcultural activities, physical loci for work, worship, leisure, education and politics and different practices within them. Because the research process itself incorporates both a locality and a set of social practices, the venue of the interview, chat or discussion is an additional dimension of the cultural field from which language flows. Since the arrival of the Internet, there are further sites for subcultural activities and for conducting research – these are the physical sites of computer use and also the virtual locale and text-based practices of cyberspace. Textual data carry knowledge of these varied aspects of field and are defined by them. Thus, we need to ask: how do FTF and CMC data carry knowledge of field and how are they defined by field?

FTF Data and Field

In FTF research, visual, aural and tactile impressions of the physical and social environment, and a participant's relationship to that environment, all contribute towards an understanding of field. For instance, researchers may grasp more fully a local meaning of 'work' if they can identify the heat, stench, noise and damp of a dark mine; the smell of coffee, soft leather sofas, clear desk and panoramic view of the penthouse office; the driving snow or blazing sun of the farm. In many FTF studies, researchers' fieldnotes provide details of physical location and other background information based on non-verbal impressions of how individuals and groups seem to experience, interpret and structure their lives. These data help to 'fill the gaps' or 'read between the lines' of what is said and how something is done.

In addition, contextual information is obtained through interviews and other interactions between participants and researchers. In qualitative research, participants are often asked to use language to describe/explain a social context. This is not a transparent process because the environment they refer to has already shaped their language use and given it meaning. For instance, the language of participants may be a culturally dominant or minority language with a particular local knowledge. Within the language, accent, dialect or intonation may point to region, ethnicity or social class. There may be other subcultural markers such as slang or some use of specialized languages (such as jargon, religious or literary language). Language use will also be responsive to the research location and practices. For instance, the choice of physical venue (is it the researcher's office? the participant's home?) may affect the formality of language. The researcher's own use of language may lead to necessary or optional adjustments. (Are questions appropriately pitched? Is the participant's language use 'foreign' to the researcher or vice versa? Is a form of translation needed? Is there sufficient consensus of language use to allow differences to be discussed? Are accents moderated and by whom? And so on.)

Finally, the meanings which participants ascribe to the research, the researcher and other participants may also affect the syntax, content, terminology and emphasis of their narratives. Language is used in different ways, for different purposes and in different situations. As previous studies have shown, participants may respond differently to different forms of research environment even to the extent of varying the ways they make sense of facts and events in different contexts (Mann, 1998).

FTF interaction offers many, varied markers of field in terms of observation, linguistic and paralinguistic cues. The potential for drawing on different senses means that there is always the possibility that perplexities and anomalies found in the field (including the research field) may be investigated by triangulation methods. Observation of action may belie report; report may throw light on observation; narratives collected in multiple contexts may evoke different insights and meanings (Mann, 1998). The final status of textual data is frequently informed by these checks and balances, even if the processes involved are often informal and intuitive.

Online Data and Field

When data are collected online, much of this contextual material is missing. In the mainly black and white world of text we lose the Technicolor of lived life and its impact on most of our senses. We may still take fieldnotes which record working hypotheses and act as a general *aide-mémoire*, but there is no longer a place for contextual understandings gleaned through non-written information. We cannot observe the world in which participants live. We cannot see them and we cannot hear them. We do not even share the same physical site for purposes of research. Even if participants are affected by the physical field of the research interaction (the computer terminal and the home, office, cybercafé or computer laboratory in which it is situated) the researcher can only know this from the evidence of, and in, the text.

Disembodiment separates the language of the researcher and participants from the social context which would give their words meaning. As a result, language has a heavy interpretative load to carry. As we have discussed in earlier chapters, a researcher sitting FTF with another person makes rapid speculative guesses about areas which might resonate in that individual's life. Initial impressions may be entirely subjective and may even mislead. As Horn rightly states, 'You don't have any more guarantees that someone is who they say they are just because you can see them. We are as often fooled by appearances as we are informed by them' (Horn, 1998: 91). Nevertheless, social and personal cues can open up possible areas for enquiry and give an initial frame for making sense of responses. Most people accept that an elderly woman and a young man, a heavily veiled woman and one with spiked hair and tattoos, a person dressed in fine fabrics and one whose shoes are in holes, will see the world in subtly or overtly different ways. The same words spoken by each might not convey the same meaning.

In CMC there are no data relating to person or place outside that detectable in the digitally generated script. The text which appears on computer screens must provide all available information about the communication as well as being the communication. It has to be both location and social context. It must 'carry the social situation, it must also carry the participants' relationship to the situation, their perception of relationships between the knowledge and objects under discussion' (Yates, 1996: 46).

Can CMC rise to this challenge? To discuss this question we consider the characteristics of CMC data in three different areas. The first two areas concern research which uses CMC to investigate 'real' as opposed to virtual communities, first in unfamiliar and then in familiar contexts. The third area is concerned with issues of field in research which focuses on online communities.

Researching Unfamiliar Cultures

Where do we draw a line if we seek to differentiate social contexts with which we are familiar from those with which we are not? There will be places we have never visited, social practices we have never experienced, language use we do not recognize – and these could be found as easily in the next street as on the other side of the world. At one level we live globally. At another level each person's 'local knowledge' is circumscribed by cultural, historical and personal histories which divide up life experience in idiosyncratic ways. All researchers can identify communities and locations about which they know very little, as opposed to those where there is sufficient shared cultural understanding to attempt to identify finely tuned differences.

With FTF qualitative research, practical factors frequently militate against investigations which cross geographical, cultural and linguistic borders. Now, the global reach of the Internet increases the potential for research on the unfamiliar (Ma, 1996); but we need to consider carefully the factors which may affect the status of the data generated by such research.

Let us suppose that, in order to widen understanding of a highly sensitive cultural issue such as dealing with death and dying, unknown people from multiple unfamiliar contexts are interviewed online. What are the issues for data here? To understand this cultural phenomenon the researchers would need to know the rules that pertain within the culture; only then could they see how language is used to describe that social world (Winch, 1988). However, working online, all data come from the perspectives of the participants, not the direct perceptions of the researcher. These data, in the form of text, are the only vehicle for transmitting understanding. Informants need to have the time, ability and inclination to explain subtle cultural practices (such as those dealing with death) using only words. This demands a high level of linguistic skill. There are no shortcuts like pointing or demonstrating.

'Indirect' communication which avoids explicit reference to delicate issues is problematic (Ma, 1996). If researchers are unfamiliar with the field, they may not know what questions to ask – nor can they be sure that they fully understand participants' responses. Sitting at a computer, set apart from the environments which create endlessly innovative rituals around dying, they would have no way of knowing whether individual participants are attaching specific meanings to language. These difficulties have led commentators such as Paccagnella (1997) to acknowledge that 'obtaining information about someone's off-line life through online means of communication - although seemingly easy and convenient - is always a hazardous, uncertain procedure'.

CMC not only gives little ethnographic context but it can also increase misunderstanding. These difficulties will be compounded when there are language differences. Even if researchers have a proficient understanding of the language of interaction, they require a cultural understanding of words (including dialect, slang and jargon) to allow for the equivalence of meaning (May, 1993). There are further difficulties when a translator is employed (see Chapter 5). For example, in the Young People and Health Risk study, equivalent meanings provided by the Chinese young women for the Australian young women revealed the dilemmas which language differences can hold, in spite of the best attempts of translation.

> Yellow Oz: what does a pretty girl look like in china, what would you call a pretty girl and a handsome boy?
> Yellow Beijing: just momont we have to translate into English.
> [different threads]
> Yellow Beijing: we call a pretty girl is "white snowprincess" handsome boy is "white horse prince"

We see here that an apparently simple linguistic exchange may have layers of ambiguity. The Australian girl may have been asking about the actual qualities which are called 'pretty' or 'handsome' in China. Even if she were only asking for the form of words which would signify that someone had such qualities the phrases she was given, with all their cultural references, may have increased rather than decreased mystification.

How would the research situation differ in FTF studies where field and participants are unfamiliar? First, if the researcher worked in person on site, a degree of exposure to field, and the participants' relationship to it, would be inevitable. Second, even if participants were seen on neutral ground, they would embody aspects of their culture and this information would be accessible to the interviewer. As we discussed in Chapter 6, the FTF interviewer might pick up clues from, for instance, body language and actions and this could assist decisions about the appropriateness of questions (vital sensitive areas), and identify clear signs of cultural or linguistic confusion.

However, there are also drawbacks to FTF investigations in unfamiliar contexts. For instance, when interviews are conducted in a real-life context and location, participants or researchers may be positioned as 'outsiders'. They may be physically near to people involved in the research but feel that their different values and social practices set them apart (Gudykunst and Kim, 1984). Participants may also feel inhibited and shy away from talking about sensitive issues. Visual social cues, relating both to the research venue and the strangers within it – the researcher and/or other participants – might trigger possibly inaccurate preconceptions of 'strange' cultural practices elsewhere or evoke feelings of embarrassment about personal traditions and rituals. Ma (1996) has carefully documented the way that the efforts of East Asian participants to save face in such stressful situations often lead to ambiguous forms of communication. These indirect forms of communication rely heavily on contexts outside the interview field to create meanings (Hall, 1976). Some FTF interaction may even be forbidden outside the participants' cultural field. For example, it might be taboo to discuss issues of death and dying FTF, or with representatives of other religions or ethnicities.

The online venue can address some of these concerns. Ma (1996) suggests that, because CMC users do not occupy a common physical place, there is no longer a host/guest distinction, so participants are immediately less bound by a particular set of cultural rules or overshadowed by the host culture. The virtual venue is, in effect, culturally neutral. In this sense it offers a familiar field for communication. Participants are on their own home ground, which might allow communication to flow with a minimum of self-consciousness and self-restraint. East Asians, for instance, see CMC as being set apart from local social networks so there is less risk of experiencing the rejection or disagreement that might lead to loss of face in FTF contexts. As a consequence, interaction in the virtual field may lead to more direct communication and greater self-disclosure even about sensitive issues (Ma, 1996). In addition, if participants are struggling to communicate in a second language, or across a wide cultural divide, the mode of written language might be more suitable than speech. Particularly with asynchronous interaction, where there would be time to compose responses about a complex and delicate subject, a participant is less likely to feel flustered or foolish and may talk in greater depth.

Conclusion

Undoubtedly, research benefits from background knowledge of cultural fields which are beyond the virtual field created explicitly for the purpose of interaction (Yates, 1996). However, as we have seen, the online environment can offer access to accounts of the unfamiliar which may not have been available, or may have been presented in less direct forms FTF. If online interviewers familiarize themselves with pertinent literature relating to specific social contexts, that would go some way towards helping them to recognize language usage and to pursue cultural references. When this kind of preparation is combined with adept online interviewing skills (Chapter 6), the researcher should be able to evoke the most meaningful data that are available, given the constraints of comparative research.

However, the deeper theoretical problems of conducting intra-societal and inter-societal studies of real-life cultures remain (see May, 1993; Reinharz, 1992). In attempting comparative research there may be a tendency to be ethnocentric in approach and, even if methodological difficulties are recognized, researchers might 'consciously ignore the many stumbling blocks of the nonequivalence of concepts, a multitude of unknown variables interacting in an unknown context and influencing the research question in unknown ways' (Øyen, 1990: 5). These problems apply to both online and FTF research and it is yet to be seen whether the technology which allows people to 'speak' across cultural boundaries will also allow them to understand each other.

Researching Familiar Cultures

There is no doubt that in situations where the field is unfamiliar, and participants are previously unknown, research is highly demanding. However, much qualitative research is conducted in a context where the researcher's own cultural knowledge contributes to processes of interpretation. Here, participants do not have to provide so much background information about the wider cultural context. This allows the researcher to focus on the specific local knowledge that is in the gift of participants. We shall now look at the value of CMC data when the research study is closer to home.

The Graduates of the Millennium project offers a useful starting point for this discussion. Here, the researcher had considerable familiarity with the phenomenon being studied. The focus of Mann's research was student experiences within a specific university and not only had she herself experienced the workings of the university as an undergraduate, postgraduate and teacher, but her research was also based in a university building and used university computer networking. Mann's local knowledge meant that she had a high level of shared cultural understanding with the current students, and this allowed her to seek deeper and more varied meanings relating to field (the university). Within a frame of shared knowledge, she drew on the perspectives of student participants who offered diverse viewpoints by virtue of differences in age, status, gender, social background, intellectual interests, personality and so on.

This familiarity with context meant that the practical advantages of CMC could be maximized. It would have been impossible for a single researcher to keep in contact with up to 200 students from a wide range of faculties, over the full course of their degrees, if a rolling programme of FTF interviews had had to be arranged, conducted and transcribed. While Mann's knowledge of the field alerted her to the range of perspectives which would enrich data, the technology allowed those voices to be heard. In addition, the speed of response allowed her to capitalize on inside knowledge by asking informed questions of the data and, if necessary, seeking immediate clarification and/or elaboration from participants.

She could also register, first hand, the possible impact of computer-based research on the data produced by a particular subculture. For instance, Mann knew that most of the students emailed from crowded, public and erratically available computer laboratories, although others could also send messages from their own College rooms – noisy social centres or quiet refuges. She and the students alike knew when parts of the email facilities were 'down' or when viruses or alerts over hackers threatened to delay interaction or raised questions over confidentiality. This shared context helped to explain sudden 'silences' (from researcher and/or students) which, as we saw in Chapter 6, can threaten rapport. It also gave insight into why individual messages might be uncharacteristically brief (the computer room was about to be locked) or low key (written in the early hours of the morning from a study bedroom) or cautious (the student newspaper had focused on hackers infiltrating the university network).

Mann could also see, as Sterne noted, that the Internet was becoming part of the fabric of many students' lives; that they saw its use as relatively 'banal', no more a break from daily experience 'than getting on a crowded elevator to move up three stories in a building' (Sterne, 1999: 258). This local information informed Mann's assessment of the impact of CMC technology on the textual data she was collecting. It suggested to her that, after early tentative usage, the students who participated in the study were quickly at ease with the medium. The technology did not cramp or inhibit their efforts at communication, so the data would not suffer from being in written rather than oral form. In addition, local knowledge enabled Mann to identify subcultural differences in the tone of communication students used in different areas of their lives. She was familiar with Cambridge students' written material in a range of real-life contexts (essays, journalistic writing, personal notes to staff), and had observed their FTF interaction with university staff. This background detail enabled her to make distinctions between their online and offline styles of communication, as well as difference in styles between student–student and student–researcher email messages. The following message was exchanged between mathematics students in the initial stages of the research (see Chapter 6) and, probably inadvertently, posted on to the researcher. Unsurprisingly, she found that student-to-student messages were different in tone to those addressed to the researcher.

> Stop sending shit mails. I suggest we stop all this spamming right now (that's replying to everyone on the list by the way) as it is not only illegal, but really irritating to find a load of messages saying nothing in particular from people you don't even know. Now, I don't mind, as I will write to just about anybody, but you lot are in serious danger of confirming the rumour that all [college] people are wankers. (GOTM student–student exchange)

Being aware of differences in the ways students used language increased the level of reflexivity that Mann could bring to bear on the data. The students' research contributions were fairly conversational in tone (without the slight formality of student–staff interaction) but they did display a seriousness and focus which, even when laced with humour, marked their messages off from casual emails sent to friends (which would probably conform to a 'student culture' email style; see McCormick and McCormick, 1992). And, while their messages were often forthright in making particular points, they did not have the campaigning tone of the student press or, if someone did get carried, away there would usually be a disclaimer ('OK I'll get of my soap-box now!!!' GOTM student). It was against this cultural background that Mann could begin to get a sense of when messages hit a 'wrong note', just as FTF interviewers are alert to changes in tone in speech. In such cases CMC allowed further enquiries to be made with great rapidity and possible problem areas could be quickly dealt with.

However, even when the context is familiar, a key problem remains. Mann sought accounts from across the student body but, working online, she had no way of knowing for sure that messages written by, for instance, engineers and classicists, were actually written by students in those disciplines. Her study set up structures (such as an initial questionnaire) through which to identify differences, but there was no mechanism to ensure that messages came from students who did fit a particular profile or that messages continued to come from the same person over time ('Please pay no attention to that "scotsjohn and bob are fab" thing – just two of my more computer literate friends messing around' GOTM student). The questions which the Graduates of the Millennium study raises, and which are relevant to a broader discussion of researching social context online, include: What is the point of acknowledging the impact of field on specific individual experiences accessed through CMC, if we have no way of connecting the text to the typist? What status can we give to the data, even when they are collected in cultures and subcultures with which we are familiar, if the identity of participants is problematic? These issues are examined next, when we turn our attention to issues of identity online.

Researching Online Cultures

We have discussed some of the possibilities and limitations for data of using virtual research to investigate real-life contexts. But researchers now have the additional option of studying 'social spaces in which people still meet face-to-face, but under new definitions of both "meet" and "face"' (Stone, 1991; Slouka, 1995). With the existence of virtual worlds the definition of field has become a key challenge for online researchers. Jones, noting that real-life researchers typically travel to material places to study culture, questions whether travel to virtual 'places' is possible – for, in cyberspace, 'is there a "there" there?' (Jones, 1999b: 18).

An additional question is: in cyberspace is there a 'person' there? For, if identities are 'flexible, swappable and disconnected from real-world bodies' (Shields, 1996), are we talking about personae rather than people? Sudweeks and Simoff define the debate about researching the virtual field in the following terms: 'Should we consider the Internet an environment in itself or should we consider it a complementary part or an extension of our own environment?' (1999: 31)

Extension of Real World

Commentators who see the virtual world as an extension of the real world do so because 'on-line experience is at all times tethered in some fashion to off-line experience' (Jones, 1999a: xii). Everyone communicating online has a physical body that remains involved in experiences separate from the interactions occurring online (Kendall, 1999). Even the most enthusiastic members of virtual communities acknowledge this connection: 'the idea that you can isolate anything, any one piece of your life, and try to define it without referring to all that is connected to it is nonsense' (Horn, 1998: 46). In fact many members of virtual communities extend relationships maintained online to real-life interaction (Stone, 1991; Turkle, 1995; Parks and Floyd, 1996; Horn, 1998).

> The WELL felt like an authentic community to me from the start because it was grounded in my everyday physical world. WELLites who don't live within driving distance of the San Francisco Bay area are constrained in their ability to participate in the local networks of face-to-face acquaintances ... I've attended real-life WELL marriages, WELL births, and even a WELL funeral. (Rheingold, 1994: 2)

In one view, a strong desire for the physical may lead new users to leave online communities if they are not offered some opportunity to meet other users in person (Argyle and Shields, 1996). This possibility was anticipated by Bennett (1998) when she interviewed men in various continents. Although the research design precluded meeting participants FTF she compensated for this by encouraging them to 'explore' her home city online, and she sent photographs and made occasional telephone calls.

> My co-investigators were also keen to try to situate me within their minds, often finding their own resources in order to see where, and how, I lived. Victor (aged 41), for example, wrote that he had found a link that will give me the Townsville weather report in one shot. 'So, before I write you I look at the weather report to see what's happening "down under"'. (Victor, 41, 10 March.,1998)

When an online world is seen as an extension of the physical world it follows that the meanings transmitted by CMC are seen to be formed by and associated with real life and to be tied by conceptual language to the embodied world. Denzin concludes that: 'Cybernarratives are grounded in the everyday lives and biographies of the women and men who write them' (1999: 108). It is also claimed that the social and political contexts of daily life help shape online behaviour. This was the theme of Kendall's comprehensive study of the interactive, text-only, online forum (or MUD) known as BlueSky. Drawing on online and FTF methods, Kendall claimed that, 'participants draw on their off-line resources, as well as understandings gained in off-line experiences, to negotiate and interpret their on-line interaction' (Kendall, 1999: 58). She concluded that, as participants come to online fora from different positions of power within society, this affects both their actions online and their interpretations of others' actions. 'Participants clearly can and do reproduce off-line power relationships in their on-line interaction' (Kendall, 1999: 67). Wakeford suggested that individuals combine meanings from real life and their online activity. Her study of student Internet use at the University of California showed how online activities were constituted simultaneously within existing forms of student culture and the conventions of Internet fora (Wakeford, 1999). The consensus for these commentators is that real life and virtual cultures both have implications for language, conceptual understanding and interaction online. Hence the data generated would relate to both.

Virtual Worlds as Separate Fields

Given these links with the everyday world, is it still possible for researchers to view cyberspace as a discrete field? Some theorists suggest that it is; that there is, indeed, a 'there' there beyond the limits of physical locale (Fernback, 1999). For Gibson, this is a fictional, psychic space where minds can fuse in a trance-like 'consensual hallucination' (1984). However, as noted elsewhere in this book, the majority of commentators do not see the virtual field as a single, homogeneous culture. Rather, the online world is seen as a collection of virtual locations. The emphasis and focus of much research is on the characteristics which make specific virtual cultures *different from* both real life and each other. Factors involved might include different levels of interactivity and variations in the purpose of, and norms of behaviour within, virtual worlds. It is a combination of these factors which creates the 'there' which is there to be investigated.

Researchers who view virtual worlds as separate fields generate data from communities of common interests and affinities, 'whose specialized meanings allow the sharing of imagined realities' (Reid, 1995: 183). Meanings may be drawn from patterns of life in real-time chat groups (Reid, 1991), BBSs (Myers, 1987), or Usenet newsgroups (Baym, 1995a; Galegher *et al.*, 1998; McLaughlin *et al.*, 1995). For instance, Baym interviewed and documented exchanges between users participating in a Usenet newsgroup which focused on television soaps (rec.arts.tv.soaps – r.a.t.s.). She concluded that the people participating had a rich, dynamic and distinctive online culture grounded in communicative practice. She saw r.a.t.s. as one of many online groups where hundreds of participants have 'voluntarily created communities rich in social information, prominent personalities, valued relationships, and behavioural norms' (Baym, 1995a: 141).

Researchers also investigate the text-based, multi-participant forms of virtual reality known as MU* environments [1]. Variations of these include a virtual university campus (DU-MOO), a meeting place for media enthusiasts (MediaMOO), and a large rambling house (LambdaMOO) offering a range of activities such as 'poetry readings, support groups, chess matches and even virtual sex' (Sempsey, 1997: *online*; see also Bruckman, 1992; Curtis, 1997). Are MUDs communities (Bromberg, 1996)? Many researchers insist that they are. For example, Correll (1995) studied an online lesbian café. The 'patrons' had constructed an elaborate virtual café which gave a context for their interaction. As in real life, the virtual café was frequented by different kinds of people, regulars, newcomers (newbies), visitors who wanted to see what went on without necessarily getting involved (lurkers), and the out of place and unwelcome (such as the 'bashers' – mainly men who send abusive posts). The shared setting created a common sense of reality constructed purely through verbal descriptions. It was not that locale was missing – it had just become virtual. Correll concluded that without the shared virtual reality of the bar the community might not be able to function. The virtual field made sense of communication, allowed valued interaction, and was much safer than any real location where 'the games are for real' (1995: 281).

Virtual worlds of all kinds are considered separate fields because they share the defining characteristics of real-life communities. For insiders, virtual communities are 'characterized by common value systems, norms, rules, and the sense of identity, commitment, and association that also characterize various physical communities or other communities of interest' (Fernback, 1999: 211). As with real communities the 'overall social climate' may evolve over time (Paccagnella, 1997). Access to many virtual fields, as with access to physical spaces, is regulated through social and cultural practice and beliefs. 'In effect, certain spaces are socialised by certain homogeneous groups who regulate and exclude unwelcome visitors. Social spaces, as found in any city, are thus contested through processes of domination and marginalisation' (Kitchin, 1998: 17). For instance, a 'newbie' might need to ask about what commands can be used, how objects are defined, what one can change about one's character. 'This is roughly equivalent to arriving in a new country and enquiring about the laws of physics' (Carlstrom, 1992).

Citizens of virtual worlds are also subject to interpersonal and institutional struggles (Wakeford, 1999). As Reid pointed out: 'The social environments found on MUDS are not chaotic, or even anarchic. There is indeed no moment on a MUD in which players are not enmeshed within a web of social rules and expectations' (1995). In one virtual setting (LambdaMOO) the inhabitants started a debate about whether their own society had been created just for fun – or whether it needed enforceable laws. Some welcomed the beginnings of a process of democratization (a voting system was established to decide the rules regarding property rights and free speech), others thought the facility irrelevant to their online life (Mnookin, 1996). Fernback concluded that issues of ideology, agency, power, ontology, roles and boundaries affect virtual communities just as they do physical communities, although power relations may focus on 'wit, tenacity, and intelligence rather than brawn, money or political clout' (1999: 213). As a consequence,

Interactions in cybercommunities can be described and interpreted just as interactions in physical communities can. (Fernback, 199: 216)

Taken overall, the evidence from studies which have focused on online cultures suggests that a virtual world may be seen as *either* an environment in itself *or* an extension of real life depending on the research interests of the investigator. For, as Schwandt reminds us, 'what constitutes data depends on one's enquiry purposes and the questions one seeks to answer' (1997: 60). Researchers can gain insights about virtual worlds through the perspectives of embodied participants in FTF interviews (Correll, 1995; Kendall, 1999). Alternatively they may work 'in situ' using CMC. If researchers interview or conduct participant observation within the field of a virtual community they may be generating data from personae. Once again questions of consistent identity of informants remain.

Online Field and Data

It seems clear that online language is embedded in and hence may provide 'local knowledge' of virtual communities. In addition, some researchers, including the authors, have used CMC to investigate real-life communities. This is not unproblematic. As we have seen in Chapter 6, researchers and participants find ways to compensate, on an interpersonal level, for the loss of embodiment. However, taken overall, available evidence suggests that CMC is indeed a 'lean' bandwidth in terms of speedily transmitting information about the embodied self and the physical environment. Such material can be conveyed online, but it may be a lengthy process and valuable research time may be taken describing details which would have been immediately obvious FTF. It may also be a hit and miss process. It assumes that researchers can make enough of an imaginative leap to ask pertinent exploratory questions while working 'in the dark'; or that participants themselves will recognize aspects of their personal and social identity which are crucial to the research and will spontaneously proffer this information.

These considerations potentially limit available data although, as we have seen in earlier chapters, this problem may be alleviated when participants fully understand and support the research aims. In this situation they would not only be more inclined to share information about themselves, but also more likely to recognize which aspects of their lives were salient to the research study. But even when these factors and the possible limitations of language skills (see Chapter 8) are taken into account, we argue that CMC can still generate useful data from familiar real-life cultures, and may offer some compensation for the loss of FTF interaction in the difficult area of unfamiliar real-life cultures.

However, whether researchers investigate real or virtual worlds, the challenge of identity remains and we consider this next.

Identity and Disembodiment

Data gathered through CMC may be interesting and insightful but – if participants are virtual – what credence can be given to information transmitted online? As Fernback suggests, concerns about validity in qualitative research are applicable to research in the virtual realm as well. Ethnographers working in cyberspace must 'develop a sense about the truthfulness and candour of their informants, just as ethnographers of the nonvirtual must' (Fernback, 1999: 216). How is it possible to defend data in a field where anonymity and pseudonymity are the norm and where participants may choose to exploit the virtuality of the medium to experiment with the presentation of self?

Boshier (1990) claims that electronic networking opens possibilities for deception because many of the cues that normally circumscribe roles and which foster or inhibit participation are not present. Unlike FTF communication where participants are largely 'known' to each other, at least on a visual level, in the online environment there is no such recognition. Users of CMC can change the way they express their personalities, can switch genders or change their age, or become fantasy characters in virtual worlds. As consistency in identity has strong associations with authenticity these possibilities have clear implications for data. According to Thu Nguyen and Alexander, the central question has become, 'without the materiality of lived existence how can one sustain responsibility for one's words, written or oral?' (1996: 104)

Self-presentation Online

Non-role-play Communities There is a large body of opinion which suggests that the differences between self-presentation in real life and in (non-role-play) online communities are far less divergent than might be expected. Wallace (1999) discussed studies which pointed to the psychological probability that self-presentation online will be an extension of the 'real' individual into a different social environment (Giese, 1998). For instance, Bechar-Israeli's (1996) research on nicknames in IRC suggested that about 8% of users used their real names, 45% chose 'nicks' that related to themselves in some way, and only 6% chose nicks of a fanciful nature. Similarly, research into Web site home pages suggests that these pages:

> Integrate the individual, make a personal statement of identity, and show in a stable replicable way what the individual stands for and what is deemed important. (Wynn and Katz, 1997: *online*)

When Mann asked Graduates of the Millennium students to reflect on possible future criticisms that their research contributions should be discounted because their identities could not be confirmed, many students were indignant.

I am not virtual. I am very, very real. To say otherwise is an absurd objection (unless someone has stolen my password). (GOTM student)

One student made clear that her real-life relationships depended upon sustaining as authentic a persona using email as any other form of communication:

'Virtual' people? If e-mail had nothing to do with the real us, our lives would fall apart; e-mail is as immediate, as common and as much to do with us as real people as talking on the telephone. (GOTM student)

This is not to say that conscious self-presentation will not be a feature of online life. Kendall (1999) points out that research participants have engaged in different presentations of self well before the existence of online fora. As Giese (1998) asks: 'Who has not agonised over the "correct" tie or skirt to wear for that special occasion?' He concludes, as do others, that 'the rituals of self-presentation' will now be transferred to a textual mode. However, as the bandwidth of CMC is relatively narrow, the scope for controlling the presentation of self increases and participants may offer 'a filtered and posed representation of reality' Whittle (1997: 193). The struggle between being 'honest' and adding a bit of extra gloss to the online persona has been well documented and has implications for data:

In cyberspace you have more control over how someone sees you. Everything begins with words. You are who you say you are. And you can make yourself sound really good. (Horn, 1998: 294)

I was very concerned with being authentic and true to my real self via this electronic persona I was projecting, though I could not resist using the cover to heighten aspects of myself that I thought a bit inappropriate in person. (Argyle and Shields, 1996: 59)

On the other hand, the students in Mann's study claimed that their written texts conveyed authentic aspects of self because their responses were often *more* accurate than they might have been FTF. There was general agreement that, FTF, the potential for being judged, or the perceived obligation to give 'expected' responses, would have led to evasiveness or a level of dishonesty. A student in the Cambridge study described a different dynamic in her experience of online research:

I am conscious that the "I" I write is not the "I" I am - writing of yourself constructs and presents a persona, necessarily - but then so does speaking of yourself - we all self-edit and self-fashion all the time ... Perhaps the difference is that in oral conversation the gaps in the self-construction show, since it would be kind of improvised; writing leaves double opportunity for self-editing. I know I would not be able to say as much - probably would not contribute to this study at all - if I had to speak directly. (GOTM student)

This quote raises all kinds of questions. If we assume that participants might prefer the 'double editing' of writing, does that mean that the resulting data are less 'close to truth' than data which arise from FTF methods? Or does it mean that a time for reflection can act as a safeguard, allowing participants to explore their thoughts and feelings more deeply and with more self-awareness than in FTF interaction? Perhaps interaction on- and offline is a balancing act where participants make decisions relating to sharing or withholding information. And perhaps, in a disembodied environment, data have their own kind of depth and authenticity because, when words can be carefully processed to avoid unwelcome self-exposure, participants may have the confidence to say more (and with more penetration) than they would risk in the *ad hoc* self-presentation that is possible FTF (see also Walther, 1996).

Finally, there are claims that CMC paves the way for identity to fracture into multiple and ever changing perceptions and projections of self. However, despite some experimentation with self-presentation online, there is a wide consensus that people still tend to perceive their identities and selves as 'integral and continuous' (Kendall, 1999: 61). For this reason it is seen to be difficult to sustain a persona which is quite divorced from the 'real' self. As Berger has argued, 'it is very difficult to pretend in this world. Normally, one becomes what one plays at' (1966: 98). Similarly Horn maintains that, 'much as we might dearly love to sometimes, we can't leave ourselves behind when we get online. Even when someone is just playing around or in disguise, something true is revealed, it is never completely invented' (1998: 6).

Role-play Communities The opportunities for experimenting with self-presentation are, however, a deliberate feature of some virtual worlds. Users in chat rooms are usually identified by a descriptive nickname that is sometimes chosen to 'promote a certain image or invite a particular response' (Newby, 1993: 35). The nickname can be used as a kind of carnival mask. It can hide identity but also give tantalizing hints about the people who have chosen masks of expressive power and imaginativeness (Ruedenberg *et al.*, 1995). In such environments, the masking and unmasking of identity is part of a general 'playful' atmosphere (Lee, 1996).

On the other hand, as nicknames are 'trademarks' recognized by friends and enemies alike (Myers, 1987), they become a badge of identity. People rarely change their 'nicks' even though it is easy to do so (Bechar-Israeli, 1996). One challenge for the status of data when researching virtual worlds is to ensure that 'nicknames' remain associated with the same persona. In this context, for a participant to have 'an artificial but stable personality' would imply that while 'you can never be certain about the flesh-person behind an IRC nickname ... you can be reasonably certain that the person you communicate with today under a specific nickname is the same person who used that nickname yesterday'

(Rheingold, 1994: 176). As netiquette decrees that appropriating another's nickname is a cardinal sin (see Bechar-Israeli, 1996; Curtis, 1997), most researchers would probably resign themselves to taking the consistency of nicknames on trust. As Reid states:

> The uniqueness of names, their consistent use, and respect for - and expectation of - their integrity, is crucial to the development of online communities. (1991)

By sustaining nicknames participants in virtual communities create relatively consistent personae and can assume social or organizational roles[2]. One research study suggested that continuity of self in virtual communities may even go beyond consistency in the use of nicknames. In BlueSky, the MUD Kendall studied, people were known by their fantasy character name but they also identified each other by known personality characteristics, a shared history with others in the group, and data concerning their offline lives (1999: 69). This study, and online norms of consistent nicknames, suggest that researchers may test 'truthfulness' against regular patterns of interaction even in virtual worlds.

Implications of Disembodiment for Research Practice

What About Active Deception?

We have considered the ways that CMC might tempt participants to garnish the truth about themselves. However, outside of communities such as role-playing MUDs, would many people deliberately present themselves as other than they are? And, in particular, would they use a research project to do so? There are FTF precedents for this kind of deception. Denzin reported how Garfinkel (1967) interviewed one participant 'Agnes' over several months. Many years later she revealed that she had duped him about the details of a sex change. As a result 'Garfinkel produced a document that told the story Agnes wanted told. He, in fact, wrote a fiction that, until Agnes' disclosure, had the appearance of truth' (Denzin, 1989: 38). On the other hand, how many participants would expend that amount of energy on deception? One Graduate of the Millennium student thought it would be a complete waste of time to do so:

> We could all be making everything up for a laugh- but I don't see why any student would feel compelled to feed you mis-truth over email - be realistic - where's the fun in sending prank e-mails to an social science researcher? Although due to time constraints they will of course not give you the whole truth! (GOTM student)

Another student found it curious that a tendency to deceive might be more associated with CMC than other forms of communication:

> I'm actually rather offended that people might think e-mail was somehow less
> genuine than things I might say if I hand wrote or talked to you personally or
> whatever. Questionnaires also have indirect contact - are they any more or less
> likely to be more or less truthful or accurate or exact? (GOTM student)

Detecting deceit is a necessary exercise in real-life as well as online
communities. As Wallace (1999: 50–52) points out, psychological research has
shown that most of us are poor judges of truthfulness. She notes that even
professionals such as police and customs officers seemed unable to improve
their deceit-detection capacities even with training (Kohnken, 1987).
Fortunately, validity checks done on self-report studies in delinquency research
suggest that the accuracy of an offender's statements is usually about 75% (see,
for instance, Jupp, 1989). This relatively high level of truthfulness in a situation
where it may often seem tempting to lie may reassure researchers (and ethics
committees) that statements made online are probably *aiming* for truth. Indeed,
checks made in qualitative market research, where the truthfulness of
participants is carefully monitored, also suggest that deliberate deception online
is unusual.

> So far, it appears that respondents are who they say they are and the threat of
> cheaters and repeaters is minimal. (Sweet, 1999)

However, as we shall now discuss, the online researcher may still be required to
defend virtual data.

Authenticity of Data

Researchers may approach the 'authenticity' of online data in a variety of ways.
In the first place they would need to make their own assessments of the
'candour' of participants. They would then need to determine the status and
significance of data generated. To a large extent the appropriateness and value
of data will depend on the purposes of the research. If the key requirement of a
study is that participants have 'informed' knowledge of a specific area then
individual identity may not be so crucial. For both O'Connor and Madge (2000)
and Hodkinson (2000) a defence of data would depend more on displaying a
participant's knowledge of the substantive issues of the research (which the
CMC-generated text could demonstrate) than giving 'proof' of personal identity.

How might researchers decide that a participant is 'sincere and aiming for
truth' (Seidman, 1991: 18)? Psychological studies point to some characteristics
which may signal lying FTF, such as

overcontrolled movements, reduced rate of speech, more vocal pauses, and higher voice pitch. It appears we have to concentrate to lie, and the effort diminishes some of the spontaneity of normal human interaction. (Wallace, 1999: 51)

It is with this kind of understanding in mind that Seidman recommended that transcripts and fieldnotes of FTF interaction be scrutinized for factors identifying sincerity and spontaneity; 'the syntax, the pauses, the groping for words, the self-effacing laughter' which would persuade the researcher of the speaker's authenticity (1991: 18). But, in the final analysis, such assessment is subject to the practised intuition of the FTF researcher. This same intuition also leads people to argue that they can gauge the sincerity, authenticity and individuality of disembodied CMC users; that 'it is definitely possible to get some "sense" of who is online and who they "really" are' (Giese, 1998). Or that online reports were trustworthy:

> Many people trusted this 'other' that I gave them of myself, and they revealed parts of themselves to me in turn. What we exchanged was *real*. I felt it in my body that they were as honest about the facts of their lives, their confusions, their dreams, as I was. (Argyle and Shields, 1996: 59)

As with FTF researchers, online researchers may also get 'a feel' for what is happening. Wallace, drawing on research into deception in online messages (see Burgoon *et al.*, 1996) reported that suspicions are often aroused by evasive and indirect answers. 'There was a tendency for truthful subjects to use words in a slightly different way compared to non-truthful ones. Their words were somewhat more likely to be complete, direct, relevant, clear and personalized.' (1999: 52). When Coomber received Web survey responses he concluded that five responses were 'spoofs'. He felt able to differentiate the apparently sincere from the apparently false: 'Characteristically, [the spoofs] tended not to finish the questionnaire, apparently getting fed up half-way through and did not attempt to answer the questions sensibly' (1997: *online*). In contrast responses 'considered reliable' answered in full 'with apparently consistent, informed and non-sensational answers'.

The difficulty with this kind of knowledge is that it offers a doubtful defence for the integrity of data. Further assurances may be needed in some kinds of study and for some audiences. For instance, there will be situations where it is essential that participants fulfil particular demographic criteria. As Bennett's (1998) qualitative study of masculinity depended upon her interviewing men, she encouraged the exchange of photographs, and made spot phone calls as a way of double-checking gender through voice. There will also be many occasions where researchers want participants to be able to talk from a particular standpoint of life experience or situation. For instance, professional focus group moderators may ask for as much demographic and psychodemographic background from virtual participants as they do from in-person groups. They may then double-check this information using on-site FTF verification (see details of the Young People and Health Risk study in Chapter 5), photo checks or screeners (Sweet, 1999).

However, the difference between focus group interaction, which is frequently a one-off occurrence, and more extended interaction is that 'reality checks' are more cumbersome and probably more likely to alienate participants when they have to be regularly repeated. Different criteria for establishing trust may be needed in longitudinal studies. Seidman, working FTF, has already alerted qualitative researchers to the reassurance that may be found in participants' reports that show internal consistence over a period of time (1991: 18). Online studies confirm that repeated interaction with participants not only establishes trust (see Chapter 6) but also compensates for the 'masking of identities'. As Bennett explained, 'I felt that for most people it is difficult to sustain untruths when involved in long-term, intensive interactions' (1998: 36). This was certainly the view of the students in Mann's study:

> Being "virtual students" might be a problem if this was just a short study. But the fact that those of us taking part have been replying for so long (not a criticism!) makes it unlikely that anyone who was concerned with being completely untruthful would have bothered to continue to respond. (GOTM student)

Researchers investigating virtual worlds may also find ways to defend data if they spend time with participants over time. They will 'learn to interpret participants' identity performances in the same way that participants themselves do' (Kendall, 1999: 70). For, in online fora 'participants actively interpret, evaluate, and react to each other's online presentations and do not recognize all such performances as equally vain or real' (1999: 66–67). Not only does such an approach give a profile of the 'continuous' online self, it also avoids a tendency for forum members to resist the attentions of researchers who only make brief visits to their sites. Kendall suggests that researchers who are seen to take a superficial approach may not penetrate the anonymity of members and the honesty of responses may be more difficult to evaluate.

Conclusion

It is clear that qualitative researchers will continue to struggle with the implications of disembodiment for as long as CMC is a mainly text-based medium of research[3]. At the moment most researchers and participants who engage in online research tend to take a fairly philosophical view of the situation. As one focus group moderator points out, there is often an unspoken belief that 'if you have the body you have mind', which is not true in the many situations where being able to contribute to research without 'leaving home' is felt to be an advantage by participants (Sweet, 1999: *online*). The potential for deception is another area where pragmatism is called for. Here, as with FTF research, human interaction is a matter of establishing trust and this is a two-way process, as a student in Mann's study made clear: 'You receive information from "virtual" students but look at it the other way round: we give information to virtual researchers!'.

This necessarily philosophical and pragmatic approach will of course always be open to criticism, and criticism that is difficult to counter without, as discussed above, resorting to the questionable defence of intuition. However, such criticism is most likely to come, we would argue, from those with little personal experience of CMC. As this experience becomes more and more common, and trust in the medium grows, it is likely that the perceived potential for duplicity in online communication will diminish until it is no greater than for communication FTF.

It is also interesting to speculate whether this criticism will be increased or reduced as qualitative research using the Internet moves beyond the confines of text. The challenges for the online researcher of the future have yet to be formulated.

Notes

1   See Sempsey (1997) for literature review. See also Marvin (1995), Mnookin (1996) and Reid (1995).
2   See for example Reid (1991), Herring (1993) and Kramarae and Taylor (1993).
3   A state of affairs which does not escape the attention of theorists who are at the cutting edge of sociology of the body (see Turner, 1996).

10 Future Directions

We have already mentioned the difficulties, and the potential for embarrassment, that face those who try to predict the future of something as unregulated and rapidly developing as the Internet. But if researchers are to invest time and effort in coming to terms with this new medium, the attempt needs to be made. Has communication via the Internet now reached some sort of plateau, or will it soon be transformed out of all recognition? Will the challenges that we have identified in this book turn out to be temporary issues or insuperable problems? And what are the implications for qualitative research?

The safest prediction to make is that the number of people with access to the Internet will continue to grow, and at a rapid pace. As it does so, the diversity of users (and uses) will increase, diluting the status of the technically proficient. Nevertheless, use will continue to be disproportionately concentrated among the better-off sections of society and the more economically developed countries; but there are signs of a recognition that correcting this imbalance is a political task and cannot just be left to market forces. US President Clinton has called for a 'goal within developed countries of having Internet access as complete as telephone access within a fixed number of years', and has said that 'developed countries should spread mobile phones and computer connections in poorer countries'[1]. It remains to be seen how, if at all, these sentiments will be turned into action.

The main barrier to more widespread use lies in the hardware and (in some countries) infrastructure costs associated with the desktop computer/modem/landline technology that currently dominates Internet access. Truly global access will require the development of other technologies, and the shape of these is becoming clear. Some mobile phones can already be used to send and receive emails (Alanko *et al.*, 1999). Email will also be offered as an offshoot of digital television (in conjunction with a telephone connection). Phones and other mobile devices such as personal organizers or 'Palm Pilots' will use wireless application protocol (WAP) to gain access to the Internet using a 'microbrowser', which displays Web pages specially formatted for tiny screens[2]. If such devices follow the pattern of mobile voice telephony we can expect that hardware costs will drop dramatically after the first couple of years (though usage costs may remain high), and that they will prove especially popular in countries (not only developing countries) where conventional telephone services are inadequate or unreliable.

For researchers, these developments offer the exciting prospect of Internet-based communication (and hence research) with a far wider spectrum of socio-economic groups and nationalities than is currently available. However, the question remains of what form of communication this will be. Although phones and the other mobile devices technically allow text messages to be entered, it is hard to imagine someone participating fully in the cut and thrust of a virtual focus group while pecking out responses on a fiddly keypad or tapping on the screen with a stylus. Even when the communication is asynchronous, the difficulty of entering text is bound to have an effect on the depth of the responses that people will provide, or their willingness to provide them. We may be forced to the realization that text-based communication for research purposes requires, if not a desktop computer, then at least a full-size QWERTY keyboard. While standard keyboards are not expensive, ports enabling them to be connected may not be fitted to mobile devices routinely (or at all). More promising (from the researcher's point of view) are infra-red keyboards that can be used, for example, to send messages via interactive television from one's armchair

But Internet communication need not be limited to text. As the capacity of the Internet itself and the connections to it increase, voice and video communication will become possible, eliminating the obstacle of the keyboard. From a research point of view, it could be argued that this will simply get us back to where we are now, because it is difficult to see any substantial differences between voice communication on the Internet and voice telephony. Video communication may be a different matter since, although the technology for non-Internet video conferencing currently exists, its inflexibility (and cost) means that it has rarely been used for qualitative research. Cheap miniaturized cameras that can stick on a monitor are already available, and it may before long become the norm to include a video feed of oneself as part of any real-time CMC. This will be clearly helpful to the researcher in terms of confirming the identity of the participant; but the reintroduction of visual status cues will also have an effect on the communication itself.

Non-text-based communication also removes one of the main practical research advantages of CMC that has been described in this book, precisely because it produces no text. Researchers who wish to analyse the communication will be forced to re-embrace the problems of transcription that we discussed in Chapter 2, and moreover in a situation where sound quality is poorer and creating a recording raises a new set of technical problems. It is here that a further technical development promises to transform research. Speech-recognition software converts spoken words into text, removing the need for a keyboard, opening up research to those who are unable or unwilling to type, and eliminating the bias in favour of the fleet-fingered in online discussions. When combined with machine-translation technology it could turn the Internet into a 'multilingual real-time intercom', making it 'possible to hold a conversation [or interview] in English with a friend in Tokyo who is reading your words in Japanese'[3]. These ideas are not new and examples of both technologies exist – examples that illustrate the problems inherent in perfecting them. Nevertheless, the benefits that they offer for simplifying communication are such that research and investment are bound to continue.

The model for Internet communication in the future seems likely to be a hybrid of various forms, with users switching between text, voice, video and graphics, and between synchronous and asynchronous communication, as circumstances dictate. One implication for research practice of these different types of communication will be the increased possibility of establishing 'who is there' at the other end of the link. Adding voice or video contact to text will not eliminate the problems of disembodiment, but it will help researchers to have more confidence that participants are who they describe themselves to be.

The multiple forms of communication that will be enabled by the 'broadband' Internet may also mean that it will be used for more things. Once broadband is common, people will be able to work together, wherever they are, on anything from planning a company merger or designing a new car to discussing evidence to use against a suspect or interpreting a patient's scan. If permission to participate in these discussions can be obtained, the researcher will simply have to 'plug in' – again, from wherever they happen to be – and a powerful new form of observation becomes available.

The final areas in which researchers need to be aware of developments concern confidentiality and privacy for information transmitted via the Internet. We described in Chapter 3 the concept of 'encryption keys' that enable messages to be coded and decoded. Their general introduction looks likely to be subject to an ongoing struggle between advocates of privacy and security agencies who are reluctant to lose the possibility of monitoring Internet communication. At the same time there will be increasing attempts under data protection legislation to ensure that the information provided for one purpose is not exploited for other ends; and while being generally sympathetic to these aims, qualitative researchers will need to be alert to ensure that laws and procedures are not drawn so tightly that valid research becomes impossible.

While we cannot be sure exactly where the Internet will lead, we are confident that its influence on our personal and professional lives will only increase over the next decade. Researchers need to be actively engaging with the issues it raises. We hope this book will help to start the debate.

Notes

1   *Guardian* newspaper, UK, 22 November 1999, p. 9.
2   *The Economist*, UK, 13 November 1999, p. 30
3   *The Economist*, ibid.

Glossary

This glossary has been compiled from the following Web sites:

www.netlingo.com
www.matisse.net/files/glossary.html
www.icactive.com/_internetglossary.html
www.webopedia.com/
www.whatis.com

Asynchronous/Non-real-time communication takes place at a different time, same place

Bandwidth refers to the range of elements involved in various communication styles. More technically, it refers to the range of frequencies a transmission line or channel can carry. The higher the frequency, the higher the bandwidth and the greater the information-carrying capacity of a channel.

Bulletin Board Systems (BBSs) are computerized meeting and announcement systems for conducting discussions, uploading and downloading files, and obtaining online information and services.

Channel is the virtual area where Internet Relay Chat (IRC) users communicate in real time.

Computer-mediated Communication (CMC) is used in this book to mean a text-based communication process involving the direct use of computers.

Conferences Also called a forum, a conference is an online public discussion area where users exchange ideas and information. A conference or forum usually has themes and topics and is controlled by a facilitator. Forum participants generally do not have to be online at the same time.

Cyberspace is a term coined by author William Gibson in his novel *Neuromancer*. Cyberspace is currently used to refer to the digital world constructed by computer networks, in particular the Internet.

Emoticons are groups of characters that produce 'icons that represent emotion'. They grew out of the need to display feeling in the two-dimensional, online, written world.

FTF – face-to-face, where the participants in an interview or discussion are physically present in the same room at the same time..

Fora See Conferences

HTML – HyperText Markup Language – the coding system used to create pages which can be displayed by Web browsers.

HTML-style tag is a tag like <h1> and </h1> which is used to structure text into headings, paragraphs, lists, hypertext links and more.

HTTP (Hypertext Transfer Protocol) is the protocol that tells the server what to send to the client, so the client can view Web pages, or other areas of the Net.

Hypertext is a system of writing and displaying text that enables the text to be linked in multiple ways, to be available at several levels of detail, and to contain links to related documents.

Internet A system of linked computer networks, international in scope, that facilitates data communication services such as remote login, file transfer, electronic mail and newsgroups. See also: www.eff.org/pub/Net_culture/internet_sterling.history.

Internet account is an account with an ISP (Internet Service Provider) that allows you to access the Internet.

IP (Internet Protocol) is a scheme that enables information to be routed from one network to another.

IRC (Internet Relay Chat) refers to a live chat area of the Internet in which real-time conversations among two or more people take place via IRC software. IRC is divided into channels. When you join a channel everything you type is visible to other people in the same channel, and everything they type is visible to you. Most channels have a topic. See also: http://www.irchelp.org/.

ISP (Internet Service Provider) is a company that provides access to the Internet. Before you can connect to the Internet you must first establish an account with an Internet Service Provider.

Mailing list is a discussion forum where participants subscribe to a list and receive messages by email.

MU* environments (including MUDS, MOOs) are multi-user, text-based, role-playing environments.

Newsgroups are a part of the Internet which allows users to 'post' and 'reply to' messages from other users. They are discussion fora similar to that found on local BBSs.

Nickname is the name or pseudonym a user selects to use in online interactions whether they be in chat, mailing lists, email, etc.

Online means being connected to the Internet. Online is used as an adjective to describe a variety of activities that you can do on the Internet, for example online chat, shopping and games.

Portal is a marketing term used to describe a Web site that serves as a starting point to other destinations or activities on the World Wide Web. Portals commonly provide services such as email, online chat fora and original content.

Protocol is the 'language' spoken between computers to help them exchange information. More technically, it is a formal description of message formats and the rules that two computers must follow to exchange those messages.

Real life (RL) refers to offline or offscreen living.

Server is a computer, or a software package, that provides a specific kind of service to client software running on other computers. The term can refer to a particular piece of software, such as a WWW server, or to the machine on which the software is running. A single server machine could have several different server software packages running on it, thus providing many different servers to clients on the network.

Software is a term used to refer to an 'end user' computer program or group of programs like database, spreadsheet, word processing and Web browser programs.

Spam (or Spamming) is an inappropriate attempt to use a mailing list, or Usenet or other networked communications facility as if it were a broadcast medium (which it is not) by sending the same message to a large number of people who didn't ask for it.

Synchronous/Real-time communication takes place at the same time and same place.

TCP/IP (Transmission Control Protocol/Internet Protocol) is a set of protocols that makes Telnet, File Transfer Protocol (FTP), email and other services possible among computers that do not belong to the same network.

Telnet is the command and program used to log in from one Internet site to another. The Telnet command/program gets you to the login prompt of another host.

Thread is a chain of postings on a single subject in a newsgroup, mailing list, BBS. Most newsreaders include a command that lets you follow the thread; that is, jump to the next message on the topic rather than display each message in sequence.

URL (Uniform Resource Locator) describes the server location (for example, www.hello.com) and access method (usually http). All Web sites have URLs. One could say a URL is to a Web site what a street address is to a house.

Usenet is a worldwide system of discussion groups, with comments passed among hundreds of thousands of machines. Not all Usenet machines are on the Internet, maybe half. Usenet is completely decentralized, with over 10,000 discussion areas, called newsgroups.

Virtual indicates simulation technology that enables the user to cross boundaries and experience something without needing its physical presence, as in virtual sex, and virtual theme parks. The Internet is a 'virtual' world.

Virtual reality (VR) is a combination of interactive databases with video and audio technology to develop a multi-sensory way to create new experiences for the purposes of education, entertainment and commerce.

Web browser is a program used to view, download, upload, surf or otherwise access documents (pages) on the World Wide Web. Browsers can be text based (meaning that they do not show graphics or images) but most display text and graphics.

World Wide Web (WWW) is a global hypertext system that uses the Internet as its transport mechanism. See also: www.boutell.com/faq/ and www.w3.org/.

Appendix A: Online Consent Form

This consent form was developed by Parkany and Swan (1999):

CONSENT FORM

Subject: Assessment and Evaluation of Electronically Generated Portfolios in On-line Coursework

Consent [IRB Protocol Number 99-052]

I would like to collect and study the assignments you complete for this course. Your identity will be kept confidential throughout this enterprise, as well as in any reporting of our findings. You do not, of course, have to allow me to include your work in the study, and your decision will in no way affect your participation in the course. All students must complete the same assignments, and no one involved with the inquiry should be able to distinguish between students who have allowed us to study their work and those who haven't.

Your decision is completely voluntary. If you have any questions concerning your rights as a subject, please contact: the Compliance Office, Office for Research, The University at Albany at (518)442-3510. Please read the following and indicate whether or not I have your permission to use your assignments in my inquiry. You can return this document by completing the test, below, as you would any other assignment.

I appreciate your kind attention very much. A prompt reply would be quite helpful. Those of you who are interested in copies of the inquiry and its representations can ask me for these materials in your journals and I will be happy to make arrangements for your receiving copies as they become available.

NOTE: You will be asked to Take a TEST on the Consent Page, don't worry, be happy!
This is just how to REPLY...
Thank you so much for your time, and I remain...
Sincerely,
Rick Parkany; ETAP426/526 Instructor

Subject: Brief Description

This is a study that will investigate the portfolios generated for an on-line teacher preparation course, ETAP426/526. It will specifically investigate: (a) the various individual portfolio entries (assignments, practica, and projects) of selected subjects in private spaces only open to individual subjects and the instructors; (b) several common public spaces (open to just the instructors and course participants) such as Meet Your Classmates, Discussion, Question, and Bulletin Board areas in Lotus Domino Workspace; and (c) threaded discourse defined in these Public Spaces. The purpose of the study is to investigate: (a) how it is that portfolios generated in such electronic spaces can be assessed by appropriate standards, thereby extending such assessments from their current criterion-based methods; (b) the nature and structure of cultural spaces in these environments; (c) instructor and peer factors influencing the development of literate discourse in these spaces; and (d) how the depth, breadth, and articulation of this electronic discourse can be improved.

Methodology

Procedures will be according to traditional discourse analysis, subject interviews, network analysis and text analyses common to existing practice acceptable in quantitative and qualitative analysis. Specifically, the electronic portfolios will be treated as individual case studies. Their contents will be examined and analyzed with respect to variables not currently assessed for determinations of grades; that is, this study's interventions by the instructor will occur in dimensions according to which they are not currently assessed, thereby removing the ethical threats otherwise inherent in such a study.

Subject Selection

Subjects are to be selected on a voluntary basis from the course roster for ETAP426/526; Spring99. No payment is provided for participation.

Confidentiality

For the purposes of this study, all portfolio materials will be coded with numeric and text based labels indicating fictitious names for purposes of readability in the final representation of the data and its analysis. Identifying details of subject names, places of work, and other situating and identifying data points present in the documentation stream will be given fictitious names, as well. Course portfolios and documents pertinent to the course are stored in password protected files on the SUNY Learning Network Lotus Notes Domino Workspace located in:
> courses/99spring/EDUCATIONALCOMP1SL2/lns9ks.nsf
> corresponding systematically generated back-up files on the same server.

Additionally, the files and portfolios are kept in password protected files in the ETAP CELA office (ED basement), on my home office computer workstation, and on a laptop provided me by CELA.

****

TEST Reply
This is the easiest test you might ever be asked to complete.

IF you consent to allowing your work to be used in my inquiry anonymously...

SIMPLY...

ANSWER, "True" if you consent; "False" if you refuse consent

THEN -----   CLICK on "Submit the Information Above" BUTTON.

That's it!

Thank you so much for your consideration and help...   ;-} rap.

1. Yes, I consent to the use of my assignments in Rick's Inquiry...
["True" = "YES"   "False" = "NO"]

****

Contact Information
Principal Investigator: Rick Parkany
rparkany@borg.com; (315)733-2015; htp://www.borg.com/~rparkany/

http://www.borg.com/~rparkany/Resources/OLPA1.htm
Powerpoint Summary of the Provaluation :
http://www.borg.com/~rparkany/Resources/ProvalPresent/index.htm

Parkany commented that:

The study was approved by the SUNYAlbany IRB (Institutional Review Board). They required that I take off the generic notice from my supervising professor that advised participants to e-mail *if they did NOT want to be involved* w/an *active document* that outlined the description of the study, etc., and required them to e-mail the approval through the Lotus Notes/Domino platform that confirmed the posts of consent by the use of user passwords that enrolled the students (1999, *personal email*).

Appendix B: An Email Text-based Survey

The example below illustrates the format of a survey designed to be sent as the text of an email. This example was created using the survey creation program SurveySolutions for the Web (see www.perseus.com). The program automatically includes the instructions to the respondent, though these can be edited by the survey designer.

Q. 1
Sex

    (Type an X between the brackets preceding your choice. Select only one choice.)

    [ ] Male
    [ ] Female

Q. 2
Date of birth

    (For each topic below, type your answer between the brackets. Don't worry about extra spaces at the end of your responses.)

    Day:
    [   ]
    Month (eg 10):
    [   ]
    Year (eg 1967):
    [   ]

Q. 3
How would you describe your ethnic origin?

    (Type an X between the brackets preceding your choice. Select only one choice.)

    [ ] Black Caribbean
    [ ] Black African
    [ ] Black Other
    [ ] Bangladeshi
    [ ] Chinese
    [ ] Indian
    [ ] Pakistani
    [ ] Other Asian
    [ ] White

Q. 4
How influential has each of the following factors been in determining your academic success?

    (For each topic below, type an X between the brackets preceding the choice you wish to select.)

Career ambitions
[ ] Crucial   [ ] Very influential   [ ] Quite influential   [ ] Not influential
Support from home
[ ] Crucial   [ ] Very influential   [ ] Quite influential   [ ] Not influential
Ability
[ ] Crucial   [ ] Very influential   [ ] Quite influential   [ ] Not influential
Very good teachers
[ ] Crucial   [ ] Very influential   [ ] Quite influential   [ ] Not influential
Fear of failure
[ ] Crucial   [ ] Very influential   [ ] Quite influential   [ ] Not influential

Q. 5
What were your main reasons for choosing to come to Cambridge?

(Type your answer between the brackets, using as much space as necessary. Don't worry about extra spaces at the end of your response.)

[   ]

Q. 6
Which societies or activities might you get involved with when you come to Cambridge? Please tick all the boxes that may apply.

(Type an X between the brackets preceding each choice you wish to select. Select as many choices as appropriate.)

[ ] Religious organisations
[ ] Drama
[ ] Sport or games
[ ] Journalism and writing
[ ] Politics/debating
[ ] Non-party political organisations

A completed survey, returned as an email reply, might look like this:

Q. 1
Sex

(Type an X between the brackets preceding your choice. Select only one choice.)

[ ] Male
[X] Female

Q. 2
Date of birth

(For each topic below, type your answer between the brackets. Don't worry about extra spaces at the end of your responses.)

Day:
[8   ]
Month (eg 10):
[9   ]
Year (eg 1967):
[1980   ]

Q. 3
How would you describe your ethnic origin?

(Type an X between the brackets preceding your choice. Select only one choice.)

[ ] Black Caribbean
[ ] Black African
[ ] Black Other
[ ] Bangladeshi
[ ] Chinese
[X] Indian
[ ] Pakistani
[ ] Other Asian
[ ] White

Q. 4
How influential has each of the following factors been in determining your academic success?

(For each topic below, type an X between the brackets preceding the choice you wish to select.)

Career ambitions
[ ] Crucial   [X] Very influential   [ ] Quite influential   [ ] Not influential
Support from home
[X] Crucial   [ ] Very influential   [ ] Quite influential   [ ] Not influential
Ability
[ ] Crucial   [ ] Very influential   [X] Quite influential   [ ] Not influential
Very good teachers
[ ] Crucial   [X] Very influential   [ ] Quite influential   [ ] Not influential
Fear of failure
[ ] Crucial   [ ] Very influential   [ ] Quite influential   [X] Not influential

Q. 5
What were your main reasons for choosing to come to Cambridge?

(Type your answer between the brackets, using as much space as necessary. Don't worry about extra spaces at the end of your response.)

[The reputation of the teaching staff in my department   ]

Q. 6
Which societies or activities might you get involved with when you come to Cambridge? Please tick all the boxes that may apply.

(Type an X between the brackets preceding each choice you wish to select. Select as many choices as appropriate.)

[ ] Religious organisations
[x] Drama
[ ] Sport or games
[x] Journalism and writing
[x] Politics/debating
[ ] Non-party political organisations

This is a 'correct' response. All questions have been answered as requested and although there is some variation in the positioning of replies within the brackets, and both upper and lower case Xs have been used, all the answers can be interpreted by automated analytical tools. However, there would have been nothing to prevent the respondent from typing answers outside the brackets or from selecting more than one option where only one was required.

Appendix C: A Web-page-based Survey

The example below shows how the survey in Appendix B might appear if presented as a Web page. This example was also created using SurveySolutions for the Web. As with the text-based version, the HTML created by the program can be edited by the survey designer.

In this example, answers where only one choice is required are presented in a drop-down list and responses to scale questions are presented as 'radio buttons'. Either drop-down lists or radio buttons can be used for both these question types.

The following screens show how a completed survey might look to the user. Depending on the script attached to the 'Submit Survey' button, the researcher might receive a file containing the question answers only, or might receive an email for each response containing the answers and some text to identify the question.

References

Acker, S. and Feuerverger, G. (1999). Hearing others and seeing ourselves: Empathy, ethics and emotions in a study of Canadian women academics. Paper given at Voices in Gender and Education Conference, University of Warwick, UK, 29–31 March.

Ackermann, E. (1995). *Learning to Use the Internet: Issues Ethical, Legal, Security, and Social.* Wilsonville, OR: Franklin.

Ackeroyd, A. (1988). Ethnography, personal data and computers: The implications of data protection legislation for qualitative social research. In R. Burgess (ed.), *Conducting Qualitative Research* (179–219). Greenwich, CT: JAI Press.

Ackeroyd, A. (1991). Personal information and qualitative research data: Some practical and ethical problems arising from data protection legislation. In N. Fielding and R. Lee (eds.), *Using Computers in Qualitative Research* (89–107). London and Newbury Park, CA: Sage.

Aikens, S. (1996). A history of Minnesota electronic democracy 1994. *First Monday, A Peer Reviewed Journal on the Internet* [Online], 1(5). Available: http:// www.firstmonday.dk/issues/issue5/aikens/.

Alanko, T., Kojo, M., Liljeberg, M. and Raatikainen, K. (1999). Mobile access to the Internet: A mediator-based solution. *Internet Research: Electronic Networking Applications and Policy*, 9(1). Available online: http://www.mcb.co.uk/cgi-bin/journal1/intr.

Allen, C. (1996). What's wrong with the 'golden rule'? Conundrums of conducting ethical research in cyberspace. *The Information Society*, 12(2): 175–187. Abstract: http://www.slis.indiana.edu/TIS/abstracts/ab12-2/allen1.html.

Anders, E. (2000). *Women with Disabilities: Higher education, feminism and social constructions of difference.* Unpublished PhD thesis, Deakin University, Melbourne, Australia.

Anderson, R. (1997). A research agenda for computing and the social sciences. *Social Science Computer Review*, 15: 123–134.

Anderson, R., Lundmark, V., Harris, L. and Magnan, S. (1994). Equity in computing. In C. Huff and T. Finholt (eds.), *Social Issues in Computing: Putting Technology in its Place* (352–385). New York: McGraw-Hill.

Aoki, K. (1994). Virtual communities in Japan. Paper given at Pacific Telecommunications Council Conference.

Aoki, K. (1995). Synchronous multi-user textual communication in international tele-collaboration. *Electronic Journal of Communication*, 5(4).

Argyle, K. and Shields, R. (1996). Is there a body in the Net? In R. Shields (ed.), *Cultures of the Internet* (58–69). London: Sage.

Aycock, A. and Buchignani, N. (1995). The e-mail murders: Reflections on 'dead' letters. In S. Jones (ed.), *Cybersociety: Computer-mediated Communication and community* (184–231). Thousand Oaks, CA: Sage.

Babbie, E. (1996). We am a virtual community. *The American Sociologist*, Spring, 65–71.

Bachmann, D., Elfrink, J. and Vazzana, G. (1996). Tracking the progress of e-mail vs. snail-mail. *Marketing Research*, 8: 30–35.

Bannert, M. and Arbinger, P. (1996). Gender-related differences in exposure to and use of computers: Results of a survey of secondary school students. *European Journal of Psychology of Education*, 11: 269–282.

Barnes, J. (1979). *Who Should Know What? Social Science, Privacy and Ethics*. Harmondsworth: Penguin Books.

Bashier, R. (1990). Socio-psychological factors in electronic networking. *International Journal of Lifelong Education*, 9(1): 49–64.

Baym, N. (1992). Computer-mediated soap talk: Communication, community and entertainment on the Net. Paper presented at the Annual Meeting of the Speech Communication Association, Chicago.

Baym, N. (1995a). The emergence of community in computer mediated communication. In S. Jones (ed.), *Cybersociety: Computer-Mediated Communication and Community* (139–163). Thousand Oaks, CA, and London: Sage.

Baym, N. (1995b). From practice to culture on Usenet. In S. Star (ed.), *The Cultures of Computing* (29–52). Oxford: Blackwell.

Bechar-Israeli, H. (1996). From <Bonehead> to <cLoNehEAd>: Nicknames, play, and identity on Internet Relay Chat. *Journal of Computer-Mediated Communication* [Online], 1(2). Available: http://jcmc.mscc.huji.ac.il/vol1/issue2/bechar.html.

Becker, H. (1996). The epistemology of qualitative research. In R. Jessor, R. Colby and A. Schweder (eds.), *Ethnography and Human Development* (53–72). Chicago: University of Chicago Press.

Bennett, C. (1998). *Men Online: Discussing lived experiences on the Internet*. Unpublished Honours dissertation, James Cook University, Townsville, Australia.

Berger, P. (1966). *Invitation to Sociology: A Humanist Perspective*. Harmondsworth: Penguin.

Bernstein, B. (1971). *Class, Codes and Control Volume 1: Theoretical studies towards a sociology of language*. London: Routledge and Kegan Paul.

Bernstein, B. (1975). *Class, Codes and Control Volume 3: Towards a theory of educational transmissions*. London: Routledge and Kegan Paul.

Biber, D. (1998). *Variations Across Speech and Writing*. New York: Cambridge University Press.

Bing, J. (1980). Personal data systems – a comparative perspective on a basic concept in privacy legislation. In J. Bing and S. Kelmer (eds.), *A Decade of Computers and Law* (72–91). Oslo: Universitetsforlaget.

Black, S. (1983). Real and non-real time interaction: Unravelling multiple threads of discourse. *Discourse Processes*, 6: 59–75.

Bornat, J. (1993). Presenting. In P. Shakespeare, D. Atkinson and S. French (eds.), *Reflecting on Research Practice: Issues in Health and Social Welfare*. Buckingham: Open University Press.

Bornat, J. (1994). Is oral history auto/biography? *Auto/Biography* (publication of the British Sociological Society Study Group on Auto/Biography), 3(1).

Boshier, R. (1990). Socio-psychological factors in electronic networking. *International Journal of Lifelong Education*, 9(1): 49–64.

Brannen, J. (1992). *Mixing Methods: Qualitative and Quantitative Research.* Aldershot: Avebury.

Briggs, C. (1986). *Learning How to Ask: A sociolinguistic appraisal of the role of the interview in social science research.* Cambridge: Cambridge University Press.

Bromberg, H. (1996). Are MUDs communities? Identity, belonging and consciousness in virtual worlds. In R. Shields (ed.), *Cultures of the Internet: Virtual Spaces, Real Histories, Living Bodies.* London: Sage.

Brown, L. and Gilligan, C. (1992). *Meeting at the Crossroads.* Cambridge, MA: Harvard University Press.

Bruckman, A. (1992). *Identity Workshops: Emergent social and psychological phenomena in text-based virtual reality.* MIT Media Laboratory (Email: bruckman@media.mit.edu).

Bruckman, A. (1993). Gender swapping on the Internet. Paper given at INET93, San Francisco.

Bryman, A. (1988). *Quantity and Quality in Social Research.* London: Unwin Hyman.

Burgess, R. (1993). *Research Methods.* Walton-on-Thames: Thomas Nelson.

Burgoon, J., Buller, D., Guerrero, L., Wallid, A. and Feldman, C. (1996). Interpersonal deception: XII. Information management dimensions underlying deceptive and truthful messages. *Communication Monographs,* 63: 50–69.

Burgoon, M. and Miller, G. R. (1987). An expectancy interpretation of language and persuasion. In H. Giles and R. N. St. Clair (eds.), *Recent Advances in Language, Communication and Social Psychology* (199–229). Hillsdale, NJ: Erlbaum.

Burkhalter, B. (1999). Reading race online: Discovering racial identity in Usenet discussions. In M. A. Smith and P. Kollock (eds.), *Communities in Cyberspace,* (60–75). London and New York: Routledge.

Cameron, D. (1996). The language-gender interface: Challenging co-optation. In V. Bergvall, J. Bing and A. Freed (eds.), *Rethinking Language and Gender Research: Theory and Practice.* New York: Longman.

Camp, L. J. (1996). We are geeks, and we are not guys: The Systers mailing list. In L. Cherny and E. R. Weise (eds.), *Wired_Women: Gender and new realities in cyberspace* (114–125). Seattle, WA: Seal Press.

Cannell, C. (1985). Overview: response bias and interviewer variability in surveys. In T. Beed and R. Stimson (eds.), *Survey Interviewing, Theory and Techniques.* Sydney: Allen & Unwin.

Carlstrom, E. (1992). Better living through language: The communicative implications of a text-only virtual environment. Research report: Grinnell College, USA.

Cavazos, E. (1994). Intellectual property in cyberspace: Copyright law in a new world. In E. Cavazos and G. Morin (eds.), *Cyberspace and the Law: Your rights and duties in the on-line world.* Cambridge, MA: MIT Press.

Chafe, W. (1994). *Discourse, Consciousness & Time: The flow and displacement of conscious experience in speaking and writing.* Chicago and London: University of Chicago Press.

Chafe, W. and Danielewicz, J. (1987). Properties of spoken and written language. In R. Horowitz and S. Samuels (eds.), *Comprehending Oral and Written Language* (83–113). New York: Academic Press.

Chamberlain, M. and Thompson, P. (1998). *Narrative and Genre.* London and New York: Routledge.

Chanfrault-Duchet, M. (1991). Narrative structures, social models, and symbolic representation in the life story. In S. Gluck and D. Patai (eds.), *Women's Words* (77–93). New York and London: Routledge.

Cherney, L. (1994). Gender differences in text-based virtual reality. Stanford University (Email: cherney@csli.stanford.edu).

Cherney, L. and Weise, E. R. (eds.) (1995). *Wired_Women: Gender and new realities in cyberspace*. Seattle, WA: Seal Press.

Cheseboro, J. and Bonsall, D. (1989). *Computer-Mediated Communication: Human relationships in a computerized world*. Tuscaloosa, AL: University of Alabama Press.

Clandinin, D. and Connelly, F. (1994). Personal experience methods. In N. Denzin and Y. Lincoln (eds.), *Handbook of Qualitative Research* (413–427). Thousand Oaks, CA, and London: Sage.

Coffman, K. and Odlyzko, K. (1998). The size and growth rate of the Internet. *First Monday, A Peer Reviewed Journal on the Internet* [Online], 3(10). Available: http://www.firstmonday.dk/issues/issue3_10/coffman/index.html.

Cohen, J. (1996). Computer mediated communication and publication productivity among faculty. *Internet Research: Electronic Networking Applications and Policy*, 6: 41–63. Available: http://www.mcb.co.uk/cgi-bin/journal1/intr.

Cohen, S. and Taylor, L. (1977). Talking about prison blues. In C. Bell and H. Newby (eds.), *Doing Sociological Research*. London: Allen & Unwin.

Cole, R. (2000). Promising to be a man: Promise Keepers' organizational construction of masculinity. In D. Claussen (ed.), *Men Wrestling with Commitment: The Promise Keepers, Masculinity and Christianity*. Jefferson, NC: MacFarland.

Collot, M. and Belmore, N. (1996). Electronic language: A new variety of English. In S. Herring (ed.), *Computer-Mediated Communication: Linguistic, Social and Cross-Cultural Perspectives* (13–28). Amsterdam: John Benjamins Publishing.

Colomb, G. and Simutis, J. (1996). Visible conversation and academic inquiry. In S. Herring (ed.), *Computer-Mediated Communication: Linguistic, Social and Cross-Cultural Perspectives* (203–224). Amsterdam: John Benjamins Publishing.

Comley, P. (1996). The use of the Internet as a data collection method [Online]. Available: http://www.sga.co.uk/esomar.html.

Condon, S. and Cech, C. (1996). Functional comparisons of face-to-face and computer-mediated decision making interactions. In S. Herring (ed.), *Computer-Mediated Communication: Linguistic, Social and Cross-Cultural Perspectives* (65–80). Amsterdam: John Benjamins Publishing.

Connelly, F. and Clandinin, D. (1988). *Teachers as Curriculum Planners: Narratives of experience*. New York: Teacher's College Press.

Coomber, R. (1997). Using the Internet for survey research. *Sociological Research Online* [Online], 2. Available: http://www.socresonline.org.uk/socresonline/2/2/2.html.

Correll, S. (1995). The ethnography of an electronic bar: The lesbian café. *Journal of Contemporary Ethnography*, 24: 270–298.

Couper, M., Blair, J. and Triplett, T. (1999). A comparison of mail and e-mail for a survey of employees in US statistical agencies. *Journal of Official Statistics*, 15(1): 39–56.

Creswell, J. (1998). *Qualitative Inquiry and Research Design: Choosing among five traditions*. Thousand Oaks, CA, and London: Sage.

Cringely, R. (1993). *Accidental Empires*. London: Penguin.

Curtis, P. (1997). Mudding: Social phenomena in text-based virtual realities. In S. Kiesler (ed.), *Culture of the Internet* (121–142). Mahwah, NJ: Lawrence Erlbaum. Available: http://www.oise.on.ca/~jnolan/muds/about_muds/pavel.html.

Cushing, P. (1996). Gendered conversational rituals on the Internet: An effective voice is based on more than simply what one is saying. *Anthropologica*, XXXVIII: 47–80.

Cutler, R. H. (1995). Distributed presence and community in cyberspace. *Interpersonal Communication and Technology: A Journal for the 21st Century*, 1.

Davis, B. and Brewer, J. (1997). *Electronic Discourse Linguistic Individuals in Virtual Space*. New York: State University of New York Press.

Daws, L. (1999). 'Cattle, Special Education, Old Hats and Rain'. Investigating rural women's use of interactive communication technologies: Issues for qualitative computing. Centre for Policy and Leadership Studies, QUT Kelvin Grove Campus, Queensland, Australia 4059 (Email: l.daws@qut.edu.au).

Denzin, N. (1970). *The Research Act*. Chicago: Aldine.

Denzin, N. (1989). *Interpretive Biography*. Newbury Park, CA: Sage.

Denzin, N. (1999). Cybertalk and the method of instances. In S. Jones (ed.), *Doing Internet Research*. Thousand Oaks, CA, and London: Sage.

Denzin, N. and Lincoln, Y. (1994). Introduction: Entering the field of qualitative research. In N. Denzin and Y. Lincoln (eds.), *Handbook of Qualitative Research*. London: Sage.

Derkley, K. (1998). Falling for the Net. *The Age* newspaper, Australia, 2 November.

Dibbell, J. (1993). A rape in cyberspace, or how an evil clown, a Haitian trickster spirit, two wizards, and a cast of dozens turned a database into a society. *The Village Voice* newspaper, New York, 23 December.

Dillabough, J. (1999). Feminist ethnography: A quest for truth or understanding? Paper given at Voices in Gender and Education Conference, University of Warwick, UK, 29–31 March.

Douglas, J. (1985). *Creative Interviewing*. Beverly Hills, CA: Sage.

Dubrovsky, V., Kiesler, S. and Sethna, B. (1991). The equalization phenomenon: Status effects in computer-mediated and face-to-face decision-making groups. *Human Computer Interaction*, 6: 119–146.

Dunne, G. (1999). *The Different Dimensions of Gay Fatherhood: Exploding the myths*. Report to the Economic and Social Research Council. London: London School of Economics.

Dyrkton, J. (1996). Cool runnings: The contradictions of cybereality in Jamaica. In R. Shields (ed.), *Cultures of the Internet: Virtual Spaces, Real Histories, Living Bodies*. London and Thousand Oaks, CA: Sage.

Elgesem, D. (1996). Privacy, respect for persons and risk. In C. Ess (ed.), *Philosopical Perspectives on Computer-Mediated Communication*, (45–66). Albany, NY: State University of New York Press.

Ferganchick-Neufang, J. (1998). Virtual harassment. Women and online education. *First Monday, A Peer Reviewed Journal on the Internet* [Online], 3(2). Available: http://www.firstmonday.dk/issues/issue3_2/fergan/index.html.

Fernback, J. (1999). There is a there there: Notes toward a definition of cybercommunity. In S. Jones (ed.), *Doing Internet Research*. Thousand Oaks, CA, and London: Sage.

Fernback, J. and Thompson, B. (1995). Virtual communities: abort, retry, failure? Paper given to International Communication Association Convention, Albuquerque, New Mexico.

Ferrara, K., Brunner, H. and Whittemore, G. (1991). Interactive written discourse as an emergent register. *Written Communication*, 8.

Ferri, B. (2000). The hidden cost of difference: Women with learning disabilities. *Learning Disabilities: A Multidisciplinary Journal*, 10.

Fetterman, D. (1998). *Ethnography: Step by Step*. London and Newbury Park, CA: Sage.

Fielding, N. (1982). Observational research on the national front. In M. Bulmer (ed.), *Social Research Ethics*. London: Macmillan.

Fielding, N. (1999). The theoretical and practical applications of IT in qualitative analysis. In M. Henry (ed.), *I.T. in the Social Sciences* (96–112). Oxford: Blackwell.

Fielding, N. and Lee, R. (1998). *Computer Analysis and Qualitative Research*. London and Thousand Oaks, CA: Sage.

Finnegan, R. (1992). *Oral Traditions and the Verbal Arts: A guide to research practices*. London: Routledge.

Finnegan, R. (1996). Using documents. In R. Sapsford and V. Jupp (eds.), *Data Collection and Analysis* (138–153). London and Thousand Oaks, CA: Sage.

Fishman, P. (1983). Interaction: The work women do. In B. Thorne, C. Kramarae and N. Henley (eds.), *Language, Gender and Society* (89–101). Rowley, MA: Newbury House.

Flick, U. (1998). *An Introduction to Qualitative Research*. London and Thousand Oaks, CA: Sage.

Fontana, A. and Frey, J. (1994). Interviewing: The art of science. In N. Denzin and Y. Lincoln (eds.), *Handbook of Qualitative Research*. London: Sage.

Forcht, K. and Fore, R. (1995). Security issues and concerns with the Internet. *Internet Research*, 5.

Foster, G. (1994). Fishing with the Net for research data. *British Journal of Educational Technology*, 25(2): 91–97.

Foster, J. (1990). *Villains: Crime and Community in the Inner City*. London: Routledge.

Foster, P. (1996). Observational research. In R. Sapsford and V. Jupp (eds.), *Data Collection and Analysis*. London and Thousand Oaks, CA: Sage.

Frankfort-Nachmias, C. and Nachmias, D. (1996). *Research Methods in the Social Sciences*. London and Sydney: St Martin's Press.

Fraser, N. (1994). Rethinking the public sphere. In P. McLaren and H. Giroux (eds.), *Between Borders* (74–99). New York: Routledge.

Frey, J. and Fontana, A. (1995). The group interview in social research. In D. Morgan (ed.), *Successful Focus Groups Advancing the State of the Art* (20–34). Newbury Park, CA: Sage.

Fulk, J., Schmitz, J. and Schwarz, D. (1992). The dynamics of context-behaviour interactions in computer-mediated communication. In M. Lea (ed.), *Contexts of Computer Mediated Communication* (7–30). London and New York: Harvester-Wheatsheaf.

Gaiser, T. (1997). Conducting on-line focus groups. *Social Science Computer Review*, 15: 135–144.

Galegher, J. *et al.* (1998). Legitimacy, authority, and community in electronic support groups. *Written Communication*, 15.

Garfinkel, H. (1967). *Studies in Ethnomethodology*. London: Routledge and Kegan Paul.

Garton, L. and Wellman, B. (1995). Social impacts of electronic mail in organizations: A review of the research literature. In B. Burleson (ed.), *Communication Yearbook*, 18: 434–453. Newbury Park, CA: Sage.

Garton, L., Haythornthwaite, C. and Wellman, B. (1999). Studying on-line networks. In S. Jones (ed.), *Doing Internet Research*. Thousand Oaks, CA, and London: Sage.

Gates, W. (1997). Keynote address, Harvard Conference on the Internet and Society. In O'Reilly and Associates (eds.), *The Internet and Society*. Cambridge, MA: Harvard University Press.

Geertz, C. (1973). *The Interpretation of Cultures*. New York: Basic Books.

Gibson, W. (1984). *Neuromancer*. London: Gollancz.

Giese, M. (1998). Self without body: Textual self-representation in an electronic community. *First Monday, A Peer Reviewed Journal on the Internet* [Online], 3(4). Available: http://www.firstmonday.dk/issues/issue3_4/giese/index.html.

Gjestland, L. (1996). Net? Not yet. *Marketing Research*, 8: 26–29.

Glaser, B. and Strauss, A. (1967). *The Discovery of Grounded Theory: Strategies for qualitative research*. New York: Aldine De Gruyter.

Gluck, S. and Patai, D. (1991). *Women's Words: The feminist practice of oral history*. New York and London: Routledge.

Good, D. (1996). Pragmatics and presence. *AI and Society*, 10: 309–314.

Graham, S. and Marvin, S. (1996). *Telecommunications and the City: Electronic Spaces, Urban Places*. London: Routledge.

Gudykunst, W. and Kim, Y. (1984). *Communicating with Strangers: An Approach to Intercultural Communication*. New York: Random House.

Haddon, L. (1992). Explaining ICT consumption: The case of the home computer. In R. Silverstone and E. Hirsch (eds.), *Consuming Technologies: Media and information in domestic spaces*. London: Routledge.

Hahn, K. (1998). Qualitative investigation of an e-mail mediated help service. *Internet Research: Electronic Networking Applications and Policy*, 8(2). Available online: http://www.mcb.co.uk/cgi-bin/journal1/intr.

Hall, E. (1976). *Beyond Culture*. New York: Doubleday.

Hall, K. (1996). Cyberfeminism. In S. Herring (ed.), *Computer-Mediated Communication: Linguistic, social and cross-cultural perspectives* (147–173). Amsterdam: John Benjamins Publishing.

Hall, M. (1998). Africa Connected. *First Monday, A Peer Reviewed Journal on the Internet* [Online], 3(11). Available: http://www.firstmonday.dk/issues/issue3_11/hall/index.html.

Hammersley, M. and Atkinson, P. (1995). *Ethnography: Principles in Practice*. New York: Routledge.

Hantrais, L. and Sen, M. (1996). *Cross-National Research Methods in the Social Sciences*. Guildford: Biddles.

Haraway, D. (1991). A manifesto for cyborgs: Science, technology, and social feminism in the 1980s. In *Simians, Cyborgs and Women*. London: Free Association Press.

Hardey, M. (1998). *The Social Context of Health*. Buckingham: Open University Press.

Harnard, S. (1992). Post-Gutenberg galaxy: The fourth revolution in the means of production of knowledge. *Public-Access Computer Sytems Review*, 2: 39–52.

Hauben, M. and Hauben, R. (1998). Netizens: On the history and impact of Usenet and the Internet. *First Monday, A Peer Reviewed Journal on the Internet* [Online], 3(7). Available: http://www.firstmonday.dk/issues/issue3_7/index.html.

Havelock, E. (1998). Orality, literacy, and Star Wars. *Written Communication*, 15.

Headcount.com (1999). Who's online by country [Online]. Available: http://www.headcount.com/count/datafind.htm?choice=country.

Heim, M. (1992). The erotic ontology of cyberspace. In M. Benedikt (ed.), *Cyberspace: First steps* (59–80). Cambridge, MA: MIT Press.

Herring, S. (1993). Gender and democracy in computer-mediated communication. *Electronic Journal of Communication*, 3.

Herring, S. (1994). Gender differences in computer-mediated communication: Bringing familiar baggage to the new frontier. Keynote talk, American Library Association Annual Convention, Miami.

Herring, S. (1996a). Two variants of an electronic message schema. In Herring S. (ed.), *Computer-Mediated Communication: Linguistic, social and cross-cultural perspectives* (81–109). Amsterdam: John Benjamins Publishing.

Herring, S. (ed.) (1996b). *Computer-Mediated Communication: Linguistic, social and cross-cultural perspectives*. Amsterdam: John Benjamins Publishing.

Herring, S., Johnson, D. and Dibenedetto, T. (1992). Participation in electronic discourse in a 'feminist' field. In K. Hall, M. Bucholtz and Moonwomon (eds.), *Locating Power: Proceedings of the Second Berkeley Women and Language Conference* (250–262), Berkeley, CA.

Herring, S., Johnson, D. and Dibenedetto, T. (1995). 'This discussion is going too far!' Male resistance to female participation on the Internet. In K. Hall and M. Bucholtz (eds.), *Gender Articulated: Language and the socially constructed self* (67–96). New York: Routledge.

Herschlag, M. (1997). Harvard Conference on the Internet and Society, 464–465.

Hess, D. (1995). *Science and Technology in a Multicultural World: The cultural politics of facts and artifacts*. New York: Columbia University Press.

Hewson, C., Laurent, D. and Vogel, C. (1996). Proper methodologies for psychological and sociological studies conducted via the Internet. *Behaviour Research Methods, Instruments and Computers*, 28(2): 186–191.

Hiltz, S. and Turoff, M. (1993). *The Network Nation: Human communication via computer*. Reading, MA: MIT Press.

Hodkinson, P. (2000). *The Goth Scene as Trans-Local Subculture*. Unpublished PhD thesis, Centre for Urban and Regional Studies, University of Birmingham, UK.

Holderness, M. (1998). Who are the world's information-poor? In B. D. Loader (ed.), *Cyberspace Divide: Equality, agency and policy in the information society* (35–56). London and New York: Routledge.

Holstein, J. and Gubrium, J. (1997). Active interviewing. In D. Silverman (ed.), *Qualitative Research: Theory, method and practice* (113–130). London and Thousand Oaks, CA: Sage.

Horn, S. (1998). *Cyberville: Clicks, Culture and the Creation of an Online Town*. New York: Warner Books.

Humphreys, L. (1970). *Tearoom Trade: Impersonal sex in public places*. Chicago: Aldine.

Johnson, D. (1972). *Reaching Out, Interpersonal Effectiveness and Self-Actualization*. Englewood Cliffs, NJ: Prentice Hall.

Jones, S. (1995). *Cybersociety: Computer-mediated communication and community*. Thousand Oaks, CA, and London: Sage.

Jones, S. (1999a). *Doing Internet Research: Critical issues and methods for examining the Net*. Thousand Oaks, CA, and London: Sage.

Jones, S. (ed.) (1999b). Studying the net: Intricacies and issues. In S. Jones (ed.), *Doing Internet Research* (1–29). Thousand Oaks, CA, and London: Sage.

Jordan, T. (1999). *Cyberpower: The culture and politics of cyberspace and the Internet*. London and New York: Routledge.

Jourard, S. (1964). *The Transparent Self*. Princeton, NJ: Van Nostrand.

Jupp, V. (1989). *Methods of Criminological Research*. London: Unwin Hyman.

Kane, P. (1994). *Hitchhiker's Guide to the Electronic Highway*. New York: MIS Press.

Katz, J. and Aspden, P. (1997). Motivations for and barriers to Internet usage: Results of a national public opinion survey. *Internet Research: Electronic Networking Applications and Policy*, 7(3): 170–188. Available online: http://www.mcb.co.uk/cgi-bin/journal1/intr.

Kehoe, C. and Pitkow, J. (1996). Surveying the territory: GVU's five WWW user surveys. *The World Wide Web Journal*, 1.

Kendall, L. (1998). Meaning and identity in 'Cyberspace': The performance of gender, class and race online. *Symbolic Interaction*, 21: 129–153.

Kendall, L. (1999). Recontextualizing cyberspace: Methodological considerations for on-line research. In S. Jones (ed.), *Doing Internet Research* (57–75). Thousand Oaks, CA, and London: Sage.

Kennedy, A. (2000). *The Internet and the World Wide Web: The Rough Guide*. London: Penguin.

Kerr, E. and Hiltz, S. (1982). *Computer-Mediated Communication Systems: Status and evaluation*. New York: Academic Press.

Kiesler, S. and Sproull, L. (1992). Group decision making and communication technology. *Organizational Behavior and Human Decision Processes*, 52: 96–123.

Kiesler, S., Siegel, J. and McGuire, T. (1984). Social psychological aspects of computer-mediated communication. *American Psychologist*, 39: 1123–1134.

Kiesler, S., Zubrow, D., Moses, A. and Geller, V. (1985). Affect in computer-mediated communication: An experiment in synchronous terminal-to-terminal discussion. *Human Computer Interaction*, 1: 77–104.

King, S. (1996). Researching Internet communities: Proposed ethical guidelines for the reporting of the results. *The Information Society*, 12(2): 119–127. Abstract available: http://www.slis.indiana.edu/TIS/abstracts/ab12-2/king.html.

Kingsley, P. and Anderson, T. (1998). Facing life without the Internet. *Internet Research: Electronic Networking Applications and Policy*, 8(4): 303–312. Available online: http://www.mcb.co.uk/cgi-bin/journal1/intr.

Kitchin, R. (1998). *Cyberspace: the World in the Wires*. Chichester and New York: John Wiley.

Kohnken, G. (1987). Training police officers to detect deceptive eye witness statements: Does it work? *Social Behaviour*, 2: 1–17.

Kollock, P. and Smith, M. (1996). Managing the virtual commons: Cooperation and conflict in computer communities. In S. Herring (ed.), *Computer-Mediated Communication: Linguistic, social and cross-cultural perspectives* (109–128). Amsterdam: John Benjamins Publishing.

Korenman, J. and Wyatt, N. (1996). Group dynamics in an e-mail forum. In S. Herring (ed.), *Computer-Mediated Communication: Linguistic, social and cross-cultural perspectives* (225–243). Amsterdam: John Benjamins Publishing.

Kramarae, C. (1995). A backstage critique of virtual reality. In S. Jones (ed.), *Cybersociety: Computer-Mediated Communication and Community* (36–56). Thousand Oaks, CA: Sage.

Kramarae, C. and Kramer, J. (1995). Legal snarls for women and cyberspace. *Internet Research: Electronic Networking Applications and Policy,* 5: 14–24. Available online: http://www.mcb.co.uk/cgi-bin/journal1/intr.

Kramarae, C. and Taylor, H. (1993). Women and men on electronic networks: A conversation or a monologue? In H. Taylor, C. Kramarae and M. Ebben (eds.), *Women, Information Technology, and Scholarship.* University of Illinois, Urbana–Champaign: Center for Advanced Studies.

Krueger, R. (1993). Quality control in focus group research. In D. Morgan (ed.), *Successful Focus Groups: Advancing the State of the Art* (65–88). Newbury Park, CA: Sage.

Krueger, R. (1988). *Focus Groups: A Practical Guide for Applied Research.* Thousand Oaks, CA: Sage.

Lakoff, R. (1975). *Language and Woman's Place.* New York: Harper and Row.

Lanham, R. (1993). *The Electronic Word: Democracy, technology, & the arts.* Chicago and London: University of Chicago Press.

LaQuey, T. and Ryer, J. (1993). *The Internet Companion: A beginner's guide to global networking.* New York: Addison-Wesley.

Larson, C. (1997). Re-presenting the subject: Problems in personal inquiry. *International Journal of Qualitative Studies in Education,* 10: 455–471.

Lawley, E. (1992). *Discourse and Distortion in Computer-Mediated Communication* [Online]. Available: http://www.itcs.com/elawley/discourse.html.

Lawley, E. (1994). *The Sociology of Culture in Computer-Mediated Communication: An initial exploration* [Online]. Available: http://www.itcs.com/elawley/bourdieu.html.

Lea, M. (ed.) (1992). *Contexts of Computer-Mediated Communication.* London and New York: Harvester-Wheatsheaf.

Lea, M. and Spears, R. (1995). Love at first byte? Building personal relationships over computer networks. In J. Wood and S. Duck (eds.), *Under-Studied Relationships. Off the Beaten Track.* Thousand Oaks, CA: Sage.

Lee, G. B. (1996). Addressing anonymous messages in cyberspace. *Journal of Computer-Mediated Communication* [Online], 2(1). Available: http://www.ascusc.org/jcmc/vol2/issue1/anon.html.

Lee, R. (1993). *Doing Research on Sensitive Topics.* London and Newbury Park, CA: Sage.

Leman, P. (1999). The role of subject area, gender, ethnicity and school background in the degree results of Cambridge University undergraduates. *The Curriculum Journal,* 10(2), 231–252.

Leman, P. and Mann, C. (1999). Research and interventions on gender inequalities in higher education. In P. Fogelberg, J. Hearn, L. Husu and T. Mankkinen (eds.), *Hard Work in the Academy.* Helsinki: Helsinki University Press.

Licklider, J. and Taylor, R. (1968). The computer as a communication device. *Science and Technology.*

Liebow, E. (1967). *Tally's Corner.* London: Penguin.

Lincoln, Y. and Guba, E. (1985). *Naturalistic Inquiry*. Beverly Hills, CA: Sage.

Lindlof, T. (1995). *Qualitative Communication Research Methods*. Thousand Oaks, CA: Sage.

Litman, J. (1996). Copyright law and electronic access to information. *First Monday, A Peer Reviewed Journal on the Internet* [Online], 1(4). Available: http://www.firstmonday.dk/issues/issue4/litman/index.html.

Loader, B. D. (ed.) (1998). *Cyberspace Divide: Equality, agency and policy in the information society*. London and New York: Routledge.

Lockard, J. (1996). Virtual whiteness and narrative diversity. *Undercurrent* [Online], 4. Available: http://darkwing.uoregon.edu/~ucurrent/uc4/4-lockard.html.

Lupton, D. (1995). The embodied computer/user. *Body and Society*, 1: 97–112.

Luttrell, W. (1999). Childhood lost and found: Unpacking the self-representations of pregnant teenagers. Paper presented at the American Anthropological Association Annual Meeting, Chicago, November.

Ma, R. (1996). Computer-mediated conversations as a new dimension of intercultural communication between East Asian and North American college students. In S. Herring (ed.), *Computer-Mediated Communication: Linguistic, Social and Cross-Cultural Perspectives* (173–186). Amsterdam: John Benjamins Publishing.

MacKinnon, R. (1995). Searching for the leviathan in Usenet. In S. Jones (ed.), *CyberSociety: Computer-Mediated Communication and Community* (12–137). Thousand Oaks, CA: Sage.

Mann, C. (1998). Family fables. In M. Chamberlain and P. Thompson (eds.), *Narrative and Genre* (81–99). London and New York: Routledge.

Mantovani, G. (1994). Is computer-mediated communication intrinsically apt to enhance democracy in organisations? *Human Relations*, 47(1): 45–62

Markham, A. (1998). *Life Online: Researching Real Experience in Virtual Space*. London and Walnut Creek, CA: AltaMira Press.

Marvin, L. (1995). Spoof, spam, lurk and lag: The aesthetics of text-based virtual realities. *Journal of Computer-Mediated Communication* [Online], 1(2). Available: http://www.usc.edu/dept/annenberg/vol1/issue2/marvin.html.

Matheson, K. (1992). Women and computer technology. In M. Lea (ed.), *Contexts of Computer-Mediated Communication*. London and New York: Harvester-Wheatsheaf.

Matheson, K. and Zanna, M. (1990). Computer-mediated communications: The focus is on me. *Social Science Computer Review*, 8(1): 1–12.

May, T. (1993). *Social Research: Issues, Methods and Processes*. Buckingham: Open University Press.

McCormick, N. B. and McCormick, J. W. (1992). Computer friends and foes: Content of undergraduates' electronic mail. *Computers in Human Behavior*, 8: 379–405.

McCracken, G. (1988). *The Long Interview*. Newbury Park, CA: Sage.

McLaughlin, M., Osborne, K. and Smith, C. (1995). Standards of conduct in Usenet. In Jones, S. (ed.) *Cybersociety: Computer-Mediated Communication and Community,* (90–112). Thousand Oaks, CA, and London: Sage.

Mehta, R. and Sivadas, E. (1995). Comparing response rates and response content in mail versus electronic mail surveys. *Journal of the Market Research Society*, 37: 429–439.

Metz, M. (1994). Computer-mediated communication: Literature review of a new context. *Interpersonal Computing and Technology* [Online], 2(2): 31–49. Available: http://www.lib.ncsu.edu/stacks/i/ipct/ipct-v2n02-metz-computer mediated.txt.

Meyer, G. and Thomas, J. (1990). The baudy world of the byte bandit: A postmodern interpretation of the computer underground. In F. Schmalleger (ed.), *Computers in Criminal Justice*. Bristol: Wyndham Hall.

Meyrowitz, J. (1985). *No Sense of Place: The Impact of Electronic Media on Social Behavior* (93–94). Oxford: Oxford University Press.

Middleton, S. (1993). *Educating Feminists: Life histories and pedagogy*. New York: Teacher's College Press.

Miles, M. and Huberman, A. (1994). *Qualitative Data Analysis: A sourcebook of new methods*. Thousand Oaks, CA: Sage.

Miller, G. (1997). Contextualising texts: Studying organisational texts. In G. Miller and R. Dingwall (eds.), *Context and Method in Qualitative Research*. London: Sage.

Mnookin, J. (1996). Virtual(ly) law: The emergence of law in LambdaMOO. *Journal of Computer-Mediated Communication* [Online], 2(1). Available: http://www.ascusc.org/jcmc/vol2/issue1/lambda.html.

Moore, M. (1993). Theory of transactional distance. In D. Keegan (ed.), *Theoretical Principles of Distance Education*. London: Routledge.

Morgan, D. (1988). *Focus Groups and Qualitative Research*. Thousand Oaks, CA: Sage.

Morgan, D. and Krueger, R. (1993). When to use focus groups and why. In D. Morgan (ed.), *Successful Focus Groups Advancing the State of the Art* (3–19). Newbury Park, CA: Sage.

Morgan, D. and Spanish, M. (1984). Focus groups: A new tool for qualitative research. *Qualitative Sociology*, 7: 253–270.

Morrisett, L. (1996). Habits of mind and a new technology of freedom. *First Monday, A Peer Reviewed Journal on the Internet* [Online], 1(3). Available: http://www.firstmonday.dk/issues/issue3/morrisett/.

Murphy, K. and Collins, M. (1997). Communication conventions in instructional electronic chats. *First Monday, A Peer Reviewed Journal on the Internet* [Online], 2(11). Available: http://www.firstmonday.dk/issues/issue2_11/murphy/.

Murray, B. (1995). *Knowledge Machines: Language and information in a technological society*. London and New York: Longman.

Murray, D. (1988). Computer-mediated communication: Implications for ESP. *English for Special Purposes*, 7: 3–18.

Murray, D. (1991). The composing process for computer conversation. *Written Communication*, 8.

Myers, D. (1987). Anonymity is part of the magic: Individual manipulation of computer-mediated communication context. *Qualitative Sociology*, 10: 251–266.

Negroponte, N. (1995). *Being digital*. New York: Knopf.

Newby, G. B. (1993). The maturation of norms for computer-mediated communication. *Internet Research*, 3: 30–38.

O'Connor, H. and Madge, C. (2000). *Cyber-parents and Cyber-research: Exploring the Internet as a medium for research*. University of Leicester: Centre for Labour Market Studies.

Ott, D. (1998). Power to the people: The role of electronic media in promoting democracy in Africa. *First Monday, A Peer Reviewed Journal on the Internet* [Online], 3(4). Available: http://www.firstmonday.dk/issues/issue3_4/ott/index.html.

Øyen, E. (ed.) (1990). *Comparative Methodology: Theory and practice in international social research.* London: Sage.

Paccagnella, L. (1997). Getting the seat of your pants dirty: Strategies for ethnographic research on virtual communities. Journal of Computer-Mediated Communication [Online], 3(1). Available: http://www.ascusc.org/jcmc/vol3/issue1/paccagnella.html.

Parkany, R. and Swan, K. (1999). A provaluation of an on-line curriculum. A representation presented at The 5th International Conference on Asynchronous Learning, 8–10 October 1999, at University of Maryland. Available: http://www.borg.com/~rparkany/Resources/ProvalPresent/index.htm.

Parker, L. (1992). Collecting data the e-mail way. *Training and Development*, 52–54.

Parks, M. and Floyd, K. (1996). Making friends in cyberspace. *Journal of Communication*, 46(1), 80–97. Also in the *Journal of Computer-Mediated Communication* [Online], 1(4). Available: http://jcmc.huji.ac.il/vol1/issue4/vol1no4.html.

Parks, M. and Roberts, L. (1998). Making MOOsic: The development of personal relationships online and a comparison to their offline counterparts. *Journal of Personal Relationships*, 15· 517–537. Available: http://psych.curtin.edu.au/people/robertsl/moosic.htm.

Parks, M. R. (1997). Communication networks and relationship life cycles. In S. Duck (ed.), *Handbook of Personal Relationships* (2nd edn.) (351–372). Chichester: John Wiley.

Patrick, A. S., Black, A. and Whalen, T. E. (1995). Rich, young, male, dissatisfied computer geeks? Demographics and satisfaction from the National Capital FreeNet. In D. Godfrey and M. Levy (eds.), *Proceedings of Telecommunities 95: The International Community Networking Conference* (83–107). Victoria, BC: Telecommunities Canada. Available: http://debra.dgbt.doc.ca/services-research/survey/demographics/vic.html.

Patton, M. (1990). *Qualitative Evaluation and Research Methods.* Newbury Park, CA: Sage.

Penkoff, D. (1994). Smile when you say that: Graphic accents as gender markers in computer-mediated communication. Purdue University (Email: penkoff@sage.cc.purdue.edu).

Penny, S. (1994). Virtual reality as the completion of the Enlightenment project. In G. Bender and T. Druckery (eds.), *Culture on the Brink: Ideologies of technology* (231–248). Seattle, WA: Bay Press.

Picardie, R. (1998). *Before I Say Goodbye.* London: Penguin Books.

Plant, S. (1996). On the matrix: Cyberfeminist simulations. In R. Shields (ed.), *Cultures of the Internet: Virtual Spaces, Real Histories, Living Bodies* (170–184). Thousand Oaks, CA, and London: Sage.

Portelli, A. (1998). Oral history as genre. In M Chamberlain and P. Thompson (eds.), *Narrative and Genre* (142–160). London and New York: Routledge.

Preece, J. (2000). *Online Communities: Supporting Usability, Designing Usability.* Chichester: John Wiley.

Rafaeli, S., Sudweeks, F., Konstan, J. and Mabry, E. (1994). ProjectH Overview: A quantitative study of computer-mediated communication. [Online]. Available: http://www.arch.usyd.edu.au/~fay/projecth.html.

Ratcliffe, J. W. and Gonzalez-del-Valle, A. (1988). Rigor in health-related research: Toward an expanded conceptualization. *International Journal of Health Services*, 18: 361–392.

Reid, E. (1991). *Electropolis: Communication and Community on Internet Relay Chat.* Honors thesis, Department of History, University of Melbourne, Australia.

Reid, E. (1994). Cultural formations in text-based virtual realities. University of Melbourne, Australia.

Reid, E. (1995). Virtual worlds: Culture and imagination. In S. G. Jones (ed.), *Cybersociety: Computer Mediated Communication and Community* (164–183). London: Sage.

Reid, E. (1996). Informed consent in the study of on-line communities. A reflection on the effects of computer-mediated social research. *The Information Society*, 12(2): 169–174. Abstract available: http://www.slis.indiana.edu/TIS/abstracts/ab12-2/reid.html.

Reinharz, S. (1992). *Feminist Methods in Social Research.* New York: Oxford University Press.

Rheingold, H. (1994). *The Virtual Community: Finding Connection in a Computerized World.* London: Secker and Warburg.

Rice, R. (1992). Contexts of research on organizational computer-mediated communication. In M. Lea (ed.), *Contexts of Computer-Mediated Communication* (113–145). London and New York: Harvester-Wheatsheaf.

Rice, R. and Case, D. (1983). Electronic message systems in the university: A description of use and utility. *Journal of Communication*, 33: 131–52.

Rice, R. and Love, G. (1987). Electronic emotion: Socioemotional content in a computer-mediated communication network. *Communication Research*, 14(1): 85–108.

Rice, R. and Rogers, E. (1984). New methods and data for the study of new media. In R. Rice and Associates (eds.), *The New Media: Communication, Research and Technology* (81–99). Beverly Hills, CA: Sage.

Rice, R., Grant, A., Schmitz, J. and Torobin, J. (1990). Individual and network influences on the adoption and perceived outcome of electronic messaging. *Social Networks*, 12: 27–55.

Rinaldi, A. (1996). The ten commandments for computer ethics. In *The Net: User Guidelines and Netiquette* [Online]. Available: http://www.fau.edu/netiquette/net/index.html.

Rodino, M. (1997). Breaking out of binaries: Reconceptualizing gender and its relationship to language in computer-mediated communication. *Journal of Computer Mediated Communication* [Online], 3(3). Available: http://www.ascusc.org/jcmc/vol3/issue3/rodino.html.

Rucker, R., RU Sirious and Queen Mu (1992). *Mondo User's Guide to the New Edge.* New York: Harper Perennial.

Ruedenberg, L., Danet, B. and Rosenbaum-Tamari, Y. (1995). Virtual virtuosos: Play and performance at the computer keyboard. *Electronic Journal of Communication* [Online], 4. Available: http://www.cios.org/getfile\RUEDEN_V5N495.

Ryan, J. (1995). *A Uses and Gratifications Study of the Internet Social Interaction Site LambdaMOO: Talking with 'Dinos'*. Unpublished thesis submitted for Master of Arts at Ball State University, Muncie, Indiana. Available: http://vesta.physics.ucla.edu:80/~smolin/lambda/laws_and_history/thesisw5.txt.

Ryen, A. (1999, email notes). *E-mail Communication as Data. A Note*. Agder University College, Norway.

Ryen, A. and Silverman, D. (2000). Marking boundaries: Private culture as category-work. *Qualitative Inquiry*, 6(1).

Sacks, H. (1992). *Lectures on Conversation*, edited by G. Jefferson. Oxford: Blackwell.

Sala, L. (1998). *The paradox: Megabandwidth and micromedia*. Paper presented at the International Sociology Conference, Montreal.

Salmon, G. (2000). *E-moderating: the key to teaching and learning online*. Kogan Page London.

Saunders, D., Forcht, K. and Counts, P. (1998). Legal considerations of Internet use – issues to be addressed. *Internet Research: Electronic Networking Applications and Policy*, 8(1). Available online: http://www.mcb.co.uk/cgi-bin/journal1/intr.

Savicki, V. and Lingenfelter, M. (1996). Gender language style and group composition in Internet discussion groups. *Journal of Computer Mediated Communication* [Online], 2(3). Available: http://www.usc.edu/dept/annenberg/vol2/issue3/savicki.html.

Schaefer, D. and Dillman, D. A. (1998). Development of a standard e-mail methodology: Results of an experiment. *Public Opinion Quarterly*, 62: 378–397.

Scheuermann, L. and Taylor, G. (1997). Netiquette. *Internet Research: Electronic Networking Applications and Policy*, 7(4): 269–273. Available online: http://www.mcb.co.uk/cgi-bin/journal1/intr.

Schiano, D. (1997). Convergent methodologies in cyber-psychology. A case study. *Behaviour Research Methods, Instruments and Computers*, 29: 270–273.

Schnarch, D. (1997). Sex, intimacy and the Internet. *Journal of Sex Education and Therapy*, 22: 15–20.

Schrum, L. (1995). Framing the debate: Ethical research in the information age. *Qualitative Inquiry*, 1: 311–326.

Schwandt, T. (1997). *Qualitative Inquiry: A dictionary of terms*. Thousand Oaks, CA, and London: Sage.

Scott, J. (1990). *A Matter of Record*. Cambridge: Polity Press.

Seidman, I. (1991). *Interviewing as Qualitative Research*. Columbia University: Teacher's College.

Selfe, C. L. and Meyer, P. (1991). Testing claims for online conferences. *Written Communication*, 8: 163–192.

Selwyn, N. and Robson, K. (1998). Using e-mail as a research tool. *Social Research Update*, 21. University of Surrey, UK. Available: http://www.soc.surrey.ac.uk/sru/SRU21.html.

Sempsey, J. (1997). Psyber psychology: A literature review pertaining to the psycho/social aspects of multi-user dimensions in cyberspace. *The Journal of MUD Research* [Online], 2(1). Available: http://journal.tinymush.org/~jomr/v2n1/sempsey.html.

Serpentelli, J. (1993). Conversational structure and personality correlates of electronic communication. Anonymous FTP: Xerox.Parc.com/pub/papers.

Seymour, W., Lupton, D. and Fahy, N. (1999). Negotiating disability, technology and risk: Towards a new perspective. Report: School of Social Work and Social Policy, Magill Campus, University of South Australia.

Shade, L. (1994). Gender issues in computer networking. *Electronic Journal on Virtual Culture* [Online], 2(3). Available: http://www.monash.edu.au/journals/ejvc/shade.v2n3.

Shank, G., and Cunningham, D. (1996). Mediated phosphor dots: Towards a post-Cartesian model of CMC via the semiotic superhighway. In C. Ess (ed.), *Philosophical Perspectives on Computer-Mediated Communication* (29–44). Albany, NY: State University of New York Press.

Sharf, B. (1999). Beyond netiquette: The ethics of doing naturalistic research on the Internet. In S. Jones (ed.), *Doing Internet Research*. Thousand Oaks, CA, and London: Sage.

Sheehan, K. and Hoy, M. (1999). Using e-mail to survey Internet users in the United States: Methodology and assessment. *Journal of Computer-Mediated Communication* [Online], 4(3). Available: http://www.ascusc.org/jcmc/vol4/issue3/sheehan.html.

Shields, R. (ed.) (1996). *Cultures of the Internet: Virtual Spaces, Real Histories, Living Bodies*. London and Thousand Oaks, CA: Sage.

Short, J., Williams, E. and Christie, B. (1976). *The Social Psychology of Telecommunication*. London: John Wiley.

Silverman, D. (1993). *Interpreting Qualitative Data: Methods for analysing talk, text & interaction*. London: Sage.

Silverman, D. (1999). *Doing Qualitative Research: A Practical Handbook*. London: Sage.

Silverstone, R. and Hirsch, E. (1992). *Consuming Technologies: Media and information in domestic spaces*. London: Routledge.

Slouka, M. (1995). *War of the Worlds: Cyberspace and the high-tech assault on reality*. New York: Basic Books.

Small, H. (1996). Enforcement of intellectual property rights on the Internet. *Internet Research*, 6(1).

Smith, C. (1997). Casting the Net: Surveying an internet population. *Journal of Computer-Mediated Communication* [Online], 3(1). Available: http://www.ascusc.org/jcmc/vol3/issue1/smith.html.

Smith, M. (1989a). Computer security – threats, vulnerabilities and counter-measures. *Information Age*, 11: 205–210.

Smith, M. (1989b). *Commonsense Computer Security: Your practical guide to preventing accidental error and deliberate electronic data loss*. London: McGraw-Hill.

Smith-Stoner, M. and Weber, T. (2000). *Developing Theory using Emergent Inquiry: A study of meaningful online learning for women*. Unpublished doctoral dissertation, California Institute of Integral Studies (E-mail: mssrn@aol.com).

Sola Pool, I. de (ed.) (1977). *The Social Impact of the Telephone*. Cambridge, MA: MIT Press.

Spears, R. and Lea, M. (1992). Social influence and the influence of the 'social' in computer-mediated communication. In M. Lea (ed.), *Contexts of Computer-Mediated Communication* (30–66). London and New York: Harvester-Wheatsheaf.

Spears, R. and Lea, M. (1994). Panacea or Panopticon? The hidden power in computer-mediated communication. *Communication Research*, 21(4):427–459.

Spender, D. (1995). *Nattering on the Net: Women, Power and Cyberspace*. Melbourne: Spinifrex Press.

Spender, D. (1997). The position of women in information technology – or who got there first and with what consequences. *Current Sociology*, 45: 135–147.

Spertus, E. (1991). *Why are there so few female computer scientists?* Cambridge, MA: MIT Artificial Intelligence Laboratory.

Spitzer, M. (1986). Writing style in computer conferences. *IEEE Transactions of Professional Communication*, 29(1): 19–22.

Sproull, L. and Kiesler, S. (1986). Reducing social context cues: Electronic mail in organisational communication. *Management Science*, 32: 1492–1512.

Sproull, L. and Kiesler, S. (1991). *Connections: New ways of working in the networked environment*. Cambridge, MA: MIT Press.

Stein, S. (2000). *Learning, Teaching and Researching on the Internet: A practical guide for social scientists*. London: Addison Wesley Longman.

Sterne, J. (1999). Thinking the Internet: Cultural studies versus the millennium. In S. Jones (ed.), *Doing Internet Research* (257–289). Thousand Oaks, CA, and London: Sage.

Stewart, D. and Shamdasani, P. (1990). *Focus Groups Theory and Practice*. Newbury Park, CA: Sage.

Stewart, F., Eckermann, E. and Zhou, K. (1998). Using the Internet in qualitative public health research: A comparison of Chinese and Australian young women's perceptions of tobacco use. *Internet Journal of Health Promotion* [Online]. Available: http:// www.monash.edu.au/health/IJHP/1998/12.

Stone, A. (1991). Will the real body please stand up? Boundary stories about virtual cultures. In M. Benedikt (ed.), *Cyberspace: First steps* (81–118). Cambridge, MA: MIT Press.

Sudman, S. and Bradburn, N. (1982). *Asking Questions*. San Francisco and London: Jossey-Bass.

Sudweeks, F. and Simoff, S. (1999). Complementary explorative data analysis: The reconciliation of quantitative and qualitative principles. In S. Jones (ed.), *Doing Internet Research*. Thousand Oaks, CA, and London: Sage.

Sutton, L. (1994). Using Usenet: Gender, power, and silence in electronic discourse. The Proceedings of the 20th Annual Meeting of the Berkeley Linguistics Society, Berkeley, California.

Sweet, C. (1999). Expanding the qualitative research arena: Online focus groups. Quesst Qualitative Research, Brooklyn, New York (Email: casey@focusgroupsonline.net).

Sykes, W. and Hoinville, G. (1985). *Telephone Interviewing on a Survey of Social Attitudes: A comparison with face-to-face procedures*. London: Social and Community Planning Research.

Tannen, D. (1991). *You Just Don't Understand: Women and men in conversation*. New York: Ballantine Books.

Tannen, D. (1994). Gender gap in cyberspace. *Newsweek*, 16 May: 52–53.

Tapscott, D. (1998). *Growing Up Digital: The rise of the net generation*. New York: McGraw-Hill.

Temple, B. (1994). The message and the medium: Oral and written accounts of lives. *Auto/Biography*, 3:1 & 3:2. British Sociological Association Study Groups Publication.

Teo, T. (1998). Differential effects of occupation on Internet usage. *Internet Research*, 8(2): 156–165.

Tesch, R. (1990). *Qualitative Research: Analysis of Types and Software Tools*. New York: Falmer Press.

Thimbleby, H. (1998). Personal boundaries/global stage. *First Monday* [Online], 3(3). Available: http://www.firstmonday.dk/issues/index.html.

Thomas, D. (1998). Legal considerations of Internet use – issues to be addressed. *Internet Research*, 8(1).

Thomas, J. (1996). Introduction: A debate about the ethics of fair practices for collecting social science data in cyberspace. *The Information Society*, 12(2): 107–117. Abstract available: http://www.slis.indiana.edu/TIS/abstracts/ab12-2/ thomas.html.

Thompson, P. (1988). *The Voice of the Past: Oral History*. Oxford: Oxford University Press.

Thu Nguyen, D. and Alexander, J. (1996). The coming of cyberspacetime and the end of the polity. In R. Shields (ed.), *Cultures of the Internet: Virtual Spaces, Real Histories, Living Bodies* (99–125). London and Thousand Oaks, CA: Sage.

Townsend, M. (1994). *Real Men: What Australian Men Really Think, Feel, and Believe*. Sydney: Harper Collins.

Treitler, I. (1996). Email for democracy? A commentary on Morrisett's habit of mind and a new technology of freedom. *First Monday* [Online], 1(3) Available: http://www.firstmonday.dk/issues/issue3/treitler/index.htm.

Tse, A. C. B., Tse, K. C., Yin, C. H., Ting, C. B., Yi, K. W., Yee, K. P. and Hong, W. C. (1995). Comparing two methods of sending out questionnaires: E-mail versus mail. *Journal of the Market Research Society*, 37: 441–446.

Turkle, S. (1984). *The Second Self: Computers and the Human Spirit*. New York: Simon and Schuster.

Turkle, S. (1995). *Life on the Screen: Identity in the Age of the Internet*. London: Weidenfeld and Nicolson.

Turkle, S. (1997). Multiple subjectivity and virtual community at the end of the Freudian century. *Sociological Inquiry*, 67: 72–84.

Turkle, S. and Papert, S. (1990). Epistemological pluralism: Styles and voices within the computer culture. *Signs: Journal of Women and Culture*, 16: 128–157.

Turner, B. S. (1996). *The Body and Society*. London: Sage.

Van Gelder, L. (1991). The strange case of the electronic lover. In C. Dunlop and R. Kling (eds.), *Computerization and Controversy: Value Conflicts and Social Choices*. New York: Academic Press.

Wajcman, J. (1991). Technology as masculine culture. In *Feminism Confronts Technology* (137–161). University Park, PA: Pennsylvania State University Press.

Wakeford, N. (1999). Alone@Campus.Edu? The intersection of student and computing cultures at the University of California at Berkeley. In M. Henry (ed.), *I.T. in the Social Sciences* (170–197). Oxford: Blackwell.

Walker, J. and Taylor, T. (1998). *The Columbia Guide to Online Style*. New York and Chichester: Columbia University Press.

Wallace, P. (1999). *The Psychology of the Internet*. New York: Cambridge University Press.

Walther, J. (1992). Interpersonal effects in computer-mediated interaction. *Communication Research*, 19(1).

Walther, J. (1996). Computer-mediated communication: Impersonal, interpersonal, and hyperpersonal interaction. *Communication Research*, 23: 3–43.

Walther, J. (1999). Researching Internet behavior: Methods, issues and concerns. National Communication Association Summer Conference on Communication and Technology, Washington, DC.

Walther, J. and Boyd, S. (2000). Attraction to computer-mediated social support. In C. Lin and D. Atkin (eds.), *Communication Technology and Society: Audience adoption and uses of the new media.* New York: Hampton Press.

Walther, J. and Burgoon, J. (1992). Relational communication in computer-mediated interaction. *Human Communication Research*, 19(1): 50–88.

Walther, J., Anderson, J. and Park, D. (1994). Interpersonal effects in computer-mediated interaction: A meta-analysis of social and antisocial communication. *Communication Research*, 21: 460–487.

Waskul, D. and Douglass, M. (1996). Considering the electronic participant: Some polemic observations on the ethics of on-line research. *The Information Society*, 12(2): 129–139.

Weber, M. (1922). *Gesammelte Aufsätze zur Wissenschaftslehre.* Tübingen: Mohr.

Weiss, R. (1997). *Learning from Strangers: The art and method of qualitative interview studies.* New York: Free Press.

Werry, C. (1996). Linguistic and interactional features of Internet Relay Chat. In S. Herring (ed.), *Computer-Mediated Communication: Linguistic, Social and Cross-Cultural Perspectives* (47–64). Amsterdam: John Benjamins Publishing.

Whittle, D. (1997). *Cyberspace: The Human Dimension.* New York: W.H. Freeman.

Wilkins, H. (1991). Computer talk. *Written Communication*, 8.

Williams, E. (1998). Predicting e-mail effects in organisations. *First Monday, A Peer Reviewed Journal on the Internet* [Online], 3(9). Available: http://www.firstmonday.dk/issues/issue3_9/williams/index.html.

Wilson, M. (1996). Asking questions. In R. Sapsford and V. Jupp (eds.), *Data Collection and Analysis* (94–121). London: Sage in association with The Open University.

Winch, P. (1988). *The Idea of a Social Science and Its Relation to Philosophy.* London: Routledge.

Winter, D. and Huff, C. (1996). Adapting the Internet: Comments from a women-only electronic forum. *American Sociologist*, 27: 30–54.

Witmer, D. and Katzman, S. (1997). On-line smiles: Does gender make a difference in the use of graphic accents? *Journal of Computer-Mediated Communication* [Online], 2(4). Available: http://jcmc.mscc.huji.ac.il/vol2/issue4/witmer1.html.

Witmer, D., Colman, R. and Katzman, S. (1999). From paper-and-pencil to screen-and-keyboard: Toward a methodology for survey research on the Internet. In S. Jones (ed.), *Doing Internet Research* (145–163). Thousand Oaks, CA, and London: Sage.

Wynn, E. and Katz, J. (1997). Hyperbole over cyberspace: Self-presentation & social boundaries in Internet home pages and discourse. *The Information Society*, 13(4): 297–328. Abstract available: http://www.slis.indiana.edu/TIS/abstracts/ab13-4/wynn.html.

Wynter, L. (1996). Business and race: Survey of black hackers shows an elite audience. *Wall Street Journal*, March 6, p. B1.

Yates, S. (1996). Oral and written linguistic aspects of computer conferencing. In S. Herring (ed.), *Computer-Mediated Communication: Linguistic, Social and Cross-Cultural Perspectives* (29–46). Amsterdam: John Benjamins Publishing.

Zakon, R.H. (1996). Hobbes' Internet Timeline [Online]. Available: http://info.isoc.org/guest/zakon/Internet/History/HIT.html.

Index